**WRITING
AGAINST
REFORM**

A Volume in the Series
Becoming Modern: Studies in the Long Nineteenth Century

EDITED BY
Elizabeth A. Fay

WRITING AGAINST REFORM

AESTHETIC REALISM
IN THE
PROGRESSIVE
ERA

ARIELLE ZIBRAK

University of Massachusetts Press

AMHERST AND BOSTON

Copyright © 2024 by University of Massachusetts Press
All rights reserved
Printed in the United States of America

ISBN 978-1-62534-771-8 (paper); 772-5 (hardcover)

Designed by Sally Nichols
Set in Minion Pro by Westchester Publishing Services
Printed and bound by Books International, Inc.

Cover design by adam b. bohannon

Library of Congress Cataloging-in-Publication Data

Names: Zibrak, Arielle, author.
Title: Writing against reform : aesthetic realism
in the Progressive Era / Arielle Zibrak.
Description: Amherst : University of Massachusetts Press, 2024. |
Series: Becoming modern: studies in the long nineteenth century |
Includes bibliographical references and index.
Identifiers: LCCN 2023013414 (print) | LCCN 2023013415 (ebook) |
ISBN 9781625347718 (paperback) | ISBN 9781625347725 (hardcover) |
ISBN 9781685750459 (ebook)
Subjects: LCSH: Realism in literature. | American fiction—19th century—
History and criticism. | American fiction—20th century—History and criticism. |
Social problems in literature. | Literature and society—United States—History—
19th century. | Literature and society—United States—History—20th century.
Classification: LCC PS217.R4 Z53 2024 (print) | LCC PS217.R4 (ebook) |
DDC 813/.08309—dc23/eng/20230726
LC record available at https://lccn.loc.gov/2023013414
LC ebook record available at https://lccn.loc.gov/2023013415

British Library Cataloguing-in-Publication Data
A catalog record for this book is available from the British Library.

Some portions of chapter 1 were previously published as Arielle Zibrak, "Writing
Behind a Curtain: Rebecca Harding Davis and Celebrity Reform," *ESQ: A Journal
of the American Renaissance* 60, no. 4 (2014): 522–56; copyright © 2024 by the
Board of Regents of Washington State University. Some portions of chapter 2
were previously published as Arielle Zibrak, "Kissing a Photograph: Reproductive
Panic in Kate Chopin and Thomas Hardy," *Criticism: A Quarterly for Literature
and the Arts* 58, no. 3 (2016): 355–74; copyright © 2017 by Wayne State University
Press, Detroit, Michigan, 48201–1309.

For Jonah, my favorite scientist and explorer:
with a little hard work, you can make anything real.

CONTENTS

List of Figures ix

Acknowledgments xi

INTRODUCTION
Hideously Political

1

PART ONE: AGAINST REFORM

CHAPTER ONE
Rebecca Harding Davis and Celebrity Reform

29

CHAPTER TWO
Kate Chopin's Art Panic

62

PART TWO: THERE IS NO OPPOSITION

CHAPTER THREE
Political Intimacy in Henry James

93

PART THREE: ART IN AN EMERGENCY

CHAPTER FOUR
James Weldon Johnson's Political Formalism

123

vii

CHAPTER FIVE
Edith Wharton at War in the Land of Letters
155

Notes 193
Works Cited 225
Index 247

FIGURES

FIGURE 1. Save the Children Contaminated Drinking Water Campaign, M&C Saatchi, October 2009.   41

FIGURE 2. "Apples" in the style of Gustave Courbet (French, second half of nineteenth century).   72

FIGURE 3. Paul Cézanne, "Apples" (1878–1879).   73

FIGURE 4. *New York Times*, November 23, 1922—American Social History Project.   150

ACKNOWLEDGMENTS

In many ways, my work towards this book began at the turn of this century in a poetry class with James Longenbach, who provided the intellectual framework on which I hang all of my best ideas. He should be cited on (but not held responsible for) every page and will always be my most cherished teacher, critic, poet, and friend.

There have been many helpful readers and interlocutors along the way. I can't imagine how anyone writes a work of scholarly criticism without having John Levi Barnard for a friend and confidante. Mary Kuhn provided me with so much inspiration and vision. Marissa Gemma is the sharpest editor I know and, in all aspects of life, has flawless style. I'm grateful to Autumn Womack, Laura Fisher, and Justine Murison for much feedback and sage counsel and to Michael Edson for his unflagging allyship and the near-complete sorting of the issues that plagued chapter 3.

Susan Mizruchi and Sacvan Bercovitch taught me so much. Their early readings of my work and kind advice paved the way to making this book a reality. Hunt Howell is the very model of what a researcher and educator should be; there are not thanks enough to give him, so this will have to suffice. Laura Korobkin has influenced so much of my thinking about nineteenth-century America and provided a profound example of how to be a responsible and generous scholar. Boston University faculty Anna Henchman, Joe Rezek, John Matthews, Anita Patterson, Lee Monk, Maurice Lee, Aaron Fogel, Tom Otten, Erin Murphy, and Julia Brown were all instrumental in the completion of this work, as were my fellow graduate students: Iain Bernhoft, Heather Holcombe, Claire Kervin, Emily Field, Emily Griffiths Jones, Heather Barrett, Christian Engley, Lia Calhoun, Lindsey Gilbert, Sheila Cordner, Mike D'Alessandro, and Jono. I am so in awe of all of you.

The research towards this book was made possible by grants from the University of Wyoming's College of Arts and Sciences and the Wyoming Institute for Humanities Research, as well as an Eberly Family special collections grant from Pennsylvania State University. I am grateful to the journals *ESQ* and *Criticism* for permission to reprint the sections of the first and second chapter that previously appeared in their respective pages as "Writing Behind a Curtain: Rebecca Harding Davis and Celebrity Reform" and "Kissing a Photograph: Reproductive Panic in Kate Chopin and Thomas Hardy." Everyone at the University of Massachusetts Press has been a joy to work with. My thanks to Brian Halley, Libby Fay, Sally Nichols, Rachael DeShano, and especially the anonymous reviewers of the manuscript for their thoughtful reports.

I have endless librarians to thank for help throughout the years, but Tracy Pressey at the Beinecke and Kajisa Calkins at Coe are two particularly good ones who have been wonderfully helpful to me. The folks at the Goodstein Library at Casper College went above and beyond in every imaginable way to get me what I needed. Without the hard work, dedication, and wry humor of Donnie Clauch, the research for this book would not have been possible. (Special thanks too to Sarah North.) Hats off to the tap dancer Alex MacDonald, who gave valuable advice in his capacity as a historian of dance; and to a fabulous scholar, translator, and friend, Marie Satya McDonough.

I owe a debt of gratitude to the wonderful colleagues who fostered my work as a post doc at Case Western Reserve University: Maggie Vinter, Jeremy Bendik-Keymer, Laura Taxel, Helen Salz, Sarah Gridley, Paul Jaussen, Eric Chilton, Denna Iammarino, Erika Olbricht, Suhaan Mehta, Jared Champion, and Michael Clune.

I have had unbelievably good fortune in the bright minds and warm hearts I have encountered at the University of Wyoming, especially Bruce Richardson, Peter Parolin, Julia Obert, Nina McConigley, Tara Clapp, Josh Clapp, Mimi Fenton, Alyson Hagy, Cliff Marks, Susan Aronstein, Caroline McCracken-Flesher, Kelly Kinney, Caskey Russell, Tracey Owens Patton, Lilia Soto, Nick Crane, Zoe Pearson, Kate Hartmann, Erin Forbes, Jason Baskin, Paul Bergstraesser, Rick Fisher, Val Pexton, Michelle Jarman, Bunny Logan, Jacquelyn Bridgeman, Cathy Connolly, Allison Gernant, Vanessa Fonseca-Chávez, Nancy Small, Maggie Bourque, Donal Skinner, Kent Drummond, and Danielle Pafunda. My colleagues at UW Casper and Casper College made living and working in central Wyoming better than I could have ever imagined: Julia Whyde, Brent Pickett, Scott Seville, Eric DaFoe, Amanda DeDiego, Masha Kuznetsova, Evin Rodkey, Patrick Amelotte, Cara Rodriguez, and Valerie Ianella Maiers.

The Edith Wharton International Society is a wonderfully collegial group to bounce ideas off of and steep in all things Wharton. I am very grateful to all of its members, especially Donna Campbell, Jay Jessee, Meg Toth, Sharon Kim, Emily Orlando, Carol Singley, Meredith Goldstein, Melanie Dawson, Gary Totten, Sheila Liming, Virginia Ricard, Shafquat Towheed, Nir Evron, Myrto Drizou, and Paul Ohler. The Kate Chopin Society also provided great feedback on early versions of chapter 2, especially Emily Toth and Bernie Koloski. Sharon Harris is not only the sage of Rebecca Harding Davis studies, she is also a supportive mentor who has created an amazing legacy in Davis studies and beyond. I am immensely grateful to you, Sherry, as well as to Mischa Renfroe and Robin Cadwallader. Adena Spingarn deserves many thanks for valuable conversations and a rich sharing of work on James Weldon Johnson—as does Werner Sollors who connected us.

The Society for the Study of American Women Writers has been an immense support throughout my career. Special thanks to Sandy Zagarell, Jennifer Putzi, Claudia Stokes, Kristin Allukian, Sari Edelstein, Faye Halpern, Laura Thiemann Scales, María Carla Sánchez, Cynthia Davis, Dawn Coleman, Debby Rosenthal, Jessica Horvath-Williams, and all the members who make our conferences so generative. C19 is another scholarly home where I've found much inspiration and guidance thanks to Dana Seitler, Stephanie Foote, Elizabeth Freeman, Koritha Mitchell, Cherene Sherrard-Johnson, Caleb Smith, Sarah Mesle, and Sarah Blackwood. Gordon Hutner, Lynne Huffer, Caroline Levine, Jack Halberstam, and Amanda Claybaugh—thank you for our conversations about this material.

My beloved FREACs, the best regional writing group going, provided feedback on drafts of the introduction and chapter 2, not to mention much cheer: Maria Windell, Daniel Diez Couch, Sylvan Goldberg, Zach Hutchins, Leslie Ginsberg, and Greg Laski. Many thanks go to Winfried Flück and the colleagues who responded to early work at the Dartmouth Futures Institute and after: Magdalena Zurawski, Sarah Salter, Melissa Gniadek, and especially the marvelous Shari Goldberg, whose insights have been invaluable to me for years. You all still make me believe in narrative.

Friends and family gave so much support throughout the long journey of this project: Alexander Southgate, Anya Kamenetz, Adam Berenzweig,

Michael Colin, Daniel and Anna Barluschke, Brandi and Vipul Shah, Scarlett Verity, Lisa Rodkey, Ben Polletta, David Singerman, Evelyn Edson, Trevor C. Pederson, and Sarah Colvert. Elise Metzger has been the best of friends since before I could read. I would choose her again in a heartbeat. Marco, Vicky, Doug, Zander, Bernie, and Karen—thank you for accepting me as a package deal. Much thanks for much understanding to my family: the Sollods, the Rifkins, and the Zibraks—Ben, Rachel, Owen, Bari, Amaya, Nolan, Cameron, Joseph, and Beverly. I love you all more than you know.

Herman, Jonah, and Charlie are the core of my support system. Like Baldwin said, love takes off the masks we fear we cannot live without and know we cannot live within. Everything I do is better and more honest because of the three of you.

I lost my brother, Jonathan Bennett Zibrak, in the middle of writing this book, but it would not exist without his enthusiasm and his humor to keep me going in its early stages; the memory of his life still makes me smile most days.

WRITING
AGAINST
REFORM

INTRODUCTION

HIDEOUSLY POLITICAL

This place is hideously political, & there don't seem to me to be three people in it who care for questions of art, or form, or taste. I am lonely & speechless. Everything around me is woolly, stuffy, literal, unspeakably Philistine.

—Henry James, letter to Theodore Child, March 8, 1884, in *Henry James: A Life in Letters*

Henry James spent the majority of the first two months of 1884 in Paris, putting off the writing of *The Bostonians* and his consequent money troubles by spending time with a bohemian group of artists and writers that included the painter John Singer Sargent—who, like James, was American born but raised largely in Europe—the Goncourt brothers, Alphonse Daudet, a group of Russian friends of the recently deceased Ivan Turgenev, and Émile Zola. Upon returning to London, James grew depressed at the change of social scene. So, he invited Sargent to visit to cheer himself up and threw a dinner for the painter at the Reform Club, a social space dominated by political talk and intrigue.[1] His assertion, in a letter to the author Theodore Child that March, that London had become "hideously political" expresses a negative aesthetic reaction to a certain kind of public discourse. Such a statement reflects one complaint he and others like him had about much of the realist fiction of the Progressive Era: its overtly political content and advocacy came at the expense of the deep and complicated emotional reactions definitive of what they thought of as high art. "Politics" was a relatively straightforward and moralizing form and, therefore, "hideous" to him.

Writing Against Reform examines the critique of reform aesthetics within the tradition of American realist literature of the late nineteenth and early twentieth centuries. The realist writers in this period who criticized reform were not necessarily apolitical, as is often supposed, nor were they conservatives maintaining a posture of political silence to conform to their artistic social circles. In fact, almost all of the writers covered in this book actively engaged in direct political work we would more readily associate with the political Left than the Right today. It is my contention, rather, that these writers and thinkers were invested in championing the aesthetics of fiction over the co-option of fiction by explicit political rhetoric. The indeterminacy of fiction that had no express purpose was, for them, the very core of its value. Such indeterminacy positioned the interpretative act as an end to itself—an aesthetic orientation that put them at odds with the overtly political realist writers that dominated their period.

Jacques Rancière identifies such a debate in the criticism of the French realism to which these American authors are so indebted, citing Flaubert's 1852 letter to Louise Colet (during the composition of *Madame Bovary*) in which he writes, "the most beautiful books are those with the least matter . . . from the point of view of Art, there is no such thing as a subject, style being solely in itself an absolute way of seeing things."[2] In this view, which these writers for the most part shared, style itself is a kind of totalizing ideology. This is not, however, to say that they thought the ideological messages of reform novels ought to be substituted for a pure style devoid of political content. Rancière rightly points out that the indifferent, meaningless prose Flaubert championed was itself a way of imagining an ideal kind of democracy.

For the writers I consider in the American context, however, the response to the genre of realist reform fiction was to adopt such subjectlessness *as* subject—to represent their various critiques of the politicization of fiction through both emplotment and rhetorical strategies that satirized or inverted the conventions of the explicitly political novels of reform. In identifying these aesthetic writers as a countertradition, I recognize that at the root of their tradition is an aesthetic protest that is political in so far as their work questions the imbedded hierarchies of realist literary style.

In illuminating this countertradition, I understand literary realism, like Fredric Jameson, dialectically—taking the antinomy of its political efficacy in relation to the twinned concept of reform as a site of rich aesthetic value. Jameson writes that realism is "a historical and even evolutionary process in which the negative and the positive are inextricably combined . . . it is to be grasped as a paradox and an anomaly, and the thinking of it as a contradiction or aporia."[3] As I will demonstrate, "reform" and "realism" are both most accurately described as sites of contestation rather than unified political and literary movements. Therefore, my focus is a contest between contests—what gets created in the space of negotiation between these doubled paradoxes.

This is not a book about reform politics, but rather about how the specter of reform politics as a topic for literary engagement was perceived as antithetical to the tradition of what Mark McGurl has called "the art novel" by a significant cadre of realist writers.[4] McGurl, along with other scholars of literary modernism, places the development of the art novel in the literary historical moment of the emergence of modernism and understands it to be a part of that aesthetic project. The period this book covers straddles that emergence, but the works it treats are decidedly realist in style and, I'll argue, their use of realism—a form these writers understood to be valuable *because* it was vexed—is central to their aesthetic and therefore political strategies.

Realist literature at the turn of the twentieth century's extensive engagement with reform politics demonstrates the pervasiveness of the political as a measure of literary value for readers and writers in the period. In this book, I'll argue that realist writers often seen as indifferent to the political currents of their time actually wrote in response to them. I understand the project of writing *against* reform to be an aesthetic one, wherein writing literary realist fiction becomes a rebuttal to the emergent notion that the explicitly political itself was a marker of literary value.

Going beyond writerly objections to the aesthetics of the genre I call "reform realism," these writers' extratextual engagements with the political suggest a belief that the aesthetic is a more fruitful sphere for effecting social change when it does not explicitly engage with politics. For them, the process of social change begins within the self, and therefore the political value of seemingly apolitical fiction lies in its ability to bridge the gaps between political subjects that ideology cannot. This belief is reflected in realist plots that expose the inefficacy of the political and dramatize the death of art at the hands of the political through the deaths, disappointments, and failures of artist characters who become embroiled in politicized circumstances. Read within the context of the aesthetic countertradition, *The Awakening*'s Edna Pontellier swims out into the sea not because she's a feminist ahead of her time, but because limited exposure to truly affecting art has left her without the tools to adequately express herself and her emergent radical ideas. The tragedy of James Weldon Johnson's *Autobiography of an Ex-Colored Man* is that the titular character, a figure for America itself—a country that denies the centrality of its African American cultural heritage—turns his back on music for political reasons.

Such plots align politicized art and literature with mass culture. Nancy Bentley has identified the relationship between mass culture and reform politics, noting that "reform fiction of all kinds . . . continued to prompt Americans to buy and consume books as reading became a more widespread form of mass social engagement."[5] As Bentley notes, writers like James, Wharton, and Howells simultaneously expressed disdain for mass culture as they understood its importance and dissected its strategies. Here, I'll suggest that reform fiction and culture (nonfiction, lectures, editorials, slogans, merchandizing, and gatherings) were not merely one category of mass culture about which these writers had such mixed feelings, but rather constituted an entire genre defined by a key set of aesthetic practices they constructed their own literary projects against. If reform fiction cultivated readerly sympathy, these writers perversely courted readerly alienation. If reform rhetoric performed its own earnestness, these writers insisted upon sarcasm and irony. They saw reform aesthetics not only as a threat to high art and literature, but also, paradoxically, as an obstacle to more durable social change as well.

SOCIAL REFORM AND LITERARY REALISM

Reform is notoriously difficult to describe or define, as it is a catch-all term for any non-revolutionary social progress movement. Within aesthetic realism, it certainly means different things at different times, but becomes an organizing principle for a politics of the popular and the palatable. Reform is at the heart of what historians mean by the sociopolitical interest in "progress" that lends the Progressive Era in the United States and the Age of Progress in Britain their names. Richard Hofstadter writes that "progressivism . . . was, to be sure, a rather vague and not altogether cohesive or consistent movement," to observe that "this was probably the secret to its considerable successes, as well as of its failures."[6] In defining the term "reform," Susan Ryan writes that, in the nineteenth century, it "enjoyed wide circulation as a generic descriptor of individuals and movements, its meanings shifted, expanded, and contracted depending on the social and political commitments of the author."[7] Reformers can just as likely emerge from what we now think of as the political Left as they can from the political Right, and indeed many Progressive Era reform movements were themselves split between camps that would, to present-day eyes, seem respectively progressive and conservative. The Social Purity movement, which I discuss in chapter two of this book in relation to the fiction and writings of Kate Chopin, was both an early feminist crusade against domestic violence and a fascistic censorship campaign bent on eliminating descriptions of sex from all art and literature, among other seemingly contradictory positions including birth control advocacy, eugenics, consent awareness, and the enforcement of the "cult of motherhood," as Laura Hapke has demonstrated.[8] These Social Purity factions may seem to be in overt conflict, but as Richard White reminds us, "nineteenth-century liberals stressed individual freedom, private property, economic competition, and small government" in a manner that does not "map easily" onto the ideology of the political Left of the twenty-first century.[9]

Over the past two decades, excellent scholarship on the literature of reform during this period has demonstrated how prevalent and influential both fictional and nonfictional works that took up specific reform causes were throughout the Progressive Era. Recently, Jon Falsarella Dawson has argued that the naturalist novels of Frank Norris, Jack London, and John Steinbeck function as works of reform fiction by depicting the tragic consequences of inequity; and Mary Chapman, Amanda Claybaugh, Laura Fisher, María Carla Sánchez, and Francesca Sawaya have all made powerful earlier arguments for the centrality of reform within the tradition of the nineteenth-century realist novel more broadly.[10] Much of this scholarship has been a project of recovery. Works of reform literature that were well known in their own time have been lost to literary scholarship today or are just starting to be recognized. As Sánchez notes,

> There is no reason why you, dear reader, should be familiar with the life-work of the Reverend James Watson of Adrian, Michigan. But . . . writings such as his help us to understand the often tense but necessary relationships between the United States' social reform movements and its literature, and that leaving such work unexplored keeps a crucial segment of American literary history from view.[11]

Sánchez uncovers figures ranging from sensational novelists who borrowed from sociological accounts to compose their salacious tales of the lives of sex workers to nonfiction reform writers who learned their techniques of representation from realist novelists. Unlike the figures in Sánchez's work, the writers who appear in *Writing Against Reform* will be familiar to most readers. The lost literary history I recover is the story of how authors we've long paid much attention to are deeply engaged in a conversation that has, for the most part, escaped our notice.

This conversation begins with the sentimental reform writers of the mid-nineteenth century. Charles Dickens and Harriet Beecher Stowe are as known for their commercial success as they are for the social engagement of their fictions. Stowe's definition of her "vocation to preach on paper" speaks to her belief in literature as "the only efficient instrument" for political change, a belief that has guided not only the composition of these works but also the composition of their criticism.[12] While Stowe and Dickens both authored works with explicit political agendas in the 1850s and 1860s, they also satirized reformers within them, most notably in Dickens's African missionary and neglectful mother Mrs. Jellyby of *Bleak House* (1853) and his Benthamite educator Thomas Gradgrind of *Hard Times* (1854); and in Stowe's racist and neurasthenic abolitionist Miss Ophelia of *Uncle Tom's Cabin* (1852). These novels pit real reformers against tepid or opportunistic ones and the plots of the satirized "bad" reformers track their *bildungs* toward the true meaning of reform. In this, the novels uphold the vision of legal reform as the best path to the moral improvement of society as whole, so long as readers come to the conclusion to support or uphold the specific laws the novels champion. Stowe's most famous novel led to a more serious nationwide conversation about the Fugitive Slave Law and perhaps, as many have suggested, to the Civil War itself. While Dickens's political legacy is less cut-and-dried (scholars argue over the extent to which the social leanings of his fiction can be tied to the passage of any specific legislation), his influence on the next generation of reform writers is inarguable. Justine Murison convincingly demonstrates how mid-century sentimental novels operated via a secularized logic of "faith in exposure," creating a market that placed a moral value on the exposé.[13] Later on, as Laura Fisher has argued, Progressive Era writers of realist reform fiction institutionalized the mandate of sentimental reform fiction that readers "feel right," to quote Stowe's famous "Concluding Remarks" to her novel, channeling these vague feelings into specific, political contexts—just as we might today suggest that "thoughts and prayers" offered on social media be transmuted into political advocacy or campaign contributions.[14]

Many of the writers of reform fiction that emerged at the end of the nineteenth and beginning of the twentieth centuries were realists convinced that their work possessed a significant political instrumentality, often with good reason. Charlotte Perkins Gilman's 1899 short story "The Yellow Wall-Paper" cast much-needed scrutiny on the misogynistic "rest cure" treatment for neurasthenia. In 1913, she published an article titled "Why I Wrote the Yellow Wall-Paper" that declared, "[m]any years later I was told that the great specialist had admitted to friends of his that he had altered his treatment of neurasthenia since reading *The Yellow Wallpaper*. It was not intended to drive people crazy, but to save people from being driven crazy, and it worked."[15] By stating, "it worked," Gilman simultaneously expresses a theory of fiction: that it can, and perhaps should, be possessed of teleological aims and demonstrable outcomes.

Upton Sinclair's *The Jungle* instigated, after an investigation into its veracity commissioned by President Theodore Roosevelt returned corroborating results, the passage of the Pure Food and Drug Act and the Meat Inspection Act, both signed into law seven months after the novel's publication.[16] Fisher documents the raft of journalists turned fiction (or pseudo-fiction) writers who went undercover to document the ills of various institutions of the era ranging from the factory to the workhouse to the asylum, arguing that, "early twentieth-century undercover authors inherited the realist principle that representing everyday regions and figures in all their particularity, authenticity, and locality held political and aesthetic value."[17] The claim to absolute veracity within these works was a central feature of their ability to put the social change their writers desired into effect.

In their commitment to providing almost scientifically accurate documentation of the social ills they protested, Progressive Era writers of reform realist fiction bore a more than a superficial resemblance to the emergent social scientific fields from which they drew—new advances in psychology, sociology, anthropology, and evolutionary biology informed their work and, in turn, the aesthetic strategies of realist fiction informed the practitioners of these new and expanding fields. The British writers sometimes called the "new journalists" of the mid-nineteenth century, who often published in the *Pall Mall Gazette*, were interested in using both literary tactics and new social scientific methods to expose true social ills.[18] Most visible among these writers was Henry Mayhew, whose bestselling sociological account of poverty in London, *London Labour and the London Poor* (1851–1861), renders in grisly, exaggerative detail the lives of the nation's most disenfranchised denizens. A key selling point of Mayhew's work was his use of illustrations that were reproductions of engravings based on early daguerreotypes of street-dwellers. These were touted as remarkably modern in their method and accuracy of depiction.

Advertisements for the series employed photography as a metaphor for the verisimilitude of the work's depiction as a whole, claiming "it would be a work of superogation to extol the utility of such a publication as 'London Labour and the London Poor,' so apparent must its value be to all classes of society. It stands alone as a photograph of life as actually spent by the lower classes of the Metropolis."[19] The "photograph" to which the advertisement refers is the work as a whole—suggesting that the technology of realist prose is of a piece with the new technologies of visual representation: both modern (evidence of scientific progress itself!) and accurate.[20] Later American writers would trade in the techniques they learned from consuming these British textual products as well. The Danish-American journalist and social reformer Jacob Riis's early work was compared in the press to Mayhew's, as well as to the novels of the influential French naturalist writer Émile Zola.[21] Riis's 1890 study of tenement conditions, *How the Other Half Lives*, enjoyed popularity in large part due to its inclusion of striking illustrations made from photographs of tenement residents and their living conditions—images which were then included in the New York Tenement House Act of 1901. That the literary realism of verisimilitude emerged alongside these social scientific disciplines and new photographic technology is a historical truth that has shaped much of realism's critical history.

Literary realism and social reform have a long-recognized sympathetic relationship. Amy Kaplan notes how the realist novel behaves like the reform movements it often describes, "engag[ing] in an enormous act of construction to reorganize, reform, and control the social world."[22] Following David Masson, whose 1859 *British Novelists and Their Styles* offers an early taxonomy of novels that deal with social reform, Amanda Claybaugh suggests four groupings of such works: those that support a specific reform, those that argue against a specific reform, and those that deal with reform as a subject matter only, which she divides into those that side with the reform they depict, and those that do not.[23] I offer a different set of categories here, as my concern is to isolate a debate that these previous critical works leave undescribed, which is along aesthetic rather than exclusively political lines. I will suggest that realist works of fiction that argue for or against specific reforms might be designated as their own genre of "reform realism" and the works that take issue with this literary genre might be considered works of aesthetic realism. I put James's *The Bostonians* (1885–1886) in this second category, for example, because I believe that novel launches a significant critique—not of the aims of the movement it represents as Claybaugh argues—but of the representational strategies of that movement, along with those of the many other novels that advocate for or against such causes.

Aesthetic realism is a response to the aesthetics of reform realism, a genre characterized by copious details of the suffering it seeks to ameliorate or prevent and a moralizing narrative tone that works to forge a sympathetic, reassuring relationship between reader and narrator, usually but not always through the use of direct address. These aesthetic conventions, as Nancy Glazener has observed, worked toward two distinct yet related purposes: "to instruct [readers] about the conditions affecting other constituencies, conditions they might be able to change through philanthropy or limited reforms . . . [and/or] to enhance their sense of cultural entitlement."[24] In order to fulfill these purposes, such works needed to reassure readers of the fidelity of their depiction, and flatter them into believing that reading a text would give them an accurate understanding of the circumstance it portrays—hence the imperative of combining works geared towards reform with a realist style of depiction.

Frame narrators often provide a convenient solution to the problem of generating a feeling of reader-narrator companionship alongside a reassurance of the account's fidelity. The 1895 short story by James William Sullivan "Cohen's Figure" begins with the narrator's confession that "a drama recently added by passing events to my mental repertory . . . repeats itself in my mind every day," then proceeds with a lengthy description of a laborer in the sweatshop where this drama takes place:

> The first operator . . . is dark and gaunt. As he runs his machine he bends far over it. With the motion of his treadle his head rapidly nods and his body slightly sways and jerks. . . . His undershirt is whitish on Monday, and the rest of the week is a deepening blackish. His dark lackluster hair stands out on end. His swart face is oily. His whiskers are a stubble. As he

> works on and on, speeding his machine, his lips are parted; he is pant-
> ing. This man is a typical figure among the operators. All of them are
> work-soiled and shabby; all curve forward at work; all pant.

After this initial onslaught of realist detail, the narrator promises that the subsequent description of the drama will be more realistic still: "The reader, when the story is reminisced to him, will have it played in full in his mind's theater."[25] Like other writers of reform realism, Sullivan relies on objectifying descriptions that paint the poor as animals or children while simultaneously offering praise for himself (for his perspicuity) and his readers (for their compassion).

This proved a highly successful strategy from a commercial perspective. As William Dean Howells's journalist character Bartley Hubbard remarks in *A Modern Instance* (1882), "there is nothing the public enjoys so much as an exposé: it seems to be made in the reader's own interest; it somehow constitutes him a party to the attack upon the abuse and its effectiveness redounds to the credit of all the newspaper's subscribers."[26] The strategy Howells outlines here as a critique of journalism was indeed adopted by many reform realist novelists of the period, many of them journalists themselves, whose works became bestsellers that attracted large audiences on both sides of the Atlantic.

The view of reform realism as a literary "instrument" is shared between works both British and American. Literary exposés of social conditions were popular fodder for the late-nineteenth-century transatlantic culture of reprinting and often such works were issued as companion volumes from each shore—for example, *Tenement Tales of New York* was advertised as "A Companion Volume to *Slum Stories of London*," another 1895 collection written by Henry Woodd Nevinson and also published by Holt.[27] These parallel traditions borrowed from and supported one another. James William Sullivan is only one example of the many American writers—Stephen Crane perhaps the most famous among them—inspired by the British tradition of sociologically minded reform realism.[28]

Just as the meaning of "reform" has a tendency to shift between each new account, the term "realism" has been used to describe many phases and iterations of fiction ranging from the "puritan realism" of Daniel Defoe's *Robinson Crusoe* (1719) and Susan Warner's *The Wide, Wide World* (1850) that Sharon Kim describes to the "speculative realism" of Salvador

Plascencia's *The People of Paper* (2005), according to Ramón Saldívar.[29] Perhaps because, like reform, the term "realism" has become so capacious, there are few narratives about its resistance that don't fall back on its eventual subordination to literary modernism—in regards not only to its innovations in form and style, but also insofar as it engages with any form of political enterprise. In some of these accounts, the opacity of modernist style emerges as a kind of deus ex machina that solves the political problems of literary realism. Brad Evans's essay in the most recent edition of the *Oxford Handbook to American Literary Realism* nicely articulates this position as one that holds American literary realism to be the "historical flyover country" between Romanticism and modernism. Evans locates the modernist affinity for the aesthetic within realism in writers who were explicitly anti-realist, who published in the "proto-modernist, fin-de-siècle magazines" known as "ephemeral bibelots."[30] These works were modernist in style but realist in historical moment. In the American context, Evans argues, aestheticism is a foreign notion incompatible with both culturally American and aesthetically realist values. Evans cites Rebecca Harding Davis's "Life in the Iron-Mills" (1861) as an example of a realist story that allegorizes the inability of the aesthete to survive within the nineteenth-century American industrial context. This assessment is an apt one, and I especially agree with Evans's conclusion that modernism is just as much a part of the tradition of American literary realism as is American Romanticism; yet, I see Davis—and her influential story—as an early entrant into a different aesthetic tradition that this book outlines.

While Henry James takes Davis's 1867 novel *Waiting for the Verdict* as an example of the very type of reform realism he condemned, "Life in the Iron-Mills" exhibits a critical, slant take on reform realist aesthetics not dissimilar to James's own much later work in *The Princess Casamassima* (1886).[31] Both texts tell, through highly ironicized narration, the story of a working-class, effeminate aesthete unwittingly caught up in a politicized encounter with their class others, which they enter through the practice of their art. Both characters' plots end in suicide. "Life in the Iron-Mills," in my reading, not only protests the impossibility of the aesthetic within the oppressive conditions of labor it depicts as Evans proposes; it also demonstrates the impossibility of the aesthetic within a politicized version of class-touristic, literary realism. "A reality of soul-starvation, of living death, that meets you every day under the besotted faces on the street," Davis's hostile narrator states, "I can paint nothing of this, only give you the outside outlines."[32] Such a confession (an inability to *paint*—not even daguerreotype, a verb often used for the process of prose description in the period, e.g. Stowe's assertion that "as [Tom] is to be the hero of our story, we must daguerreotype [him] for our readers") suggests that the medium of fiction is unable to communicate the actual, day-to-day "reality" of subaltern lives to bourgeois readers.[33] The narrator's refusal to stand behind her own depiction is a direct affront to the promise of reform realism to accurately render the scenes of oppression it describes and a gauntlet thrown down to readers who believe that by accessing such fictions they are able to know, understand, or aid its subjects.

Aesthetic realism is therefore marked by a rejection of the realist claim toward mimetic accuracy and an ironic relation to its own political content which is alternately tragic (the deaths of the revolutionary failed artists Hugh Wolfe, Edna Pontellier, or James's Hyacinth Robinson) and comic (the satirical depictions of "bad" reformers like Chopin's hack journalist Miss Witherwell or Wharton's Pauline Manford of the 1927 novel *Twilight Sleep.*) The dualism of irony is a mark, in their minds, of both high thought and high art. (Recall that among James's complaints to Child is the observation that the political animals of London are "literal.") In *The Art of Fiction*, her manifesto on writerly values, Wharton states, "the chief difference between the merely sympathetic and the creative imagination is that the latter is two-sided, and combines with the power of penetrating into other minds that of standing far enough aloof from them to see beyond, and relate them to the whole stuff of life out of which they but partially emerge."[34] This is necessarily a political vision—one that resists the presumption of similarity required by the structures of sympathy in favor of a "two-sidedness," a sentiment uttered repeatedly in works of aesthetic realism, as when Rebecca Harding Davis insists "the man who sees both sides of the shield may be right, but he is most uncomfortable"—and indeed an uncomfortable, ironic relation to her subject matter marks much of Davis's own writing.[35] As Matthew Stratton suggests, though the political criticism of the mid-twentieth century defanged irony as a serious political method, the use and concept of irony within literature nonetheless allowed for a "specifically amoral and nonetheless ethical and activist politics predicated upon literary aesthetics changing individual and collective dispositions towards facts and values."[36] The frequently ironic positions of narrators and characters in works of aesthetic realism have produced critical readings that disavow any political energy within the fiction, even when the fiction seems to be dealing with political themes. Adopting this ironic stance within the realist tradition, aesthetic realists attempted to change what Stratton describes as "individual and collective dispositions towards facts and values" within the political conversations of literary realism that have long been understood to have played a significant role in inventing the very facts that needed changing. William Dean Howells famously claimed that "the very highest fiction is that which treats itself as fact," and, given its commitment to accuracy in representation and its emergence alongside the social scientific disciplines that, as David Shi and others have noted, traded in the new cultural value of the fact itself, literary realism has long been seen as having engaged in literal sociopolitical work—alternately for the better and for the worse.[37]

Early critical approaches to political, realist literature celebrated its efficacy as a political tool and its contribution to a version of liberal politics that largely aligned with the goals of the twentieth-century American university. From the vantage point of 1927, the influential critic Vernon L. Parrington saw realism as an optimistic genre productively engaged with world changing, possessed of a "confidence in the power of men to alter the world that they live in," and in contrast to literary naturalism, which he thought understood the world as "generally unresponsive."[38] At the mid-century, Lionel Trilling would argue that it is the faculty of imagination that makes a realist writer like James, in his strategic indeterminacy, superior to a naturalist like Theodore Dreiser, whose explicitly Marxist agenda had made him a critical darling of the liberal academy.[39] For Trilling, "liberalism," like "realism" and "reform" for so many writers and critics, was both what he championed and argued against. In the wake of the ascendancy of the hermeneutics of suspicion that defined a school of literary criticism throughout the 1980s and 1990s, the dominant literary critical position on social realism shifted yet again, as scholars like Mark Seltzer and Amy Kaplan began to describe realism as a tool of social control masquerading as social criticism. The popularity of Michel Foucault and his best-known metaphor, the Benthamite panopticon, within American literary circles solidified this period's critical association between many Progressive Era reform movements and their roots in the reform movements of British utilitarianism. In 1993, Kaplan observed in her foundational work *The Social Construction of American Realism* that "changes in the historical understanding of realism have accompanied the reevaluation of realism's political stance, from a progressive force exposing social conditions to a conservative force complicit with capitalist relations."[40] I identify the genre that aesthetic realists were writing against as "reform realism" because, as I have described, the success of instrumentalized reform texts was so often rooted in their adherence to the techniques of verisimilitudinous realism. Hence the objections of aesthetic realism are to the reformist use of realist tactics of representation, and to realist tactics of representation that traffic too heavily in the politics of reform.

WRITING AGAINST REFORM

"Reformers: A Hymn of Hate," a satirical poem by Dorothy Parker, first appeared in a 1922 volume called *Nonsensorship*, a collection of works by writers protesting both artistic censorship and prohibition. The yoking of the two concerns addressed by the collection is telling, and Parker's "nonsense" poem underscores a more widespread perceived connection between the rise of reform and the decline of literature and the arts. As Parker writes of reformers: "Their aim is to keep art and letters in their place . . . They will never feel really themselves / Until every theatre in the country is razed."[41] Such satires tip us off to a deep-seated antipathy between the social movements of the period and some of the producers and defenders of its arts and literature. Parker, who would later go on to become an activist for civil rights and antifascism, is nevertheless highly critical of any social movement that impinges upon artistic freedom or attempts to reconceive of the function of art along political lines. This is an anti-reform position that transcends the political content of the debates of reform themselves. Susan Ryan writes that "[political] opponents of particular reform movements characterized their adherents as radicals committed to undermining the stability of the nation"—an accurate description of political actors who opposed specific reforms (and reformers) on political grounds. The aesthetic critique of reform differs in that it tends to depict fictional reformers who are not radical but vain and often comically ineffective, like Mrs. Spear in Wharton's *Hudson River Bracketed*, who creates gatherings of "dowdy middle-aged conformists" she "still called revolutionaries."[42] Their fear is not that the aesthetic and rhetorical strategies of reform will work—it's that they feel convinced they won't. The suggestion in the depiction of these fictional characters is that their very impotence in the guise of action will undermine the aesthetic power of literature, not that their danger lies in a radicalism that may rend the national fabric through radical political action.

Their rejection of reform was both a negative reaction to its aesthetic tendencies and mass popularity as well as a defense of the primacy of aesthetic experience to their own understanding of personal and social change. Rather than producing timely literature that would stake its claim in the debates that captured the imagination and conscience of their moment, these writers—in different ways—all took a literary stand against the incursion of such dualistic political debates into the culture in general and into literary fiction in particular, revealing a skepticism towards the political efficacy and artistic integrity of work that explicitly champions political causes. They were individualists who believed that social change comes from personal development rather than collective persuasion and contrarians who rejected the binaristic logic of American politics.

Aesthetic realists tend to take a dialectical course in response to seemingly all questions rather than concede to a definitive position. For example, when a journalist asked Kate Chopin if she smokes cigarettes, she responded: "Suppose I do smoke cigarettes? Am I going to tell it out in a meeting? Suppose I don't smoke cigarettes. Am I going to admit such a reflection upon my artistic integrity, and thereby bring upon myself the contempt of the guild?"[43] Chopin's sarcastic reference to "the guild" is also typical of her feelings about belonging echoed in her review of Zola's *Lourdes*: "It is hard to understand in Mons. Zola this persistent desire to be admitted to the Academy. One would suppose he would be content, even proud, to stand outside of its doors."[44] Indeed, all of the authors in this study stood, to varying degrees, outside of the doors of clubs and institutions. "I never belonged to a club nor any kind of society," Rebecca Harding Davis wrote, "I never made a speech and never wanted to do it."[45] They rejected politics on the grounds of its aesthetic poverty and therefore, counterintuitively, its inability to affect durable change.

At the center of the revelation of this countertradition lies the question of what it means to criticize the direct political use of literature. Kenneth Warren identifies two approaches to the relationship between literature and social protest in the African American literature of this period: the "instrumental," work that directly opposes a social order predicated on white supremacy; and the "indexical," work that highlights black cultural achievement. Seeing these categories as neither mutually exclusive nor totalizing,

Warren nevertheless does not directly consider how an indexical view of the relationship between literature and social progress might also serve as a critique of the instrumentality of art and literature in its own right.[46] The writers who appear in *Writing Against Reform* would certainly be far closer to the camp of the indexical in Warren's model, in that they consciously resist making overt arguments for political causes within the context of their fiction and prefer to make visible their own aesthetic genealogies through allusion, reference, and the composition of literary criticism. Several conditions unite their points of view:

1) a desire to remain apart from organized movements or coherent political positions
2) a reverence for history and the cultural works of the past
3) a tendency to cultivate a complex narrative strategy that unsettles rather than comforts their readers
4) a resistance to the idea of literature as instrumental
5) a rejection of the notion of "progress" as an objective good.

It was the popular and powerful idea of progress itself that the writers I discuss here most uniformly rejected—an idea that mobilized not only the social reform projects of the period but also its literary realism. As Louis J. Budd writes, "nineteenth-century science undercut the ancient theories that humankind moves in recurring cycles; instead, the doctrine or myth of progress sprang into many-faceted dominance."[47] The aesthetic realist rejection of the notion of progress was, first, on the grounds that such an idea is too closely linked to consumer capitalism. As Rebecca Harding Davis wrote in a 1902 editorial, "The National progress of which we boast so loudly just now does not mean advance in science, in art, or learning, or in the nobility or distinction of individual life, but simply commercial progress."[48] Despite her own tendencies toward prejudice and intellectual snobbery, Edith Wharton rejected the concept of "progress" because she saw how it was only applicable to a select few. As Carol Singley notes, "Wharton differed from her elite group in her rejection of [an] upper-class, secular, self-justifying view of progress ... [that] conveniently ignored vast numbers of individuals for whom 'progress' did not mean improvement."[49] Furthermore, as I demonstrate in the fifth chapter of this book, Wharton worried that the devotion to progress within the context of literature would make second-class citizens of history and cultural tradition, a view she shared with James Weldon

Johnson. Johnson asked the important question of how social progress can be measured—and what dangers will arise from poorly considered metrics. He defined a distinction between progress in "thought-power" and progress in "numbers-power and wealth-power," recognizing that "a people may increase in both numbers and wealth, and yet not make real progress."[50] Johnson was concerned that the race movement's single-minded political crusade might diminish or sideline the importance of literature and the arts—the "thought power" of African American people and the nation as a whole. He feared that if African American literature came to be understood as an explicitly political project that protested the conditions of Jim Crow America, Black writers would be segregated from the canon and too closely tied to the present moment rather than a longstanding and durable tradition. Still another concern was that such a focus would further obscure the vast contributions African Americans had already made to what was falsely understood to be a white American culture. For Johnson, the political progress African Americans sought shouldn't come at the expense of the recognition of the African American cultural tradition. A future that did not contain this past was simply another injustice to him.

In its rejection of the notion of progress, aesthetic realism bears some relation to what T. J. Jackson Lears calls the antimodern tradition. His study *No Place of Grace* (1981) describes what might be thought of as a variety of antimodern types, from the Arts and Crafts-era artisan/businessman who fetishizes medieval design like Gustav Stickley, to the back-to-the-earth therapeutic movements of the late nineteenth century championed by medical professionals like Silas Weir Mitchell, to the fetishization of the masculinist archaic warrior ideal by men like Henry Cabot Lodge and Frank Norris. Yet Lears also has a tendency to conflate aesthetic and political conservatism, ultimately arguing that "the most profound radicalism is often the most profound conservatism," a statement which, I think, elides its qualifying terms, which I imagine might read like this: "the most profound radicalism *in culture* is often *linked to* the most profound conservatism *in politics*."[51] His is an accurate and compelling account of how reactionary politics emerged among elite populations in the Progressive Era, but other kinds of stories from this period lie beyond its scope. Lears's keen observation that oftentimes the reembracing of past aesthetic values can be a radical gesture doesn't necessarily, however, signal a concomitant return to past politics. The main protagonists of Lears's antimodern world are almost exclusively well-heeled white men using a connection to the past to hold on to the power they sensed to be slipping away from them, and indeed, the currents of the period's rabid nativism run through almost all of his examples. In Lears's account and the accounts of the rise of modernist aesthetics alongside the rise of fascism, a privileging of aesthetics over or as politics is often associated with regressive or reactionary political orientations. For subjects who do not fall into politically dominant categories, however, an aesthetic return to the past and/or a belief in the power of aesthetics to effect social change takes on a decidedly different significance.[52]

Aesthetic realism consists largely—if not entirely—of writers who fall outside of American white male heterosexuality. Frequently criticized for being overly "Europeanized," which is often a turn-of-the-century code word for non-heteronomative orientations (indeed, the only mention of Henry James in *No Place of Grace* is to note that Van Wyck Brooks considered him "the personification of 'feminized' European aestheticism,") aesthetic realists understood their own alterity in relation to an aesthetic tradition that valued the quality of the art produced over the identity of the producer at a time when realism, with its commitments to regionalism and fiction representative of racial and ethnic types, encouraged the primacy of sociopolitical identity.[53] This is both a sociopolitical and an aesthetic stance, as the nature of their alterity extends to a long-held assumption about American literary realism, which is that, as Kaplan describes this position, it is "an inherently flawed imitation of a European convention."[54] If American realism was, as Howells imagined, designed to offer a democratic representation of every class and type of American, these aesthetic realists—more invested as they were in the aesthetic strategies of their European counterparts—created new and different forms of realist representation that would account for the essentially non-democratic nature of American democracy. In a complex and imperfect way that, I hope, will be gradually revealed over the course of the examples that populate the body of this book, the privileging of the aesthetic over—and *as*—the political allowed these writers to envision a sense of community beyond the boundaries of sociopolitical identity.

James Weldon Johnson saw his work to be of a piece with that of Henry James and Edith Wharton, and their work to have been, in turn, influenced by Alexandre Dumas. Wharton described herself as a "citizen in the Land of Letters," a nation which we can imagine included Marcel Proust, an author about whom she wrote prolifically and with unabashed admiration in spite of her well-documented personal anti-Semitism.[55] I do not seek to weave together or endorse the individual political positions of the authors I use as my examples, but instead try to delineate their critiques of the guiding notion of reform realism that social change is best achieved through the explicit politicization of literature. I identify in the structures of their thought what I believe to be a profound argument for the value of a literary tradition that exists outside of the confines of liberal understandings of value.

Though the authors treated in this book by no means constitute the entirety of what I'm calling aesthetic realism, I have decided to use authorship as an organizing principle, centering each chapter primarily on a single writer to allow for a holistic consideration of their theory of the relationship between aesthetics and politics, the literary and the social. The writers I've chosen were all actively engaged in the work of literary criticism as well as that of fiction writing throughout their careers. In studying the idiosyncrasies of their critiques and distinctions between "good" and "bad" realisms, I discovered how what "realism" means to an individual author is deeply indicative of that author's sociopolitical worldview.[56] Rebecca Harding Davis's journalistic work—much of it about the literature of her period as well as its social causes—gives us an unusual lens through which to process her fiction. So, too, does the well-known criticism of Henry James and Edith Wharton. Kate Chopin's work as a reviewer and student of literature is lesser known but, I would argue, likewise crucial to any complex understanding of her thought. And James Weldon Johnson's writings not only on the history of American literature in his capacity as an educator, but also on the value of the aesthetic in his many essays and addresses on what he calls "the art approach to the negro problem" lend depth to any interpretation of his only novel. I orient myself, with these writers, as a theorist of fiction but one—and certainly not the only one—who contends that fictions quite frequently theorize themselves. I agree with Rancière's assessment that often "the explanatory models" critics use "to tell the truth about the literary texts are models forged by literature itself."[57] Recent interlocutors in post-critique debates have called for a movement away from critique as the hegemonic mode of criticism. Rita Felski writes,

> The literary text is not a museum piece immured behind glass but a spirited and energetic participant in an exchange—one that may know as much as, or a great deal more than, the critic. This text impinges and bears on the reader across time and space; as a mood changer, a

reconfigurer of perception, a plenitude of stylistic possibilities, an aid to thought.[58]

Felski's admonition broadens our sense of what literature does and reminds us that both literature and politics are engaged in similar endeavors: representation, world-making, and social connection. While I do not wish to stake a claim in the rich debates of critique per se, I do applaud the way in which post-critique critics like Felski have urged a return to the centrality of the literary text and especially to the view of the text as a living, changing thing. This I learned not, initially, from reading the criticism—but from my experience of the fiction itself.

My method here positions each writer as having formed a theory of fiction that is evidenced across the breadth of their work—both fictional and non-fictional. I understand these theories, because of the historical moment in which these writers were imbedded, to be most visible and compelling in their relation to political reform and the popularity of its depiction in and advancement through realist literature. I want to think with, not strictly about, these writers. Though I focus on certain key texts that most clearly engage with the issues this book takes up, I look at their oeuvres holistically, treating them as theorists in the longue durée of the attempt to unpack what Bentley calls "the Gordian knot" of aesthetics and politics: "culture is aesthetic because it is beyond politics, and therefore political precisely because it is aesthetic."[59]

Though this work of criticism, like most others, draws in critical backgrounds and occasionally turns to relevant theorists of the questions these writers take up, it does not do so to explain their work or say what they could not. The furthest-reaching stakes of this project are to seek a way of imagining a different critical relationship to literature and the assertion of its value beyond determining whether it is liberatory or oppressive, reflective of progressive or conservative ideologies. Furthermore and especially, I want to avoid using extra-disciplinary sources as test cases for the values of the literature itself. We might suggest that to understand the position on aesthetics asserted in *The Autobiography of an Ex-Colored Man*, we must turn to Schiller; and yet a close reading of that novel alongside Johnson's own essays would yield similar conclusions. The constant gesturing outward that has long been a hallmark of literary studies may unintentionally imply that literature is not enough, that in its indirection it cannot be used seriously to understand our most pressing questions, and that it must merely function as a complex set of examples that can illustrate insights generated elsewhere. In perpetuating such a method, we concede to fiction's fiercest critics, buying into the idea that it is merely play or documentation (accusations most frequently lodged at realist texts)—not serious thought in its own right. But, as Peter Brooks reminds us, the art of realist fiction is akin to the art of scale model and, as such, offers us a unique chance to "play" at the world in miniature.[60] I agree with Brooks that such play cannot be dismissed as idle distraction or entertainment; nor, I will argue here, does it require the explicitly political to lend it the seriousness realists since Howells and James have demanded it deserves.

All of the writers in this study have been identified as vanguards of new genres. Rebecca Harding Davis is widely cited as a significant, early pioneer of American naturalism; Kate Chopin and Edith Wharton, as perhaps most famously described by Elizabeth Ammons in 1992, are often thought to be the earliest examples of a transition within American female writers from popular sentimentalism to high-cultural authorship.[61] Countless critics have identified Henry James as the key transitional figure between both British and American realism and modernism. James Weldon Johnson is, on the contrary, often overlooked as an author in critical works because his own poetry and fiction predate the Harlem Renaissance he was central to producing. In a sense their avant-gardism (or, in the Case of Johnson and Wharton, both avant-gardism *and* perceived belatedness) signal a general atemporality that comes from engaging with a broad range of aesthetic influences long in scope rather than an adherence to a particular literary or thematic style that more clearly references the concerns of the present moment. But this is not to imply that they wrote shuttered in libraries, unaware of the powerful currents that were shaping the physical world in which they lived—only that the volumes on their shelves were as significant a part of that world for them as the action in its streets. It's a position that should not, I think, feel alien to anyone who has used the present tense to write about a text written many years before they were born. This book argues that these literary advances were possible in large part because of their authors' rejection of dominant modes of understanding the relationship between aesthetics and politics.

My first chapter reads the work of Rebecca Harding Davis against the emergent celebrity cultures of political reform and authorship. While Davis is frequently cited as a social agitator and a pioneer of protest fiction, a closer consideration of her oeuvre reveals a deep resistance to the triangulated relationship between consumer capitalism, authorial celebrity, and political reform projects. Davis writes against reform through satirical and even villainous portrayals of reformers. Her critique of celebrity culture is of a piece with her depiction of spectacular sites of reform like the rostrum or the titular progressive colony depicted in her novel *Berrytown* (1873). Such sites are aligned with spaces of industrial capitalism like the factory and the World's Fair—spaces she positions in opposition to libraries and artistic workrooms. Davis's struggling artist characters, like the sculptor Hugh Wolfe of "Life in the Iron-Mills" (1861) and the titular pianist of her story "Blind Tom" (1862), are oppressed by many forces: slavery, industrial capitalism, the marketplace, and the rhetoric of reform itself. While the subjects of reform realist fiction are depicted as passive objects representative of broader suffering, Davis repeatedly casts her subaltern characters as artists, emphasizing that aesthetic representation—not reform rhetoric—holds the potential for shaping more egalitarian worldviews. Her ironic realism resists the notion that fiction can provide an accurate depiction of social realities, pitting the mimetic strategies of reform writing against more literary depictions that actively engage the subject of art.

Like Davis, Kate Chopin saw an opposition between artistic work—fiction she considered to be of literary merit—and reform realism. The second chapter demonstrates Chopin's critique of the censorship campaigns and moralistic fiction associated with the Social Purity movement. Chopin's own fictions depict mimetic artists incapable of sexual or artistic expression. *The Awakening*'s Edna Pontellier is a copier rather than an innovator—a dilettante artist whose subjects (a Bavarian peasant, a basket of apples, a "young Italian character study") are deliberately clichéd references to mimetic realism.[62] Chopin's 1897 review of Thomas Hardy's 1895 *Jude the Obscure* exports the language of the Social Purity reviewers of the novel, who composed histrionic attacks on its depiction of extramarital sex, to mount a criticism of how such reviewers—more than one themselves Social Purity novelists—changed the landscape of realist fiction. It was Chopin's view that the genre of reform realism was formulaic and unimaginative, that the commercial success of such works could be attributed to its ties to the highly visible sex panic of Social Purity reformers rather than to literary skill or innovation. In the second chapter, I argue that Chopin's response to the sex panic of her moment constituted an "art panic" of her own—a fear that the Social Purity movement would drive innovative work connected to the literary traditions of the past out of the marketplace, tracing this art panic through her novels and stories, which satirically portray bad artists incapable of either depicting or experiencing authentic sexual relationships and bad reformers bent on foiling works of art.

While Davis and Chopin saw an opposition between political writing and artistic writing, Henry James set out to destabilize any discourse that would hold art and politics in opposition. James's use of realist style in the mid-period novels I consider in the third chapter draws attention to the primacy of subject matter in contemporary realist works motivated by reformist impulses. His fictions and criticism demonstrate how both reform and realism are possessed of an insidious anti-aesthetic that purports to be transparent or disinterested. I argue that, in *The Princess Casamassima* (1886) and *The Bostonians* (1886), novels that chart the failure of anarchist and woman movement goals, James protests a specific form of reform realism that I call "demographic realism," wherein the use of an individual character as a stand-in for a subjugated group of people renders that individual flat or inhuman. James uses the plot of *The Bostonians* to expose the problems of demographic realism through the reformer Olive Chancellor and her anti-reform cousin Basil Ransom's sexual competition for the women's rights lecturer Verena Tarrant. Olive and Basil's battle for Verena's love and attention is a representation of two models of intimacy that allegorize different aesthetic strategies of courting the reader within the realist novel itself: one that operates via earnest political content and another that operates via a self-negating, sarcastic style. I argue that in depicting Basil's victory over Olive, James advocates for a political style modeled on a mode of relating Candace Vogler has described as "depersonalizing intimacy," which he sees as a more powerful spark for social change than political rhetoric or the accretion of realist detail. Read in this way, the novel is not a stopgap on the way to a full-fledged modernist repudiation of realist techniques, but its own significant form of realism that undertakes an engagement with—rather than an outright rejection of—the form and politics of the reform realist novel.[63]

The final two chapters of *Writing Against Reform* consider writers who not only—like Davis, Chopin, and James—engaged with reform realist conventions in innovative ways, but also leveraged their commitment to the broader field of arts and letters to mount social projects that responded to the political emergencies of their period without sacrificing the autonomy of the aesthetic sphere. The fourth chapter describes an effort by James Weldon Johnson that spanned various media and venues to promulgate new works of African American literature and culture that would simultaneously be artistically innovative and educational—teaching the public the value and significance of the African American cultural past. In addition to his political work for the NAACP, Johnson gave lectures across the country, tracing popular American artistic forms executed by white artists to their roots in African American culture. This formal project was a deeply political act for Johnson, a figure who many critics and scholars have dismissed as insufficiently political.[64] Contrary to this view, I suggest Johnson understood American political discourse, unlike American artistic culture, to be organized around a set of white ideas and principles. During his unsuccessful fight in the halls of the nation's capital to pass a federal anti-lynching bill, Johnson came to the conclusion that African Americans must use what they themselves pioneered in the realm of art to develop a new aesthetic language of protest politics formally unmoored from the race movement's antecedents in white abolitionism. I demonstrate the ideological links between his only novel, the 1912 *Autobiography of an Ex-Colored Man*, his research into lynching for the NAACP, his anthologizing of black spirituals and poetry, and his orchestration of the 1917 Negro Silent Protest Parade—an event that pioneered the stirring performative social protests of the twentieth-century civil rights movement as well as those of today. Johnson learned what he used from his reading and practice in the realm of high literary culture to engage in more effective political activism, rather than treating literature itself as a site of political work.

Edith Wharton likewise learned to separate her political projects from her literary work while leveraging her literary knowledge and connections to reformist ends. The final chapter demonstrates her ultimate rejection of reform realist aesthetics, visible in the tensions between style and content in her early social problem novel *The Fruit of the Tree* (1907) and her unflattering and withering fictional and non-fictional portrayals of reformers. As Jennie Kasanoff notes, "Since 1921, when Vernon L. Parrington dismissed Wharton as a 'literary aristocrat' who was preoccupied with 'rich nobodies,' Wharton's conservative politics have been treated as an obstacle to literary analysis." Instead of reading Wharton's rejection of reform politics as evidence of her conservatism or her removal from political engagement,

I show how the history of her volunteerism during the First World War resists this interpretation. Her 1914 establishment of the American Hostels for Refugees, her 1915 establishment of the Children of Flanders Rescue Committee, her organization of a tubercular hospital for soldiers, and her volunteerism across the continent for the Red Cross all bespeak a deep engagement with philanthropic and humanitarian projects.[65] I argue that the anthology she produced to fund the charitable organizations she herself founded, the 1916 *Book of the Homeless*, stands as a model of practical literary engagement with the political that eschews the structures of sympathy enacted by the reform realist novel, which she saw as both aesthetically and politically problematic. At the end of the chapter, and in conclusion, I consider how the techniques of reform realism inform the cause-related marketing efforts and performative activism of today's reform movements.

I do not, in illuminating the countertradition to reform realism and tracing its legacy to the present day, mean in any way to diminish the import and positive good of the many accomplishments of the political reform movements of the Progressive Era themselves. Nor, it should be underscored, did aesthetic realists broadly criticize the political aims of reform. Indeed, as this book will demonstrate, many engaged in extensive, non-radical political activism on their own terms. Their critique is, for the most part, of the representational strategies that the movements employed, strategies bound up with the techniques of literary realism that entered into how their aims were enacted to create long-lasting, often negative, side effects. Writing this book has reminded me that representation is an action with real consequences of the most durable sort and, therefore, the writing and reading of fiction can be more than a means of achieving social good. It is a social good in itself.

PART ONE
Against Reform

CHAPTER ONE

REBECCA HARDING DAVIS AND CELEBRITY REFORM

What have aimless imagination and temporizing policy to do with the Advancement of Mankind?

—Rebecca Harding Davis, *Kitty's Choice; or, a Story of Berrytown*

Though her national career began in 1861 with the publication of "Life in the Iron-Mills" in *The Atlantic*, Rebecca Harding Davis has been critically tied to literary movements we tend to associate with later periods. Following an early interpretation by Malcolm Cowley, "Life" is most frequently read as deterministic fiction invested in the principles of social Darwinism and stripped of the moralizing markers of the sentimental realism of her peers—most notably that of Elizabeth Stuart Phelps, to whom she's often compared.[1] But the effect of her stylistic omissions and additions is also entirely different from that of the writers we traditionally associate with American naturalism—writers like Stephen Crane, Frank Norris, and Theodore Dreiser. The critically uncomfortable between-ness of "Life" (neither wholly naturalist nor sentimental) is perhaps most visible in the story's ending, which is often noted to be incongruous with its naturalistic style throughout.[2] In the final pages, Davis adopts a spiritual tone, rescuing her downtrodden heroes through the intervention of a disinterested Quaker patroness. The "years of sunshine, and fresh air, and slow, patient Christ-love" offered to Deb, the only one of the two protagonists who survives at the end of the story, strongly suggest a sentimental Christian reading.[3] The other protagonist, Deb's cousin Hugh, a talented sculptor, kills himself in prison. By focusing on his plot, critics have been able to retain the characterization of Davis as a pessimistic determinist.[4] Those who focus on the Deb plot to emphasize the story's interest in spiritual redemption place Davis more squarely within the sentimental tradition of its time. This chapter will suggest that the Christian spirituality of the Deb plot is just one of the many generic conventions Davis employs to gesture towards the liberating potential of art.[5] Dana Seitler argues that the story's straddling of multiple genres constitutes a "foregrounding of the aesthetic problem of what forms of representation exist or do not exist at any given moment that make imaginable new forms of personhood or even social change."[6] I'd like to suggest that this aesthetic problem, first posed in "Life," began a decades-long career of confronting the strategies of representation developed and popularized by reform realist fiction and reform movements themselves. I begin with an examination of Davis's career and her relationship to reform realism because not only does her career span the period between the Civil War and World War I during which the majority of the issues this book will take up are most relevant, she is also remarkably early to address the polarization between an overvaluation of aesthetics that would look like an art-for-art's-sake aestheticism and a liberal reform realism that, I argue, define the central oppositional terms of literary culture at the end of the century. Neither a sentimental realist, nor a Darwinian naturalist, nor a proto-modernist aesthete, Davis negotiates the complex relationship between art and politics during this crucial period in modern transatlantic print culture.

What makes Davis's mode so distinct, beyond its protonaturalism or even protoaestheticism, is its rejection of the tenets of identity- and property-based culture that are so central to the ideology of the transatlantic sentimental fiction of the period. Jeff Nunokawa's study of mid-century British fiction, *The Afterlife of Property* (1994), argues that property and its associated values of domesticity and security provide a refuge from "the mean streets of the cash nexus."[7] Yet Davis was early to see the problems of constructing the self through property inheritance and ownership. The very security offered by the spoils of marriage and the ownership of the home also limit the self to a discrete set of identifications—ways of being that enforce not only what one says or does, but more significantly how those actions will be interpreted by society at large. Furthermore, the securing of property for the purpose of inheritance is at the root of the injustices of class stratification to which Davis's work so strongly objects. What emerges as a solution in her oeuvre is a belief in the power of art to liberate individuals from the oppressive categories of identity and the limitations on self-development enforced by property-based society.

Davis's fictions reflect a preoccupation with the limitations that the artist's individual body (and its concomitant implication of a single, coherent identity) pose on his or her work. In multiple fictional portrayals of artist characters, authorial identity is divided between representations of artist, artwork, and spectators that thematize the often-contradictory needs and desires of the producer of literature within the socially conservative and highly competitive world of nineteenth-century publishing. As speaking engagements and international tours became a part of the job description of major transatlantic authors like Charles Dickens and Harriet Beecher Stowe, so too did the negotiation of a successful public persona which was just as much a part of the creative enterprise of nineteenth-century authorship as was the production of texts. Sarah Ruffing Robbins describes how Stowe negotiated competing demands to appear in public as a successful author/reformer without sacrificing her femininity by bringing her family with her on speaking tours and maintaining a posture of feminine demureness that Robbins identifies as a hallmark of "the traveling benevolent lady celebrity," connecting Stowe's public work as an author/reformer to twentieth-century "traveling benevolent lady celebrities" like Oprah Winfrey, Princess Diana, and Angelina Jolie.[8] Not only was celebrity like Stowe's itself a cultural commodity, but such celebrity also occasioned the production of physical commodities whose sales padded authors' reputations, if not always, prior to international copyright, their pockets. Many studies have focused on the ways in which *Uncle Tom's Cabin* became a merchandizing juggernaut.[9] But Stowe herself also became a large part of the culture industry her work produced. Barbara Hochman describes how the 1898 Appleton edition of *Uncle Tom's Cabin*, which included two portraits of Stowe within the text and a third portrait of the Maine home where she wrote *Uncle Tom's Cabin*, presents the novel as "a book that provides a reliably documented historical perspective on a famous author."[10] In 1899, *The Connecticut Magazine Company* offered readers who delivered five new subscribers to the magazine the reward of a "Harriet Beecher Stowe Souvenir Spoon," which they promised "is a work of art and makes a beautiful historical souvenir."[11] Brenda Weber describes how Fanny Fern, following the success of her bestselling novel *Ruth Hall* (1854), had "perfumes, steamboats, babies, and cigars named after her."[12] By this time, the persona of the author was inseparable from her work. This was especially true of author/reformers because their public persona was the link that bound their fiction to their public activism.

Loren Glass examines the emergence of the modern American celebrity author, a phenomenon she ties directly to the changing nature of author/reader binaries as a result of the proliferation of nineteenth-century print culture, observing that "the national mass public came to consist of potential authors and cultural producers; readers became theoretically interchangeable with the famous authors whose texts they read."[13] Glass positions this as a perilous development for the author, productive of anxiety and even bad art. At times, Davis openly expressed her concerns about the power of an emerging literary middle class; yet, she also found powerful tools for her literary activism in the ever-expanding base of readers and the increasingly ambiguous position of the author in the production and distribution of texts. Within her works and outside of them, in her strategies of publication, Davis's career epitomizes the decay of a clear self/other or inside/outside relationship that Glass describes. By rejecting the culture and generic conventions of celebrity reform authorship, Davis envisions the work of art as a means through which multiple individuals can identify without the constraints of adherence to a single, coherent identity. Such a rejection of the reification of authorial identity amounted to a protest of both the increasing commercialization of literature and, perhaps even more significantly, of the celebrity-driven political reform industry.

SUBMERGED RENOWN

Though she published more than five hundred stories, essays, and novels in some of the most prominent national periodicals in the United States throughout the second half of the nineteenth century, almost nothing was known about Rebecca Harding Davis's life by the public. Throughout her career, Davis would take careful measures to prevent a public association between the different personae she would adopt as a writer and her biographical identity. She refused to be interviewed and photographed on multiple occasions, and even the autobiography she reluctantly published in 1904 after much urging from editors—as its title, *Bits of Gossip*, suggests—deals far more with the details of the lives of the many famous individuals in her circle than it does with the details of her own life.[14] Though she was a bestselling author and a regular fixture of the elite Philadelphia literary circles in which her family moved, only one known photograph of Davis survives today.[15]

Scholars have begun to examine the significance of nineteenth-century writers' reluctance to be profiled or photographed. Michael Kearns's study of Emily Dickinson and Herman Melville makes the unlikely link between those two authors on the basis of their mutual disinterest in highly commercial publication and self-promotion. Both writers, Kearns points out, would not supply photographs upon request. For Kearns, this refusal is consistent with a desire to separate the body of the author from the reception of the work as well as distaste for the seemingly de rigueur cultivation of an authorial brand. Kearns identifies how the author photograph located the work in a distinct temporal moment: "for a writer with an eye toward immortality," he writes, "Melville and Dickinson felt, photographs were a mark of failure."[16] For Davis, photographs not only tied an author to his or her own era, but also to a single, embodied existence that fixed boundaries on the interpretation of their texts. The image of a single author's body would limit the varied professional identities Davis actively cultivated in print.

In his autobiography, Mark Twain recounts an exchange with Robert Louis Stevenson, wherein the two authors speculate about the role of fame in the production of literature. They decide that the prolific author who purposefully does not cultivate fame has secured his own success most firmly:

> We struck out a new phrase—"submerged renown" . . . a surface reputation, however great, is always mortal, and always killable if you go at it right . . . but it is a different matter with the submerged reputation . . . their idol may be painted clay, up there at the surface, and fade and waste and crumble and blow away, there being much weather there; but down below he is gold and adamant and indestructible.[17]

Down below, Rebecca Harding Davis labored to get her writing into print and therefore into the hands and minds of readers without the threat of being discounted for her personal identity. Davis's evasion of "surface reputation," read alongside the theme of the unacknowledged, subaltern artist in her fiction, demonstrates not only a different attitude towards celebrity authorship in the nineteenth century, but also her refusal to adopt the rhetoric of a brand of reform realism that I call "celebrity reform," one that distanced readers from the beneficiaries of reform as it elevated the author/narrator's own role as celebrity author. While it is true that authors—especially female authors—at the mid century were highly susceptible to scandal on the basis of the public nature of their lives, Susan Ryan reminds us that such scandals may have been less of a crisis than much scholarship claims. Citing highly publicized scandals respectively involving Stowe, Lydia Maria Child, and even James Fenimore Cooper, Ryan concludes:

> The severity and longevity of such crashes have been much exaggerated. After their immediate public relations debacles had passed, these authors and others similarly disgraced continued to publish books with well-regarded, mainstream houses and they subsequently garnered positive reviews, at least in some venues and of some titles. And all enjoyed marks of high status within the literary field: publishers' advertisements listed their names and book titles alongside those of unequivocally esteemed authors; magazines named them as important, audience-attracting contributors; and early chroniclers of US literature identified them as key figures in the formation of the nation's corpus.[18]

Given these truths which precede even her own period of activity, Davis's reasons for shielding her private life can neither be reduced to a fear of scandal nor to a gender-based prohibition on public authorship. Instead, I'll argue, Davis saw both the political and artistic power of maintaining an obscure profile and simultaneously objected to the consumerist culture to which the emergent culture of authorial celebrity responded.

As an Appalachian woman writing for a mixed-gender, transatlantic audience in the second half of the nineteenth century, Davis's work was ripe for generic marginalization to the realms of sentimentality or regionalism—a fate she clearly wished to avoid.[19] In her essay "Women in Literature," she writes a paean to American female writers who "give us pictures of the race in its decadence . . . with fidelity equal to any other photographs of dying men," and praises them for having "omitted local peculiarities in their work," making clear her views on popular generic traditions that rely heavily on social and political identity in order to connect to their public.[20]

Her decision to deny an eager public biographical details or images of her body was not merely a tactic to preserve her personal privacy. Her separation of the work from the contextual details of her life forced readers to judge her literature more seriously on its merit alone. The lack of information about Davis meant that journalists who wished to write about her would have to focus on either the content of her writing or its interpretation.

In a light-hearted birthday tribute page published in *Life* magazine shortly before Davis's death, she is notably the only woman among the six celebrities profiled. Hers is also the only profile that runs unaccompanied by a photograph. While the other profiles share chatty details like their subjects' birthplaces, their educational pedigrees, and the names of their relatives, the text under Davis's name is largely a reconsideration of literary history: "If an exact summary of American literature . . . should be made, it is probable that in weight of learning and depth of popularity the women would out-number the men."[21] Davis's contribution to the culture at large underscores the importance of a greater population of which she is a part and destabilizes the notion that women are less capable of producing high quality work.

For Davis, personal identification with one's creative works was anti-thetical to the aims of art. Not merely shying away from publicity, she rather actively sought to fight against it. She openly disdained the intrusion into the personal lives of artists, authors, and members of society that the peri-odicals to which she herself contributed, writing:

> It is undeniable that a morbid curiosity concerning the personal affairs of individuals prevails and is openly acknowledged in all classes of American society. Every morning the best and the worst papers in the country serve carefully prepared food for this curiosity. No man can now curtain his life.[22]

Her peculiar use of the word "curtain" here echoes the most memorable image from "Life in the Iron-Mills," suggesting we might also read that image (the curtained sculpture of a naked woman) as a warning against the dangers of exposure.

While Davis may have curtained her personal identity, she exploited the repetitive and fragmented form of the periodical to increase the visibility of her work. When "Life" was accepted by *The Atlantic* editor James Fields in January 1861, the story was published anonymously and, for the next six years, the majority of her *Atlantic* contributions would be attributed to "The author of 'Life in the Iron-Mills.'" This tactic allowed the work to advertise itself. Readers who admired her writing were able to connect her various pieces together without the distracting or perhaps limiting presence of an embodied author to interfere with their appreciation. Davis only began to publish under her name in *The Atlantic* in 1867, when the story "George Bedillion, Knight" was attributed to Mrs. R. B. Davis—using her middle name Blaine, rather than her maiden name, Harding, to retain a degree of anonymity. In 1873, "A Faded Leaf of History" was published in *The Atlantic* and attributed to Rebecca Harding Davis, as were the next (and last) two pieces she published there. When her articles were not attributed to "the Author of 'Life in the Iron-Mills,'" they were either unsigned or, as in the case of two 1862 stories—"David Gaunt" and "John Lamar"—attributed to "The author of 'Margret Howth,'" a novel also published in *The Atlantic* earlier that year.[23] As *The Atlantic* continued to publish her work, Davis began a parallel career publishing mystery tales and novels in *Peterson's Magazine*. Initially, she published anonymously and then under the pseudonym "the author of 'The Murder in the Glen Ross,'" following *The Atlantic* pattern of referencing the first story published in that magazine.[24] After the publication of her serial novel *The Second Life* in *Peterson's* in 1863, many of her contributions were linked to that work. In the 1880s and 1890s, Davis would contribute to *Peterson's* as both Rebecca Harding Davis and "The Author of *The Second Life*." Several editorial features of the magazine include both identities— Rebecca Harding Davis *and* "The Author of *The Second Life*"—in a list of frequent contributors, maintaining the impression that these were separate individuals.[25]

Davis's array of attributions separates the different registers of address she adopted in her writing and creates the illusion that her large body of work was the product of multiple semi-obscure authors—submerging her renown but broadcasting her message. Critics have often thought of Davis's various readerships as distinct demographics. David Dowling, for example, observes that in her literary efforts towards asylum reform, Davis "utilized the high-brow venue of *The Atlantic* for access to the power brokers of elite culture in tandem with the popular *Peterson's*, which provided an indispensable link to the masses."[26] Addressing distinct populations is certainly one function of publishing in different registers, but it is not unlikely that an "elite" *Atlantic* reader might also enjoy the sensational tales to be found in *Peterson's*.[27] Such a reader would encounter Davis works in multiple venues without necessarily knowing that a single author was behind them. We might also consider how Davis's strategy allowed her not only to access different kinds of readers, but also to access the same readers on multiple occasions—creating a platform wider than the span of a single, individual writer. As Michele Mock suggests, Davis was "a textual activist [who] perceived art not as an elusive and elitist form but rather as a participative and dialogic expression of social activism."[28] By creating and sustaining the illusion of multiple subjectivities, Davis more closely approximates the effect of an issue that concerns many within the mode of its representation; instead of the author acting as an individual portal through whom the problems of many are brought to many, the author reproduces herself in different contexts.

Her publication strategy relied not only on accessing the maximum number and variety of readers, but also of accessing those readers on multiple occasions in different authorial guises and contexts. The writer Jenny Derby, a character in Davis's 1874 novella "Earthen Pitchers," is "on two or three papers. Writes book notices, and a woman's column . . . [s]ame thing over and over; roast, hash, and ragout; you have it again week after week, and, 'pon my word, you don't recognize it."[29] While there's a sense of humor here about the kind of literary repurposing such Jenny Derbys do for profit, Davis clearly believes it is possible and even unobjectionable, given the skill, to rework the same material.

Such reworked publications in Davis's own oeuvre have been characterized as insignificant acts or even embarrassing gaffes rather than a bid to disseminate ideas more widely and decentralize authorial identity.[30] A particular incident has received multiple critical dismissals. In July 1865, Davis was accused of plagiarizing herself when her fictional story "Ellen" was published in *The Atlantic*. Two years prior she had published a nonfiction profile of Ellen Carroll, on whom the fictional story was based, in *Peterson's*. Jane Atteridge Rose assumes that Davis was "apparently ignorant of the professional impropriety [when] she published essentially the same weird-but-true story in two journals," and Sharon Harris surmises that "she did not remember using the material earlier; or she felt so pressured to supply both journals with manuscripts that she simply hoped the coincidence would go unnoticed."[31] The only paratextual evidence of this incident is a letter from Davis to Ticknor and Fields—the original now lost—reproduced in the unpublished 1947 dissertation of Helen Woodward Shaeffer, an intimate of the surviving Davis circle. In the letter, Davis clearly explains that she acted intentionally, and does not find her actions in any way objectionable:

> In 1863 I myself made use of the incident of Ellen Carroll's search for her brother as groundwork for a story I wrote for Peterson. Last year Mr. Fields requested me to furnish you with a series of sketches of real places or events which had fallen under my notice, and I stated the bald facts of her history in the paper called "Ellen," thinking them interesting

and hoping in that way to obtain some clue to her fate. My doing so did not appear to me then irregular, nor does it now.[32]

The cunning and politic writer/activist responsible for the career of Rebecca Harding Davis, who was also half of the writing syndicate David Dowling has called "Davis, Inc.," made a deliberate decision to reuse her material because she felt it was in the best interest of the work and its message to do so.[33] Why should the anonymous *Atlantic* author and "The Author of *The Second Life*" (her *Peterson's* identity during this period) be barred from mutual access to the same source material? To readers of both *Peterson's* and *The Atlantic*, the two distinct contexts and authorial identities would raise the profile of the case under the impression that it was being covered twice. Publishing the same story in different genres and venues can be seen as a deliberate attempt to increase the reach and range of Ellen Carroll's ordeal. As both "The Author of 'Life in the Iron-Mills'" and "The Author of *The Second Life*," Davis grants breadth to Ellen Carroll's postwar trauma—an experience that was neither Davis's own nor unique to Carroll herself—and more widely disseminates a story that she hopes will elicit a response, a "clue to her fate."

Another incident of Davis's literary repurposing that has been frequently raised is the marked similarity between "Life" and Charles Dickens's *Hard Times—For These Times* (1854). However, the differences between these two works and their authors are far more telling than their similarities. The example of Dickens—arguably the most successful celebrity reform writer—demonstrates Davis's objection to the genre. Dickens quickly learned that an explicit tie to reform and a public involvement in its campaigns would grant more visibility to his fictions. Amanda Claybaugh writes that "In the 1840s . . . Dickens began to identify himself publicly as a reformer, and only sometime after that he began to write in a straightforwardly reformist mode himself."[34] From that point on, his careers as novelist, reformer, and speaker were inextricable constituents of the public entity known as Charles Dickens. An integral part of this strategy was to make himself as visible to his public as possible. As Juliet John observes, "Dickens demonstrably mythologized or marketed his own personality and his relationship with his audience in order to create an idea of personal and social wholeness."[35] Dickens's mode of authorial construction is at odds with Davis's own fragmented and obscured identity within the periodical press, as well as her anti-celebrity stance. While critics have historically thought of Davis as a reform writer like Dickens, the details of her career and the asides made in her fiction itself suggest a different interpretation. Davis's work represents a genre of fiction that objects to the reform realism that predominated the period.

REFORM INDIVIDUALISM

Davis's primary objection to reform and the literature it produced has to do with the way that both endeavors (reform campaigning and the composition of reform literature) conceive of their subjects. She was in some sense "an individualist," as Rose claims, "[who] never involved herself in any organized cause," resisting identification with reform groups and preferring to act alone.[36] Davis's lack of participation in these movements, however, should not be taken as an endorsement of individualism as a celebration of the self. In fact, as Jean Pfaelzer argues, Davis's characters often "remain mired in conflicts" that, in their failure to achieve narrative resolution, dramatize her own resistance to "the nineteenth-century novel's paradigm of the unified self."[37] Her stories do not instruct their readers on becoming coherent social subjects. Instead they expose the futility of coherent identity as such, given the competing demands of our ideas, longings, and allegiances. In this view, organized social reform movements and the literature that adopted their rhetoric were simultaneously too reductive of individual character and too emphatic on the primacy of the individual in the field of social change. We might consider, through Davis's eyes, how celebrity reform can be seen as *the* individualist approach to social change: a movement that emphasizes sympathy for the individual victim while elevating the cultural status of its proponent.

Davis was particularly sensitive to the class tourism that reform realist texts offered. In "Life," she incorporates the stock details of the social problem text in an overtly self-conscious way that calls attention to the hypocrisy of the genre. Her narrator goes the extra step of making the disgust her descriptions elicit explicit: "I want you to hide your disgust, take no heed to your clean clothes, and come right down with me,—here, into the thickest of the fog and mud and foul effluvia."[38] By imagining the reader integrated into the scene she depicts, rather than removed through several layers of representation, and calling attention to the disgust that literary class tourism encourages, she reveals how such texts dehumanize the supposed objects of reform, and presents her readers with a straightforward if implicit question: should they be disgusted by those they purport to be interested in "saving"?

The narrator of "Life" is no friend to the reader. As many critics have observed, the narrative tone is nothing short of hostile.[39] Instead of conspiring with the reader to pity the victim of oppression, Davis stresses the inability of the storyteller or the reader to understand the "reality" of the workers' lives: "A reality of soul-starvation, of living death, that meets you every day under the besotted faces on the street,—I can paint nothing of this, only give you the outside outlines."[40] This refusal to stand behind the depiction is a direct affront to the promise of reform realist texts to accurately render the scenes of oppression they describe. In contrast to the narrator of *Uncle Tom's Cabin's* friendly offer; "as [Tom] is to be the hero of our story, we must daguerreotype [him] for our readers."[41] The narrator of "Life" offers no clear picture, underscoring the impossibility of truly "seeing" the reality of someone whose life is so vastly different from one's own. Davis was explicitly critical of both Dickens's and Stowe's brands of celebrity reform fiction. In "John Lamar," a character who purportedly "enlisted to free the Uncle Toms and carry God's vengeance to the Legrees" is so concerned with garnering attention for himself that he fails, in the end, to help the enslaved Ben.[42] Davis's narrators do not claim to offer readers a chance to assuage their guilt over inequity through cultivating a posture of accurate understanding—the narrator of "John Lamar" admits "neither you nor I can ever know" what it means to Ben to be enslaved.[43] Her work urges us to consider the potential for greatness in those whom we cannot know rather than to cultivate a surface understanding of others through the accretion of realistic detail.

The descriptions of poverty that we now instinctively associate with reform-based realist or naturalist writing proved to be very effective rhetoric for mobilizing initiatives to improve the conditions of the poor through the creation of the modern welfare state. Such rhetoric continues to be incorporated into the philanthropic discourse today in the form of images of disease, starvation, filth, and disfigurement that accompany the pleas for donations often made by celebrity sponsors. This approach is popular with readers and viewers and productive of a certain kind of social awareness— one that marginalizes as it calls for aid. For example, a 2009 advertising campaign for the non-profit organization Save the Children depicts children in developing nations as artifacts encased in glass boxes accompanied

FIGURE 1. Save the Children Contaminated Drinking Water Campaign, M&C Saatchi, October 2009.

by museum-style explanatory cards that read things like "Contaminated Drinking Water; Mandera, Northern Kenya ©2009."

Literally rendering the subject of the reform effort an aesthetic object, the advertisements declare, "We must make this a thing of the past." The advertisements urge viewers to unite as a privileged "we," duty-bound to save the helpless victims of poverty. They are also a mandate to construct a certain narrative of history: poverty existed until "we" eradicated it. The African encased in a glass box plays no role in their own salvation. Their representation as an aesthetic "thing" wearing rags and surrounded by trash is a product of the phenomenon Keith Tester calls "common-sense humanitarianism." Common-sense humanitarianism does not seek to alter the relationships of power that create the inequalities it attempts to assuage. Its logic is, to adopt Tester's analogy, that everyone deserves a bed for the night; with "no requirement to ask precisely why this particular person has no bed."[44]

Studies like Tester's interpret the marginalizing rhetoric of common-sense humanitarianism as a relatively new cultural development, tied to the post-internet rise of celebrity culture.[45] I would argue that while the proliferation of highly publicized, celebrity-endorsed philanthropic endeavors ranging from the Live Aid concerts of the 1980s to the Save Darfur campaign of the first decade of this century were in many ways unprecedented in both form and scope, they nevertheless have deep roots in the representational strategies of nineteenth-century reform realism.[46]

According to Tester, the object of humanitarianism is an "anti-celebrity," someone who represents by merely existing, rather than by being possessed of any special skills, talents, or even a distinct personality.[47] These "anti-celebrities" serve to buoy the positive celebrity of reformers. As Christianson has noted, nineteenth-century reformers often saw their writing "as a means of redefining social relations while also authorizing their own cultural work as professionals."[48] Reform writing demonstrates the cultural agency of the author as it describes the lack of agency of its objects. The tendency of reform writers to play a public role in politics was particularly objectionable to Davis. In an 1893 *Independent* article about the Women's Exhibition at the World's Fair, she laments how the modern woman

> seized on the world's fair as an opportunity to exploit herself. If she had her own way it would have degenerated into a game of brag. She besought every woman in the country who had ever written a paper in a magazine or invented a mousetrap to send her paper and her trap, her portrait and her autograph for exhibition. . . . It was fitting and right that women should take part in the management of the Fair, and that the papers, the shoes, and the mousetraps should be shown, But, in the name of decency, why should the private lives and faces of their makes be given up to the starving millions? . . . No one questions the value of their achievements nor their just causes for triumph. They are so strong and wise that one wonders that they are not wise enough to see that their work and not their words should recommend them.[49]

It is both the connection to identity (why should women's work be celebrated as such and not simply as worthy work?) and the boastful publicity to which she objects here. Elsewhere, she expresses skepticism about the sham fashions and superficial culture of reform-based liberalism. In her autobiography *Bits of Gossip*, she skewers "abolition men": "Why, because the good folk wanted to free the slave, should they refuse to cut their beards, or to eat meat . . . or to run after new kinds of fantastic medicines or cookery?" and even insists in "Life" that "many a political reformer . . . had gone among [the poor] with a heart tender with Christ's charity, and come out outraged, hardened."[50]

In her 1878 novel, *A Law Unto Herself*, the reformer Pliny Van Ness sets out to establish a "home for friendless children" as a scheme to appropriate funds and boost his own reputation. Van Ness is the story's villain, using his performative social goodness to obscure his financially opportunistic and sexually sadistic plots against the story's heroine, Jane. Early on in the novel, Van Ness's nefarious aims are suspected by the literary editor Bruce Neckart, who surmises, "The philanthropists I know work for principles, liberty, education and the like: they don't care a damn for the individual Tom and Jerry. The chances are, that your reformer is a cold-blooded tyrant at home."[51] In the end of the novel, Neckart marries Jane and is able to establish the children's home in New York, through the profits of his financially successful magazine. Without attracting attention to himself nor compromising the integrity of his journalistic work, Neckart accomplishes more social change than the overt reformer.

A Law Unto Herself is not the only Davis work to depict a moral contest between literary endeavors and reform work. Davis's novel *Kitty's Choice; or, a Story of Berrytown*, first published in volume form in 1874, features a bookshop at the heart of a utopian reform community called Berrytown. The misguided aims of the Berrytown elite are heavily satirized in the story, but perhaps their greatest offense is their lack of regard for literature:

> Book-shops full of old plays, and a man who talked of Scott's width of imagination and Clay's statesmanship, were indigestible matter which Berrytown would gladly have spewed out of her mouth. "What have aimless imagination and temporizing policy to do with the Advancement of Mankind? Dead weight, sir, dead weight! Which but clogs the wheels of the machine." Any schoolboy in Berrytown could have so reasoned you the matter.[52]

For the sarcastic Davis, the kind of "aimless imagination and temporizing policy" one learns from literature is exactly what schoolboys interested in the advancement of mankind ought to be focusing on. She positions the study of literature as a means of achieving a depth of social thought, whereas the faddishness of reform politics is equated with the soullessness of industrial capitalism—"the wheels of the machine." Rather than a politics of compassion, Davis saw reform as a reflection of the inequity of the capitalist system it grew out of: an opportunity for reformers to elevate themselves both financially and socially by standing on the platform of their causes. Instead of engaging in reform as a way to solidify her own public identity or social ties, she preferred an approach that mobilizes literature for sociopolitical gain without compromising its artistic integrity by having too explicit a "purpose."

THE EXAMPLE OF DICKENS

In many ways, Davis's model of social reform through periodical literature is most directly influenced by Charles Dickens. Davis modeled many elements of her first published work on *Hard Times*, itself inspired by *Mary Barton* (1848). The descriptions of Dickens's Coketown and Davis's unnamed mill town are both picturesque and starkly naturalistic, marked by an ever-present, blackening soot. The two works also tackle the same social issues: the living conditions of workers and their lack of access to educational resources. In *Hard Times*, the workers are called "Hands," a metonymic naming principle carried into a critique of the distribution of labor: "the multitude of Coketown, generically called 'the Hands'—a race who would have found more favor with some people, if Providence has seen fit to make them only hands, or, like the lower creatures of the sea-shore, only hands and stomachs."[53] Davis imagines Dickens's hard-hearted "some people" explicitly in the character of the mill owner Kirby, who offers, "If I had the making of men, these men who do the lower part of the world's work should be machines,—nothing more,—hands. It would be kindness."[54] Eric Schocket suggests that readers of *The Atlantic* would specifically recall *Hard Times* in reading Davis's story. This deliberate referencing on Davis's part has been read as an homage rather than, as I read it here, a rejoinder.[55]

As in Dickens's Coketown, smoke and soot blacken the persons and objects of Davis's unnamed Virginia mill town to form a monochromatic industrial landscape wherein little distinction is made between even the animate and the inanimate. The descriptions of the towns and their inhabitants, both picturesque and starkly naturalistic, are remarkably similar. A pervasive theme of similitude is created throughout both works by the leitmotif of smoke and the dissolution of temporal structure that feature so prominently in these passages. Both works highlight class oppression through the use of racialized language. Coketown's buildings are an "unnatural red and black like the painted face of a savage," while Davis's narrator "used to fancy a look of weary, dumb appeal upon the face of the negro-like river slavishly bearing its burden day after day."[56] Schocket argues that Dickens's removal from actual "savages" is a simile, whereas for Davis it references the presence of subjugated labor "[of] antebellum America [that] cannot so easily be contained in the landscape."[57] Yet for neither author is the slave or savage landscape entirely contained. By giving the buildings and the river the same blackened faces of the human laborers, Dickens and Davis create a setting that is all subject—and all accusatory gaze—from the moving parts to the static features. This is a realism that goes one step beyond projecting the characteristics of individual characters onto the environment. It highlights—like Harriet Beecher Stowe's "man that was a thing"—the objectification of laborers and, furthermore, the coextension of that objectification with the destruction of the natural landscape. Davis would ultimately be more successful than Dickens in identifying an overarching narrative strategy for the protest of racial oppression.

Dickens's 1842 visit to the States certainly destroyed any sense of safe removal from American slavery that he may have previously had. He was so disturbed by his confrontation with it in Virginia that he cancelled the majority of the planned Southern leg of his journey, forgoing Charleston for St. Louis.[58] It also proved to be the most difficult topic to address in his *American Notes for General Circulation* (1842), not only because of his attenuated stay in the South, but because he seemed to be unable to capture the brutality of the institution within the confines of his own personality-driven mode of authorship. Instead of writing a chapter on the American South into his travel narrative as he had intended, Dickens tacks on a seventeenth chapter before his "Concluding Remarks"—titled simply "Slavery." The chapter begins with Dickens's promise that he "shall not write one word [on slavery's atrocities] for which I have not ample proof and warrant."[59] Indeed, though the chapter begins with his impassioned yet abstract reflections, it quickly resorts to a technique of montage wherein unidentified periodical articles and advertisements for runaway slaves are reproduced in extract from Theodore D. Weld's 1839 "American Slavery As It Is"; the same pamphlet later used by Stowe in creating the fragmented views of slavery that occur outside of the central plot lines of *Uncle Tom's Cabin* (1852).[60] The promise of Dickens's "ample proof and warrant" is fulfilled in the form of plagiarized text, a somewhat hypocritical choice for inclusion in a volume whose very title was a calculated jab at the American resistance to international copyright. His prefatory statement suggests that his decision to ostensibly step down as author in regards to the topic of American slavery is in deference to the importance of maintaining truth and authenticity in its portrayal. The montage technique produces this desired effect by adopting local and journalistic voices at odds with the personal, narrative, and distinctly English style of the rest of *American Notes*. These voices thicken the population of the text, as they do in *Uncle Tom's Cabin*, lending the issue the weight of multiple subjectivities.

Though the use of confessional or outside voices was a common abolitionist tactic, it was a rare strategy for Dickens, whose authorial voice and public persona united his fiction and nonfiction works alike. As John notes, "Exposure and visibility were key techniques in the establishment of 'the Dickens industry.' He was highly aware of himself as a brand, promoting the image of Dickens from his first fame onwards."[61] Dickens offered himself as a familiar authorial and editorial presence for readers, a notion that grew out of a long tradition of British print culture. According to John Forster, Dickens's friend and early biographer, *Household Words*, the first periodical that Dickens edited, was explicitly conceived in the image of Addison and Steele's *Spectator*. In the first issue of the *Spectator*, Joseph Addison wrote a sketch of the character he called the Spectator, the voice of the paper, a narrator who promises to "open the work with my own history." While various characters appear in different issues of the *Spectator* to take over narrative control, they are always introduced as members of the Spectator club, *friends* of the Mr. Spectator whose ever-present personality unites them.

Instead of a fictional "Mr. Spectator" character, Dickens installed himself, trading on his already established reputation as a beloved and family-friendly storyteller to build a literary empire. In the first number of *Household Words*, Dickens promises "to be the comrade and friend of many thousands of people, of both sexes, and of all ages and conditions," and his voice in the paper serves as a guide to the journalistic miscellany that bombarded the mid-century reader.[62] While *Household Words* published everything from recipes, to how-tos, to poetry and fiction, as well as opinionated essays on the issues of the day, most articles included a brief introduction from Dickens. Rarely is any name but Dickens's listed in attribution. Dickens's periodicals, first *Household Words* (1850–1859) and then *All the Year Round* (1859–1895), were also outlets for his own fiction, which was inevitably their most popular fare. When sales of *Household Words* began to lag in 1854, he began serializing a new novel of his own, *Hard Times*, more than doubling the paper's circulation. Given the publication context and Dickens's characteristic voice, well-honed by this time, it would be impossible for the readers of *Household Words* in England and abroad not to associate the narrator of *Hard Times* with Dickens himself.

Though Davis read Dickens avidly and found inspiration in his work, she also felt that his career was marked by an emotional and artistic shallowness she sought not to replicate in her own. After seeing him speak in 1868, she wrote "when it comes to simple pathos—unmixed with any comic element, his voice and manner had no effect upon me—one was metallic and the other artificial."[63] Just three years before Davis would make her own entrance into the transatlantic publishing scene, Dickens fell under attack after the dissolution of his marriage to Catherine Hogarth when he published a shocking notice, somewhat ironically titled "Personal," in *Household Words* announcing, at length, "some domestic trouble of mine."[64] Many readers first learned of Dickens's marital strife through this notice, and still more were offended by his decision to so publicly air the troubles that beset him and his family.[65] In a letter to Charles Eliot Norton about her new novel *North & South*, Elizabeth Gaskell writes that she hoped to serialize in *The Atlantic*, but, because of work owed to Dickens, it seemed likely to end up in his new venture, *All the Year Round*: "Mr. Dickens happens to be extremely unpopular just now, (owing to the well-grounded feeling of dislike to the publicity he has given to his domestic affairs,) & I think they would be glad to announce my name on their list of contributors. And I would much rather they did not. . . . I know it is fated to go to this new Dickensy periodical & I did so hope to escape it."[66] Perhaps most revealing here is Gaskell's sense that *All the Year Round* is too "Dickensy"—that the outsized and coherent personality of Dickens would subsume the entire contents of the periodical.

Davis's use of the periodical as a fragmented form that might obscure authorial identity can be seen in contrast to Dickens's excessively author-driven model, which set the standard for transatlantic authorial success. Her publication of the story that she called "Blind Tom" in both *All the Year Round* and *The Atlantic* demonstrates how fears like Gaskell's played out. When the story appeared in October 1862 in *All the Year Round*, Dickens changed the title of the piece to "Blind Black Tom" and added an introduction, which stated, "we have received the following remarkable account from a valued friend in Boston, Massachusetts. It will be published in that city within a few days after its present publication in these pages."[67] That November, the story was published anonymously in *The Atlantic* as "Blind Tom," with no introduction, save an unattributed epigraph from Tennyson.

The emphasis on framing the work in terms of social identity—both the identity of the subject (Black) and the identity of the author (a friend from Boston)—separate the Dickensy publication strategy from the Davisy. Dickens utilizes his renown to encourage interest in social issues on his behalf, like a friend asking a favor of the reader. In the context of *All the Year Round*, readers are given signposts that they should view "Blind Black Tom" as an abolition tale that paints a particular portrait of the injustices of slavery, through the addition of the word "Black" and the association of Boston with the abolitionist movement.[68] By removing the identity of the artist from the equation and connecting her story to a literary tradition with the epigraph, Davis encourages the reader to identify aesthetically with the story's prose and the protagonist Tom's music. In *All the Year Round*, "Blind Black Tom" is a straightforward work of reform fiction; in *The Atlantic*, "Blind Tom" is a portrait of an artist. Though the text of the story remains the same, the context of this second version asks us not to oppose slavery out of pity for its subhuman victims, but to celebrate the genius of a man unfairly subjected to a barbaric system. We should not act because of who tells us to act any more than we should extol or condemn a work because of who created it.

THE BLIND ARTIST

Davis's fictional depictions of artists like Blind Tom and the iron worker Hugh Wolfe, both underappreciated because of their subaltern social status, suggest a view that an artist's—or an author's—visibility could only hinder the pure appreciation of his or her work. "Blind Tom" critiques the marginalizing genre of the abolition story while celebrating the haunting music of an enslaved artist. The story depicts the inability of Southern spectators to understand an enslaved person as a virtuosic composer and pianist. Thomas Bethune, or "Blind Tom Wiggins," as he is sometimes known, was a real-life pianist from Georgia who Davis saw perform in Baltimore.[69] The content of Davis's story is an astonished and precise explanation of the nature of Tom's gifts. Beginning with an almost mythical account of the seven-year-old prodigy turning out "the most difficult exercises usually played by [his master's] daughters" when left alone with the drawing room piano for the first time, the story outlines the emergence of Tom's extraordinary musical genius.[70] His capacity for mimicry is excellent: "his memory is so accurate he can repeat, without the loss of a syllable, a discourse of fifteen minutes in length, of which he does not understand a word. Songs, too, in French or German, after a single hearing, he renders not only literally in words, but in notes, style, and expression."[71] Davis, however, quickly prevents readers from assuming that Tom is a mere mimic. She describes how he can accompany accomplished players without prior rehearsal or the use of sheet music:

> The mere repetition of music heard but once, even when, as in Tom's case, it is given with such incredible fidelity . . . demands only a command of mechanical skill, and an abnormal condition of the power of memory; but to play secondo to music never heard or seen implies the comprehension of the full drift of the symphony in its current,—a capacity to creat, [sic] in short.[72]

In Davis's telling, Tom is an original artist compelled to perform parlor tricks and feats of banal memorization for the benefit of paying audiences. Davis insists that Tom is a genius misunderstood by crude owners who see him merely as a means for generating profits.

> There was hardly a conception . . . in the minds of those who heard him, how deep the cause for wonder lay. The planters' wives and daughters of the neighborhood were not people who would be apt to comprehend music as a science, or to use it as a language; they only saw in the little negro, therefore, a remarkable facility for repeating the airs they drummed on their pianos.[73]

Though the value of Tom's art is underappreciated by his audience, Davis nonetheless gestures towards its liberating potential, marveling at Tom's ability to *keep* creating under such marginalizing scrutiny and exploitation. As he performs, Tom seems unaware of how his spectators—Davis's narrator included—view him. Her description of his physical appearance evokes the objectifying gaze of the crowd. He has "great blubber lips and shining teeth" and approaches the piano "like an ape clawing for food."[74] She trots out the worst of the audience and readers' potentially prejudicial views of Tom rather than trying to sentimentalize his portrait by suggesting he is physically attractive or, worse, Anglo-Saxon in his features. This is a challenge to her readers to confront their assumptions. Not one to draw conclusions based on physiognomy or race, Davis delights in pointing out the incongruity of appearance with personality or acuity—such gestures are direct assaults on the racist and eugenicist physiognomic theories of personality that found wide acceptance in her period. For example, she suggests that the kindly Quaker woman in "Life in the Iron-Mills" is "a homely body" with a face of "the stuff out of which murderers are made."[75] Her implication in "Blind Tom" is that Tom is exactly the kind of person the reader and the spectators at the performance would wrongly dismiss as worthless. Throughout the disturbing catalogue of his body, we are reminded that Tom himself focuses on the piano—not the censorious audience. Neither Tom nor the narrator expresses pity for his fate; the narrator seems to find in him a kindred creative spirit.

Davis's depiction of Tom is another instance of her use of a portrayal of an artist to consider her own vexed relationship to authorial identity. Neither the writer nor the blind musician can see their audience, a situation that allows them freedom of expression—even when other freedoms are denied them. The original compositions Tom creates are, according to Davis, unfit for the music hall: "uncertain, sad minors always, vexing the content of the hearer,—one inarticulate, unanswered question of pain in all. . . . Even the vulgarest listener was troubled."[76] The description of these sorrowful melodies recalls her *Atlantic* editor's complaints about her own writing. After the success of "Life," Davis sent a full-length novel to James T. Fields entitled *The Deaf and the Dumb*. Fields initially rejected the novel, which most likely later became the work we now know as *Margret Howth* (1862). Although his letter has not been found, his grounds for the initial rejection are sufficiently clear from Davis's response. She writes, "Whatever holier meaning life or music has for me has reached me through the pathetic minor. I fear that I only have the power to echo the pathos without the meaning."[77] Like Tom, Davis's "sad minors" vex her hearer—her pathos lent the work too dark a tone for Fields, who was looking to women writers to provide popular, lighthearted fiction to boost the sales of a periodical whose esoteric, male-authored, nonfiction pieces were not attracting enough subscribers.[78] Fields's rejection reinforced that Davis's gendered identity would prescribe the kind of work she would be expected to produce. Davis resisted this restriction from the very beginning of her national career, creating an ambiguously gendered narrator in "Life in the Iron-Mills."

Much has been written on the narrator of "Life," from heated speculations about the unspecified gender identity of the voice to formalist attempts to locate its rhetoric within the naturalist genre.[79] By applying Malcolm Cowley's dictum that "irony—like pity, its companion—is a spectator's emotion" to Davis's story, Sara Gooding Britton argues that the narrative style is Davis's way of deliberately distancing herself from readers.[80] I'd like to add that Davis is not only distancing herself from readers, but, more broadly, from a sentimental mode of identification, in the model of Dickens, that asks the reader to see the narrator as an avuncular friend who invites the reader to join in spectating the story's pitiful subject. By refusing the sentimental mode of identification, the reader is forced to confront the systemic problems that "Life in the Iron-Mills" raises, rather than to simply experience sympathy for its characters as individuals.

THE FLESH-COLORED FIGURE

Davis's depictions of the objects of reform as artists and her own refusal to have her work determined by her political identity reverse the celebrity reform paradigm. Her texts encourage readers to care about her subjects through neither pity for the horrors of the characters' circumstances nor identification with a familiar narrator, but by encouraging appreciation for the art that the characters produce. "Life" is ultimately not a story about industrial labor so much as it is a story about the power of art: how we come to value it, what it is meant to do and—above all—who has the right to make it.[81] Wolfe, the story's protagonist, is a starving, tubercular furnace tender in a West Virginia iron mill and an amateur artist whose works in "korl," a local word for an industrial waster particulate, "show a master's hand."[82] The sculpture that he makes stands at the center of the text: naked, unsettling, and aggressive. "The korl woman," which is the story's original title as well as its central subject, is not to be ignored. The exposure of the korl woman leads to Hugh's death, but the sculpture itself survives, relegated to a corner of the narrator's study where it is awkwardly hidden behind a curtain. Though Wolfe dies an anonymous criminal, his artwork is somehow preserved. The sculpture made of waste by an industrial worker—a member of a supposedly disposable population—carries on in perpetuity.

The narrator of "Life" is less interested in the politically charged story of the ironworker Hugh Wolfe than he or she is in the remarkable sculpture Hugh produces, which is carefully guarded in the thirty-year interval between the story's events and its telling. As discussed at the beginning of this chapter, critics often reference the ending of the story—the proper burial of Hugh and the rescue of his cousin from the mills by the Quaker woman—in order to connect Davis's quixotic work to a tradition of social action rooted in Christian charity. But the text does not end with the Quaker's good deed, Hugh's funeral, nor even Deb's redemption. It ends with the sculpture. The final paragraphs follow the narrator's gaze from a tender meditation on the sculpture to a survey of the room that contains it and back to the sculpture again:

> Nothing remains to tell that the poor Welsh puddler once lived, but this figure of the mill-woman cut in korl. I have it here in a corner of my library. I keep it hid behind a curtain,—it is such a rough, ungainly thing. Yet there are about it touches, grand sweeps of outline, that show a master's hand. Sometimes,—to-night, for instance,—the curtain is accidentally drawn back, and I see a bare arm stretched out imploringly in the darkness, and an eager, wolfish face watching mine: a wan, woful face, through which the spirit of the dead korl-cutter looks out, with its thwarted life, its mighty hunger, its unfinished work. . . . The gas-light wakens from the shadows here and there the objects which lie scattered through the room: only faintly, though; for they belong to the open sun-light. As I glance at them, they each recall some task or pleasure of the coming day. A half-moulded child's head; Aphrodite; a bough of forest-leaves; music; work; homely fragments, in which lie the secrets of all eternal truth and beauty. Prophetic all! . . . While the room is yet steeped in heavy shadow, a cool, gray light suddenly touches [the] head [of the korl woman] like a blessing hand, and its groping arm points through the broken cloud to the far East, where, in the flickering, nebulous crimson, God has set the promise of the Dawn.[83]

The korl woman is only one of several aesthetic objects in this room. This tableau has been read as a scene of bourgeois comfort that separates the narrator from Wolfe. Both Lawson and Pfaelzer categorize the art objects as the dilettantish trappings of a cozy domestic interior.[84] I see these objects— "homely fragments"—as the narrator's works-in-progress. Like Seitler, I think these objects communicate that the narrator is also an artist.[85] They signify the narrator's connection to Hugh on a basis that transcends sympathy or pity, class or gender identification. It is fitting that the narrator's library is also their workshop—the voice that tells Hugh's story is deeply rooted in the aesthetic traditions of the past that the books represent. Like the dusty bookshop in the center of Berrytown, the library is a retreat from the dehumanization of industrial capitalism. The korl woman sculpture inspires the narrator to keep making, to keep creating, to try to refine the message that "the spirit of the dead korl-cutter" communicates in his own "unfinished work."

Hugh's creative work surpasses his historically specific identity and his "spirit" remains animated through the art it continues to inspire.[86] In the narrator's final summation of his life, Wolfe is a "korl-cutter," not a Welsh immigrant or an ironworker. The narrator acknowledges that Wolfe's personal story, outside of his artistic career, is unexceptional and perhaps even unworthy of notice: "I cannot tell why I choose the half-forgotten story of this Wolfe more than that of myriads of these furnace hands."[87] The circumstances surrounding the selection of this tale within the narrator's frame are made to seem arbitrary and have little to do with the narrator's interest in the details of Wolfe's life. The purpose of the narrator's story is neither to relay the biography of Hugh Wolfe, nor even the plight of specific mill workers. Its purpose is to elevate the work of art, to keep passing its spirit forward in time. The story itself is a kind of "half-moulded child's head," a nascent vision to be carried out indefinitely in the aesthetic future. As Seitler writes, "this is not a call for politically engaged art, but an argument for the unfinished project of the politics of aesthetics."[88] Davis emphasizes how artistic skill and style are what make a subject worthy of our attention. In a reversal of the popular nineteenth-century formula that puts literature in the service of social campaigns, Davis's argument for an end to social injustice hinges on the import of art. The message is that we shouldn't pity Hugh Wolfe the ironworker because of his suffering; we should bear witness to the force of the art born out of his oppression and take it as an obligation to examine the system that hinders his aesthetic expression.

Davis's work demonstrates how so many talented individuals are disenfranchised not only through social systems that prevent them from accessing education and basic necessities, but also through representational systems that omit their subjectivity. The ironworker Hugh Wolfe creates the korl woman in an act of artistic protest that mirrors Davis's own. The culmination of an aesthetic vision long in the making, Wolfe's sculpture is a representation of working-class anger worthy of its subjects.[89] As the narrator describes:

> Wolfe had not been vague in his ambitions. They were practical, slowly built up before him out of his knowledge of what he could do. Through years he had day by day made this hope a real thing to himself,—a clear, projected figure of himself, as he might become. Able to speak, to know

what was best, to raise these men and women working at his side up with him.[90]

The sculpture is angry, and its anger vividly confronts the bourgeois visitors to the mill that encounter it. "What do you mean by it?" one of them asks, to which Wolfe answers, "She be hungry . . . not hungry for meat . . . [but] summat to make her live, I think,—like you."[91] Viewing the sculpture prompts men who seem to have never considered the issue before to engage in a debate over workers' rights. Mitchell concludes that no one of them can do anything to help workers like Wolfe, because "Reform is born of need, not pity. No vital movement of the people's has worked down, for good or evil; fermented, instead, carried up the heaving, cloggy mass. . . . Some day, out of their bitter need will be thrown up their own light-bringer."[92] Mitchell scarcely realizes that this is precisely what Hugh has done, "carried up the heaving, cloggy mass" of korl to craft a light-bringer rather than serve as the light-bringer himself—the revolutionary figure is the art, not the artist.

These visitors, like the readers of reform realism, come to the mill seeking shock and titillation. Andrew Silver describes their trip to the mills as an example of picturesque travel—excursions to ruins, industrial sites, and slums that offer the curious a whiff of the Burkean sublime.[93] This is a practice that would only gain popularity throughout the Progressive Era. Davis's tourists bring among them a journalist who is "getting up a series of reviews of the leading manufactories" and the others come along primarily to be entertained and, perhaps, inspired.[94] But instead of encountering the miserable lives of the workers as raw material for their own aesthetic visions, they see that the work of representation has already been accomplished by one of the workers himself. Wolfe depicts life in the iron-mills as the workers see it, in the korl woman's image of strength and peculiar beauty. The details that Davis includes in her story like the rank pork the workers eat or the pile of rags they call their beds are the kind of information that the visitors, and the story's readers with whom they are identified, might have come looking for: aesthetic pleasures *about* the workers rather than *by* them. The evaluative dialogue that ensues among the visitors reinforces their resistance to both Hugh's potential value and the value of the work of art. As Seitler argues, "their dismissal of Hugh demonstrates the nondifference between extreme capitalist apathy and the middle class's paltry efforts at reform—based in sympathy as opposed to action."[95]

Davis elaborates on the "non-difference" Seitler dismisses in her staging of the role of each visitor. The mill owner Kirby is the utilitarian industrialist—his concern is for profits and he has little interest in improving labor conditions beyond maximizing production. Dr. May is more empathetic to the plight of the laborers; a town physician who is representative of the middle class, May pities men like Wolfe but is unwilling to make any personal sacrifice, no matter how small, to better their circumstances. When Wolfe explicitly asks for May's help, his response is unequivocal: "I have not the money, boy."[96] Mitchell poses the most nuanced position because of his sensitivity to the aesthetic value of Hugh's work. He seems convinced of the sculptor's talent and attuned to the real possibility of revolution. At first, Hugh feels confident that Mitchell will recognize the work's artistic merits: "[he] glanced appealingly at Mitchell, who saw the soul of the [sculpture], he knew. But the cool, probing eyes were turned on himself now,—mocking, cruel, relentless."[97] For a moment, the worker is able to see himself as an artist through Mitchell, but this moment passes as soon as he perceives himself rather than his art to be the object of the spectator's gaze.[98] Mitchell is himself a proto-aesthete:

> He was an amateur gymnast,—hence his anatomical eye; a patron, in a *blasé* way, of the prize-ring; a man who sucked the essence out of a science or philosophy in an indifferent, gentlemanly way; who took Kant, Novalis, Humboldt, for what they were worth in his own scales; accepting all, despising nothing, in heaven, earth, or hell, but one-idead men; with a temper yielding and brilliant as summer water, until his Self was touched, when it was ice, though brilliant still. Such men are not rare in the States.[99]

The story implies his fashionable nihilism is as bad, in the end, as the hypocritical concern expressed by May and the indifference of Kirby, who are both insensitive to the merits of the sculptor's work. May admires the depiction of "the muscles in the arm and the hand," the latter suggests that Wolfe learned anatomy from his exposure to the "half-naked figures" working around him in the hot mill.[100] Kirby's initial reaction upon seeing the sculpture is to note that it is "Not marble, eh?"[101] The very material out of which the sculpture is made is deemed valueless, as is the body of the artist himself. It is nevertheless significant that the only moment in the story in which the upper-class characters seriously discuss the question of social change is a moment of art criticism.

Though the sculpture is the story's primary figure of social change, Hugh's own alterity is one of the ways in which Davis signals an aesthetically minded activism. Hugh is "one of the girl-men: 'Molly Wolfe' was his sobriquet," referencing the seventeenth and eighteenth-century term for an effeminate man.[102] While Hugh's femininity signals his outsider status, calling him a "molly" also hints at his revolutionary potential; the molly is a figure aligned with class instability. Allan Bray notes that "the society of the molly houses did not follow class lines but rather tended to dissolve them."[103] Just as the upper-class mill visitors cannot accept Hugh as an artist because his class position is lower than their own, the other workers reject him because, to them, he bears the marks of class elevation. There is a "taint of school-learning on him;" he possesses "foreign thoughts and longings" and a "loving poet's heart."[104] Hugh's alterity is connected to his artistic sensibilities and his ability to see beyond class and gender binaries.

Mollies often flouted class convention through acts of creative self-presentation: "lower-class mollies enjoyed affecting a stylish, aristocratic manner . . . at the risk of being thought insolent."[105] This is also true of the nineteenth-century iteration of the molly: the dandy. Though the dandy is most frequently associated with the upper class, Richard Dellamora reminds us that this was not always, or even usually, the case, pointing out that "although some aristocrats were dandies, the 'dandy' as a popular phenomenon is middle-class" and that dandyism "was associated with middle-class uppityism."[106] The dandy as a challenge to the upper class can also be seen in Baudelaire's 1863 essay "The Painter of Modern Life," where he explicitly references the dandy of North America:

> Dandyism appears above all in periods of transition, when democracy is not yet all-powerful, and aristocracy is only just beginning to totter and fall. In the disorder of these times, certain men who are socially, politically, and financially ill at ease, but are all rich in native energy, may conceive of the idea of establishing a new kind of aristocracy, all the more difficult to shatter as it will be based on the divine gifts which work and money are unable to bestow.[107]

For Baudelaire, dandyism is the mark of revolutionary instability and the movement away from property-based identity formation towards an artistic and merit-based cultural elite. It is precisely this brand of dandyism in Hugh that Mitchell, himself a dandiacal figure, recognizes.

Hugh Wolfe, along with dandiacal characters in Chopin and Wharton I'll discuss later, show how writers whose work is often identified as literary naturalism utilized the figure of the dandy, primarily associated with aestheticism, as a destabilizer of both gender and class binaries. Davis, who was fluent in French, may likely have become acquainted with the European version of these ideas through works like Balzac's 1830 *Traité de la vie élégante* or Jules Barbey d'Aurevilly's 1845 *Du Dandysme et de Georges Brummel*, both of which read the visionary regency dandy George Brummel as a revolutionary—d'Aurevilly calls dandyism "the revolt of the individual against the established order."[108] Hugh Wolfe is an ambiguously gendered figure who conscientiously objects to class stratification and voices his protest through the creation of art.

When Kirby mocks the workers' misunderstanding of their own circumstances by boasting to the visitors that he easily manipulates them into voting for his own candidate at election time and asserts that "there's something wrong with these men that no talk of 'Liberte' or 'Egalite' will do away," Davis connects Mitchell's sympathy for Hugh to a threat of class revolt.[109] Hugh's sophisticated and thoughtful mode of self-stylized protest is undermined by the more literally minded Deb who, upon hearing Mitchell sarcastically declare that money is "the cure for all the world's diseases," steals a purse from his pocket.[110] When she gives it to Hugh, he is horrified by the crime but decides to keep the purse for an evening to think over this new possession and the terms of its acquisition. He begins to reflect that there is essentially no difference between himself and the "rightful" possessor of the money, "God made this money—the fresh air, too—for his children's use. He never made the difference between poor and rich . . . What, in that world of Beauty, Content, and Right, were the petty laws, the mine and thine, of mill-owners and mill hands?"[111] Davis's previous association of Mitchell with Hugh—their mutual identification through exchanged gazes, dandyism, and revolutionary vision—finds its conclusion in Hugh's possession of Mitchell's money. How is it more Mitchell's than his own?

The tragic irony of the story is that Hugh keeps the money neither as a hostile, revolutionary gesture nor because he decides to disregard a law he deems unjust. He keeps the money because, in the clarity of vision that comes from his lack of education and socialization, he can't understand how it could possibly be denied him. Davis's point is that he's right. Ultimately,

Hugh is arrested for the theft—a fact shared through the newspaper report of his arrest and sentencing. Baudelaire writes, "[a] dandy can never be a vulgarian. If he committed a crime, it would perhaps not ruin him; but if his crime resulted from some trivial cause, his disgrace would be irreparable," and it is indeed the disgrace from the crime—which he did not actually commit (it is Deb who stole the purse)—that ruins Hugh.[112] In rendering the fallout, Davis is keen to focus on Hugh's ignominy, wrapping the narrative information in layers of reception. His punishment is printed in a newspaper, which Doctor May reads aloud to his wife;

> "Oh, my dear! You remember that man I told you of, that we saw at Kirby's mill?—that was arrested for robbing Mitchell? Here he is; just listen:—Circuit Court. Judge Day. Hugh Wolfe, operative in Kirby & John's Loudon Mills. Charge, grand larceny. Sentence, nineteen years hard labor in penitentiary. Scoundrel! Serves him right! After all our kindness that night! Picking Mitchell's pocket at the very time!" His wife said something about the ingratitude of that kind of people, and then they began to talk of something else.[113]

The revelation of Hugh's grossly unfair punishment is contained within a critique of the charitable tendencies and false morality of the middle class—a group epitomized by their newspaper-reading habits and their taste for the prying kind of gossip journalism to which Davis explicitly objected.

That Hugh should achieve notoriety for his crime is made more poignant by his lack of expectation for recognition or remuneration for his art. Hugh often discards what he makes, preferring the act of creation to the end result: "[sculpting] was a curious fancy in the man, almost a passion. The few hours for rest he spent hewing and hacking with his blunt knife, never speaking, until his watch came again,—working at one figure for months, and, when it was finished, breaking it to pieces perhaps, in a fit of disappointment."[114] This kind of work is also at odds with Hugh's paid labor. As a puddler, he is given a set wage to produce endless identical rails, which are then sold for profit. Hugh's sculpting is a "passion"—something he does off the clock. Despite his inevitable disappointment, we can assume from his repetition of the act that it gives him some pleasure. In this highly structured industrial milieu, "the vast machinery of system by which the bodies of the workmen are governed," designed to cater to the demand of the consumer-driven marketplace, Hugh asserts his own desire by producing art (though he is not a trained artist) out of korl (though it is a waste substance).[115] Regina Gagnier argues that "the dandy artist . . . becomes the bestower of value where value need not imply production: it is sufficient that he mirror negatively the hopeless reification of others' lives."[116] Because Hugh is able to derive pleasure outside of the nullifying vices of his fellow workers and the consumption-based behaviors of the mill visitors, the korl woman comes to represent desire beyond the market. Hugh is a problematic figure who the mill visitors and the readers must resolve by examining their own norms.

The solution Hugh devises to free himself is suicide. He mortifies his own flesh as he had previously carved the flesh of his art, symbolically aligning his biological body with the counter-market body of the abandoned sculpture. I agree with Caroline Miles when she argues that "the only way Wolfe can overcome the biological body is through self-destruction," but disagree with her conclusion that "Davis's text participates in the same non-representation of laboring men as the national rhetoric she criticizes."[117] Hugh's death may be an erasure of his biological identity, but it is hardly an erasure of his message. The korl woman he creates is the most enduring image—and the last body standing—at the close of the story. It exists in perpetuity—not as an individual, biological worker, but as an artistically embodied representation of all workers.

The inscrutability of what—or who—the sculpture represents is its clear strength as a discursive work of art. Hugh's laboring body is linked with the sculpture throughout the story, but it does not represent him alone. Sheila Hassell Hughes reads the korl woman as a representation of his cousin Deb, arguing that her "body, as a sign of her labor, is unsexed and unlovable. . . . It is also dehumanized, as the wolfishness of *her* image, the korl statue, indicates."[118] The physical strength of the sculpture must also, however, be reconciled with Deb's frailty as well as with the equally compelling argument for an association with Hugh: his face, "a meek woman's face," and his name, Wolfe—the sculpture is "wolfish."[119] By complicating these characteristics and going so far as to assert that all Welsh puddlers share the same, sculptural features—"slight angular bodies and sharply-cut facial lines"—Davis positions the korl woman as a figure for multiple identities.[120] As Davis substitutes a generalized authorial identity for a specific one, the sculpture is *all* workers. Because Hugh's art emerges as the agent of social change, rather than he himself serving as an individual political figure, the entire group of laborers is granted equal representation. The korl woman is

Hugh's attempt to bring awareness to the injustices of class oppression by representing a mass of people in a single, compelling work of art. Davis's message here is that there shouldn't be a single hero to any political story nor a single beneficiary of charitable feelings. Her work encourages readers to care about the plight of workers not through pity for the horrors of their circumstance, but by encouraging appreciation for their art.

At the end of the story, the korl woman's flesh-colored, larger-than-life body—previously described as "a woman, white, of giant proportions"—is awkwardly tucked away in the narrator's chamber; "I have it here in a corner of my library. I keep it hidden behind a curtain,—it is such a rough, ungainly thing." It's a strange image. The curtain specifically erected to hide the naked female body in the narrator's library, the place of artistic labor, is deliberate yet ineffective; "Sometimes,—ton-ight, for instance,—the curtain is accidentally drawn back, and I see a bare arm stretched out imploringly in the darkness."[121] The work of art composed to represent the complex network of interrelations that artistic and industrial production both require is possessed of its own individual body, a body whose nudity and outstretched arm simultaneously assert the need to address the problem it represents and the vulnerable position of the artist. So that while the korl woman constitutes and posits activism on a mass scale, it is also fettered by its own individual, embodied existence.

Hugh leaves his sculpture in place of a biological descendant and the fact that the narrator lives in the house that was once the Wolfes' suggests an artistic legacy instead of a hereditary inheritance. The story ends with the work of visual art as the focus of the work of literary art—an affirmation of art over property and inheritance, just as the artistic workshop stands in the place of the bourgeois home. This theme demonstrates the superiority of a cultural legacy to society at large over the disbursement of strictly financial legacies to biological heirs.

Davis frequently wrote against the market-driven aspects of cultural production and the financial exigencies she saw deeply enmeshed in issues of gender. In addition to several articles written in the late 1880s and early 1890s denouncing consumerism and the perils of "the huge accumulation of wealth," which she calls a "noxious disease," she devoted a 1902 article in *The Congregationalist and Christian World*, "Ingenuity in Earning a Living," to the particular problems of surviving as a female breadwinner.[122] In her 1866 *Peterson's* story "In the Market," which tells the story of two girls' paths toward marriage, her character Clara articulates the double-bind of female professionalism: "If a woman attempts a man's business, hear the outcry that follows her! What am I to do with my girls?"[123] The inevitable answer is to marry them well, with only the vague hint of liberation at the story's closing phrase, "there is no prison from which there is not a means of escape."[124] The bars of this prison are the demands of property-based culture: one must possess—or be possessed—in order to be at all.

By depicting those denied equal participation in society—women, working-class whites, and enslaved African Americans—as artists, Davis attempts to highlight their subjectivity, which the predominant reform literature tended to obscure. Her portrayals of unappreciated artist characters in her fictions and her nonfiction prose, which derided the cultivation of celebrity, propose art itself as an alternative mode of social change that is not reliant on the structures of identity required by the aesthetics of reform realism. Davis saw privileged reformers on both sides of the Atlantic become famous by campaigning on behalf of the populations they objectified in their fictions. Her work reveals to us how triangulated reform, celebrity, and authorship became in the second half of the nineteenth century and how the aesthetics of reform realism—so central to how middle and upper-class Anglo Americans came to think of their relationships to those who did not benefit from their systems—was seen by some as problematic from its very beginnings.

CHAPTER TWO

KATE CHOPIN'S ART PANIC

> Moral panics rarely alleviate any real problem, because they are aimed at chimeras and signifiers.
>
> —Gayle Rubin, "Thinking Sex," *Pleasure and Danger: Exploring Female Sexuality*

> There are many things in books besides isms and ologies. The world has always its poets who sing.
>
> —Kate Chopin, "Mrs. Mobry's Reason," in *The Complete Works of Kate Chopin*

The story of the revival of the author Kate Chopin as a significant literary figure of the nineteenth century is inextricable from the story of the second wave feminist movement of twentieth century. In her own time, Chopin's works appeared in popular periodicals aimed largely at female readers like *Fashion and Fancy*, *Vogue*, and *Century*. After feminist scholars began the project of her recovery in the 1960s, it was fitting then that her first major reemergence was in the women's magazine *Redbook*, which reprinted *The Awakening* (1899) in its entirety in the November 1972 issue with an accompanying introduction that positions the novel as a grand feminist gesture ahead of its time: "its reception broke her heart and destroyed her as a writer . . . acquaintances cut her, friends deserted her . . . *Redbook* presents 'The Awakening' now so that a brave woman and a fine writer will finally have the large audience she deserves."[1] Twentieth-century lay readers were introduced to Chopin as a feminist martyr. The rise in popularity of *The Awakening* within scholarly journals and course syllabi during the same period coincided with calls to add female authors to the canon and women's studies to the curriculum. As Barbara Ewell writes:

> The recovery of *The Awakening* in the 1970s, which rode the second wave of the women's movement and the new women's studies, occasioned a reevaluation of both the literary canon and the nature of its construction. Kate Chopin became a poster child for the neglect that mainstream critics imposed on works of art that failed to match their own, often individual biases.[2]

Though she may be thoroughly (and accurately) historicized as a part of the second wave of American feminism, Chopin distanced herself from the first wave of the women's movement that occurred during her own lifetime. Her son Felix recalled that she was "not interested in the women's suffrage movement," and, read in the context of short stories that more openly caricature New Woman figures like "Miss Witherwell's Mistake"(1891) and "Wiser Than a God" (1889), both to which this chapter will return, *The Awakening* may indeed be more of a send-up of the popular concept of female liberation that preoccupied the New Woman fiction of her time than an example of it.[3]

The heroine of Chopin's first novel, *At Fault* (1890), Thérèse Lafirme, is a kind of anti–New Woman. The owner of a southern plantation, she convinces the man she loves, David Hosmer, to remarry his former wife as an act of matrimonial duty. Her almost saint-like nature is contrasted with that of Hosmer's sister, Melicent, another New Woman caricature. Melicent is flighty, capricious, and caught up with the latest fashions all under the guise of a modern femininity the novel treats as shallow. Her entire personality amounts to a recurring joke in the novel, as when David tells Thérèse he has a "weighty" letter from Melicent:

> "Melicent talking weighty things? That's something new," said Thérèse interested.
> "Is Melicent ever anything else than new?" he enquired.[4]

As Ann Heilmann writes, "if the transatlantic New Woman movement is conceived as the cultural and literary arm of first-wave feminist activism, with the underlying objective of many writers being the use of literature as a political tool for social change, Chopin was certainly not a straightforward New Woman."[5] While it is not the case, as the last two chapters of this book will demonstrate, that it is impossible to be an activist who writes against reform fiction, the study of Kate Chopin is a dramatic illustration of how a writer who kept a considerable distance from the progressive movements of their own time might nevertheless produce fiction that would spur others to political action along the lines of those same movements.

I will suggest in this chapter that the reform writing Kate Chopin most closely criticized was not the New Woman novel or women's rights more generally, but another movement with which it overlapped: Social Purity. Chopin took aim at Social Purity for aesthetic, not political, reasons because its activists had first entered into the field of literary criticism. Their critique was one of content while Chopin's was one of style. Ultimately, Chopin criticized the conflation of morality with literary value and envisioned a form of realist fiction that would broaden the minds of its readers through the conveyance of impressions rather than data, of ideas rather than arguments.

PHOTOGRAPHIC RÉALISME

Chopin has been associated with both the realist and the naturalist traditions in American literature, but she also had specific complaints about various iterations of these movements. Donna Campbell identifies Chopin as an "unruly naturalist":

> unruly naturalism . . . pushes the boundaries of naturalism past conventional limits [and] provides a different way of looking at pervasive strains existing in the background rather than the foreground of classic naturalism, including issues of waste and abjection, disability and age, structural unevenness or excess, sentimentalism and melodrama, social reform, and women's use of technology.[6]

Many critics have associated Chopin with naturalism on the basis of the social determinism of her two published novels; she is also frequently connected to the literary realism associated with writers like Henry James and William Dean Howells.[7] Nancy Bentley locates Chopin's literary realism in her "scalpel-like style," but acknowledges that "literary realism likely had different compass points for Chopin from those it had for most northeastern writers," citing her deep affiliation with the French literary tradition.[8] Whether "unruly naturalist" or Franco-realist, Chopin's relationship with conventionally defined American literary movements is an uneasy and idiosyncratic one. Though Chopin was a Southern American writer who is often associated with the local color movement, Chopin scholarship has also long acknowledged the broad range of her international influences. Emily Toth identifies the short fiction of Guy de Maupassant as the influence for one of her earliest short stories, the 1891 "Mrs. Mobry's Reason."[9] Susan Wolstenhome reads the same story as having been primarily influenced by the Norwegian playwright Henrik Ibsen's 1881 *Ghosts*.[10] Both are likely right—Chopin was widely read in continental European literature and preferred it to the fiction of her fellow writers in English.

What is clear is that Chopin found fault with works of realism that were overly bent on accuracy. In a review of Émile Zola's *Lourdes* (1894), she laments how the author buries his narrative "beneath a mass of prosaic data."[11] Campbell writes that "Zola's methodically detailed naturalism was antithetical [to Chopin's]."[12] Flaubert and Balzac—French realists that heavily influenced Chopin but whom she also set out to improve upon stylistically—were subject to criticism that their work was too mechanical. The discourse of their time labeled this brand of realism as photographic: a mechanized reproduction devoid of the soul of the painter. The novelist Jules Barbey d'Aurevilly called the new French realism "l'école du daguerreotype" and of Flaubert, he wrote:

> If machines to narrate or analyze were forged in good English steel in Birmingham or Manchester—machines that functioned by themselves according to unknown processes of dynamics—they would absolutely function like Mr. Flaubert. In these machines we would feel as much life, soul, and human guts as we do in the man of marble who wrote *Madame Bovary* with a stone pen.[13]

The critic and historian A. A. Cuvillier-Fleury wrote in 1857 that "in the novel such as it is written today, with the techniques of photographic reproduction, the man within the painter disappears: only a steel plate is left."[14] As Jill Kelly explains of the aesthetically conservative French critics of their mid-nineteenth-century novelists,

> the camera objectified for the conservative critic all the sins of the realists: all the excesses of observation, of the use of the details of physical reality, of the indiscriminate cataloguing of the visible, of mechanical impersonality, of the immoral use of base materialism as subject. The dominance of a mechanical process was incompatible with true artistic goals; therefore, these literary "daguérreotypeurs" were not true artists.[15]

Chopin voices her own critique of overly exacting realism through bad artist characters that copy rather than innovate, record rather than invent. She casts Edna Pontellier, the heroine of *The Awakening*, as a congenital copier rather than a true artist who might represent the brave innovator's struggle against the demand for sexual propriety in the literary marketplace. *The Awakening* begins with the image of a parrot, mindlessly "repeating over and over" overheard phrases, prefiguring the characterization of Edna as a dilettante artist whose subjects (a Bavarian peasant, a basket of apples, a "young Italian character study") are deliberately clichéd, and whose prose is derivative: "Her most intimate friend at school had been one of rather exceptional intellectual gifts, who wrote fine-sounding essays, which Edna admired and strove to imitate."[16] When Madame Ratignolle praises one of Edna's sketches, she proclaims, "This basket of apples! Never have I seen anything more lifelike. One might almost be tempted to reach out a hand and take one."[17] Edna earlier attempts a sketch of her friend and is "greatly disappointed to find that it did not look like her," eventually throwing it away on account of her failure to produce an exact likeness, despite the praise the sketch garners from others.[18] Such devotion to verisimilitude is implied to be Edna's artistic weakness. When she pronounces to Mademoiselle Reisz that she is "becoming an artist," Reisz seems highly skeptical, and warns Edna that "the artist must possess the courageous soul . . . that dares and defies."[19] Edna's wrongheaded notions about art are precisely the reason why her rebellion against social norms has so often been deemed a failure.[20] Only art that is, according to Chopin's judgments, original—that is to say, passionate, expressive, and of the body—can produce the necessary reaction to effect social change. Likewise, as Rebecca Harding Davis's fiction argued before hers, social oppression can prevent the production of such original art.

One symptom of the lack of aesthetic originality in *The Awakening* is that Edna spends the near entirety of the novel quite bored. Often, she is bored to the point of somnolence, as when she grows sleepy reading Emerson. Authentic displays of artistry in *The Awakening*, like the emotional piano solos performed by Mademoiselle Reisz, move Edna in ways she can scarcely understand: "The very first chords which Mademoiselle Reisz struck upon the piano sent a keen tremor down Mrs. Pontellier's spinal column . . . the very passions themselves were aroused within her soul, swaying it, lashing it, as the waves daily beat upon her splendid body. She trembled, she was choking, and the tears blinded her."[21] Though Edna is capable of such deep affective responses to true artistry, her aesthetic sensibilities are more generally dulled by the culture of cheap entertainments and empty commodity consumption that surrounds her.[22] Chopin positions the singular, passionate work of a true artist like Reisz over the legions of sheet-music amateurs and hack writers who populate her age of cheap reproductions.

We might compare the scenes of Edna's response to Reisz's playing with her boredom induced by the banal *soirees musicales* at the Ratignolles', which consist of performers "with various degrees of taste and agility." She is likewise bored by the repetitive piano duets of the treacly Farival twins at Grand Isle. At the beginning of the novel, the twins are "playing a duet from 'Zampa' on the piano," which is described as "noise," and by chapter nine, they're still playing "a duet from 'Zampa,' and at the earnest solicitation of every one present follow[ing] it with the overture to 'The Poet and the Peasant.'" "Zampa" (1831) was a popular comic opera by the French composer Ferdinand Hérold that was widely recognized as derivative of Mozart's "Don Giovanni" (1787). It was later copied by Mérimée in his "La Vénus d'Ille" (1837). "The Poet and the Peasant" (1846) by Franz von Suppé was based on Karl Elmar's 1846 comedy of the same name. Mrs. Highcamp's mechanical performance of Greig is another major aesthetic disappointment at Grand Isle: "She seemed to have apprehended all of the composer's coldness and none of his poetry. While Edna listened she could not help wondering if she had lost her taste for music"—a complaint whose language echoes the criticisms of photographic réalisme lodged by the French critics.[23] Coldness without poetry implies, as d'Aurevilly wrote of Flaubert, a lack of the warm-bloodedness, of the passions, that both the French critic and the Southern U.S. writer saw as deadly to the production of truly effective fiction.

For Chopin, the passions of the body and the heart were linked to those of the mind and the pen. Love and art often seem dichotomous in Chopin's fictions. This theme has contributed to a reading of her works as feminist along the lines of Elizabeth Stuart Phelps's *The Story of Avis* (1877), wherein Avis tries—and fails—to negotiate between the demands of being a wife, mother, and artist. No one ever stops Chopin's characters from making art. Edna is never made to choose between her new artistic desires and her marriage. She is not prevented nor even hampered when she moves into the studio space she calls "the pigeon house"—her husband Léonce only works to reframe the situation to make it more palatable to onlookers. While

Léonce is without a doubt an insufferable male chauvinist, he is hardly a tyrant. I think the point of his depiction is how he demonstrates Edna's own lack of imagination in choosing and then tolerating him. If *The Awakening* is a book that teaches, by negative example, how to imagine, it is equally devoted to imagining both better art and better love.

Paula Von Stoltz, the German-American heroine of Chopin's 1889 short story "Wiser than a God" is forced to play cheap, imitative music at social gatherings in order to support herself and her ailing mother while she prepares for a career of playing professionally in Europe. The night of a gig at the wealthy Brainards, Paula reflects that their chosen program of popular waltzes will offer nothing "to tempt me into flights of originality; there'll be no difficulty in keeping to the hand-organ effect." As the evening progresses, the party allows Paula to attempt a richer and more challenging piece than the waltzes on the program: "the magnificent 'Jewel Song from "Faust."'"[24] The explanation of her expertise in playing this particular piece offered by Chopin's narrator suggests the author's belief in true artistry as a mix of practice and originality:

> How little did [Paula's] auditors appreciate in the performance the results of a life study, of a drilling that had made her amongst the knowing an acknowledged mistress of technique. But to her skill she added the touch and interpretation of the artist; and in hearing her, even Ignorance paid to her genius the tribute of a silent emotion.[25]

When George, the eldest son of the Brainard family, later proposes to Paula, she's practically offended by his suggestion that she—a true artist—would be content to be a wealthy society wife:

> "What do you know of my life," she exclaimed passionately, "What can you guess of it? Is music anything more to you than the pleasing distraction of an idle moment? Can't you feel that with me, it courses through the blood of my veins? That it's something dearer than life, than riches, even than love?"[26]

This isn't a choice between a life devoted to true, non-imitative art and the promise of love—even though Paula *does* admit that she loves George Brainard. It's a rejection of a love that's not quite up to the standards of her art. At the end of the story, it is implied that Paula has entered into a romance with a fellow musician in Germany—someone with enough originality and inspiration to provide a proper partnership.

Chopin's characters often turn to art when there isn't passion to be found anywhere else. Edna Pontellier is sexually aroused by art and representation (music, fiction, paintings, letters—and photographs) rather than the bodies of other characters. This tendency has been noted by Nicholas Gaskill, who suggests that "Chopin draws upon the affiliation between music and the erotic to express the paradoxical way in which the aesthetic, like sex, uses the rhythmical movements of corporeal experience to produce an ecstasy imagined to move beyond the boundaries of the self."[27] While scenes of actual sexual intercourse are implied in the novel, as in the final line of chapter twenty-one when Edna "become[s] supple to [the] gentle, seductive entreaties" of Alcée Arobin, they are always elided.[28] The most explicitly sexual passages are to be found in Edna's responses to the representational. It is ironic, then, that the anonymous reviewer of the novel for the *Chicago Times-Herald* laments that "it was not necessary for a writer of so great refinement and poetic grace to enter the overworked field of sex fiction," when the moral outrage *The Awakening* is meant to stir up is not directed towards bad sexualities, but rather towards bad art. This reviewer might have more keenly read the passage where Edna herself encounters such a fiction being passed among the guests at her *pension* in the resort community of Grand Isle: "she felt moved to read the book in secret and solitude, though none of the others had done so,—and to hide it from view at the sound of approaching footsteps. It was openly criticized and freely discussed at table. Mrs. Pontellier gave over being astonished, and concluded that wonders would never cease."[29] Edna's Kentucky-Presbyterian recoiling at the public intimacy of Creole culture is not the only reason that her response to the sexually explicit novel differs from that of her fellow resort-goers. Its other readers understand it as a diversion—an aesthetic construction—whereas, for Edna, the aesthetic *is* the sexual.

Edna's male love interests are uninspiring to her because they tend towards the artificial and the hackneyed. She reviews her history of sexual longing for a soldier, a tragic actor, and other masculine heterosexual clichés in her youth. The relationship with the tragic actor, the most detailed example, is entirely engaged through her interaction with his publicity photograph:

> The picture of the tragedian stood enframed upon her desk. Any one may possess the portrait of a tragedian without exciting suspicion or comment. (This was a sinister reflection which she cherished.) In the presence

> of others she expressed admiration for his exalted gifts, as she handed the photograph around and dwelt upon the fidelity of the likeness. When alone she sometimes picked it up and kissed the cold glass passionately.[30]

Edna justifies the existence of the framed photograph in her collection through the claim that she admires its representational qualities, the "fidelity of the likeness." She feigns enthrallment with the "gifts" of the man represented in the frame, but, in her solitude, it is revealed that the photograph itself is the object of her longing. What she values is not a successful representation, but an erotic object on which she can safely project her inchoate sexual desires. When she kisses the glass—the description of the glass as cold simultaneously reinforces the sensual delight of the act and the lifelessness of her partner—she is engaging in erotic play with an idealized representational object, not fantasizing about engagement with an actual man. Edna's relationship with the photograph also distances her from the "others" mentioned in the passage through behavior that she self-identifies as deviant, evidenced by her categorization of her "reflection" as "sinister." Walter Benn Michaels writes that "Edna's possession of the portrait marks a public not a private relation with the tragedian . . . you don't have to be loved by him to be able to buy his picture."[31] While Edna is obviously unloved by the tragedian and still able to perform her love, his fame does not make her relationship with him public nor is her love directed towards the tragedian himself. The public love for the tragedian is the lie that masks her more illicit, intensely private love for the representational image.

Her later affairs with Robert Lebrun and Alcée Arobin continue the pattern of her preference for the banal representations formed in her youth. Arobin is a surface character who produces nothing but abstract desire. His kiss is "not the kiss of love," but it nevertheless "inflamed her." Just as his kiss is not the kiss of love, but is able to produce a similar effect as we might imagine the kiss of love would, he is emblematic of what is to Chopin the most pernicious brand of realism: "his manner was so genuine that it often deceived even himself." Arobin is as close as one can come to being a photographic human, happy to be merely the simulacrum of a lawyer. His "personal friend" Laitner, of "Laitner and Arobin, lawyers . . . permitted Arobin's name to decorate the firm's letterheads and to appear on the shingle that graced Perdido Street," because, as Arobin quips in a Wildean appropriation of Shakespeare, "one is really forced as a matter of convenience these days to assume the virtue of an occupation if he has it not."[32] The "evidence" of Edna and Arobin's romantic intrigue that Robert finds is a photograph of Arobin. Edna uses the photograph, at Arobin's suggestion, to finish a drawing of him rather than having her subject sit for the portrait. This mode of reproduction from reproduction (drawing from a photograph) contrasts with the mode in which Edna produces the sketch of Adèle that she discards on account of its failed realism. That sketch is taken from life.

Edna's penchant for photographically mimetic art not only marks her preference for the representational ideal over the real in life, but also draws attention to the stodgy conservatism of her style more generally. Madame Ratignolle's praise for the realism of Edna's apples specifically marks both the subject and style of her work as *après garde*. Though the still life has always been a popular subject for representational painters, during the second half of the nineteenth century, apples enjoyed an unprecedented vogue. Mid-century realists like Gustave Courbet, who devoted most of his early career to the photorealistic depiction of laborers and peasants, made a surprisingly impressionistic turn in his depiction of apples in the 1870s, anticipating those more famous fruits of Cézanne and Degas, the former of whom was lifelong friends with Zola and the subject of his 1885 naturalist novel *L'Oeuvre*, and the latter of whom was living in New Orleans at the same time as Chopin.[33]

Courbet's earlier paintings, most particularly his 1849–1850 *A Burial at Ornans*, were influential for their revolutionary subject matter rather than an originality of technique.[34] *A Burial at Ornans* is almost hyperrealistic, demonstrating Courbet's influence from the Dutch school. The turn in his later work is therefore striking. His 1871 *Red Apples* are not only a drastic departure from the portraits and tableaux that made his name, stylistically they dissolve into a far more abstract impressionism.

The innovations in technique that marked the 1870s through the 1890s had a profound impact on the symbolic significance of what was often very banal subject matter. As Meyer Schapiro suggests, "in Cézanne's habitual representation of the apples as a theme by itself there is a latent erotic sense, an unconscious symbolizing of a repressed desire."[35] In her compulsive need to produce exact reproductions, Edna allows for none of the interpretive freedom that permeates Cézanne's still lifes to be expressed. Edna's art lacks the originality and passion that would make it meaningful or expressive of her rebellious desires.

FIGURE 2. "Apples" in the style of Gustave Courbet (French, second half of nineteenth century). H. O. Havemeyer Collection, Bequest of Mrs. H. O. Havemeyer. Courtesy of the Metropolitan Museum of Art.

Chopin's interest in visual art reappears throughout her writings and the word "impression" is a key one for her.[36] She praises Hamlin Garland's writing on Impressionism in painting in an 1894 essay and, in another essay on Zola, she suggests that Impressionism offers a deeper truth than realism, a sentiment she echoes in praising Maupasssant:

> I read his stories and marveled at them. Here was life, not fiction; for where were the plots, the old-fashioned mechanism and stage trapping that in a vague, unthinking way I had fancied were essential to the art of story making. Here was a man who had escaped tradition and authority, who had entered into himself and looked out upon life through his own being and with his own eyes; and who, in a simple and direct way, told us what he saw. When a man does this, he gives us the best that he can; something valuable for it is genuine and spontaneous. He gives us impressions.[37]

While Chopin herself has moved far past the mechanical, photographic realism of mid-century fictions and paintings, Edna has not. Her mid-century mode of depiction is clearly not up to the progressive political aims of her late-century moment nor aligned with Chopin's own tastes in art.

FIGURE 3. Paul Cézanne, "Apples," 1878–1879. The Mr. and Mrs. Henry Ittleson Jr. Purchase Fund, 1961. Courtesy of the Metropolitan Museum of Art.

Robert's praise of Edna's less realistic work might be suggestive of a more progressive aesthetic position. His surname, Lebrun, is quite possibly a reference to the seventeenth-century court painter Charles Le Brun, a reading supported by Robert's tendency to pay homage to the courtiers of Grand Isle.[38] The popularity of the Paris Salon exhibits of the Académie Royale de Peinture et de Sculpture in the late nineteenth century occasioned a host of articles, in both high and low periodicals, presenting the history of that venerable institution, which referenced Le Brun and the debates he organized at the Académie in 1667. A seventeen-page illustrated spread about the debates by Henry Tyrrell appeared in July 1893's *Frank Leslie's Popular Monthly*, a magazine to which Chopin documents submitting her short story "A Shameful Affair" in June 1891.[39] Tyrrell's history includes an account of the struggles Lebrun faced, prior to the establishment of the Académie, in keeping the atelier he shared with his colleagues warm enough in the winter months to allow for the use of nude models, a practice he believed was essential to the production of fine paintings.

The subject of the 1667 debates was the balance between imitation and innovation, as many were beginning to fear that the mode of art education through copying the masters would lead to overly imitative styles.[40] Paul Duro notes that Le Brun argued that the ancient Greeks wore loose-fitting clothing that "in no way spoiled the visible form of their limbs."[41] Along with being able to study at will near-naked slaves and athletes, painters and sculptors of the classical age were thereby offered a natural advantage over artists of a later, less-favored, age, who were forced to reference ancient art in order to have access to nude models. In Le Brun's estimation, the sexual conservatism of the late seventeenth century was an indirect cause of that era's perceived decline in artistic innovation. Artists of that period were forced to copy other representations rather than produce from life.

Nathaniel Hawthorne similarly longs for the sexual freedom of the Greeks in comparison with his own less-favored age in *The Marble Faun* (1859), a novel rife with moments of art criticism like Robert and Edna's. Hawthorne's Miriam points out that a nineteenth-century artist

> cannot sculpture nudity with a pure heart, if only because he is compelled to steal guilty glances at hired models. The marble inevitably loses its chastity under such circumstances. An old Greek sculptor, no doubt, found his models in the open sunshine, and among pure and princely maidens, and thus the nude statues of antiquity are as modest as violets, and sufficiently draped in their own beauty. But as for Mr. Gibson's coloured Venuses, (stained, I believe, with tobacco-juice,) and all other nudities of to-day, I really do not understand what they have to say to this generation, and would be glad to see as many heaps of quick-lime in their stead![42]

Miriam's "nudities of today" are ineffective not only because they are copies of copies but because they are produced in a culture from which the body has been removed. So the depiction of sexuality, or even simply the human body, must be reduced to provocative contexts. Chopin's writing is clearly not a version of "coloured Venuses," but an attempt to chip away at the edifice of prudery casting shadows over the production of art that attempts to depict a more well-rounded representation of the human experience. The modesty Miriam notes in the Greek sculptures is redolent with the kind of innocence and authenticity characterized by heroines like Edna. For Chopin, these depictions of sexuality were consonant with real-world experience, representations of life from life, rather than sanitized imitations of previous works.

THE TWO PANICS

Chopin's fiction connects the earlier French critics' aesthetic concern that literary realism could, in its worst iterations, be too "photographic" with British and American Social Purity activists moral concern that photographs could be too "real." The Social Purity activists' disdain for technological reproducibility found its most formidable enemy in the photographic print—which, therefore, became a potent symbol of their politics. The National Vigilance Association in Britain demanded before the House of Commons that the law pertaining to "indecent pictures and prints" be "vigorously enforced and, if necessary, strengthened."[43] In the American context, Molly McGarry shows how the Social Purity activist Anthony Comstock's disgust for the "lewd photographs" among his collection of "abominations," paralleled anxieties about photographs represented in the larger cultural sphere of the mid-nineteenth-century popular periodical, which frequently printed stories about a hero or heroine's moral decline perpetuated by a photograph. The protagonists of such tales would replace a human lover with a photographic love object, a "double" with "a unique ability to disrupt an ordinary, heterosexual love plot. In this sense, the copy encoded a certain kind of sexual transgression, troubling marriages and redirecting female desire away from proper, 'real' lovers."[44] The Social Purity concern over the proliferation of what its reformers called sex fiction, often produced in inexpensive volumes that made their contents more readily accessible to all classes of readers, was as much paranoia about the increased ease of *textual* reproduction as it was about the depiction (or indirect implication) of acts of *sexual* reproduction. Anthony Comstock's New York Society for the Suppression of Vice (NYSSV) made a special distinction, for example, between expensive editions of potentially vice-ridden "classics" like the *Decameron* for "literary or educational purposes" and those "sold by certain parties as 'rich rare and racy books,' 'amorous adventures,' 'spicy descriptions,' 'love intrigues on the sly,' etc."[45] Cheap, mass-produced copies of works even Comstock would admit possess a literary value are cast as dangerous contaminants when made available to the masses.

The Social Purity movement, embodied by such organizations as the NVA in England and the American Purity Alliance (APA) in the United States, was a highly visible reform movement in the late century that, like the New Woman movement, engaged in a reciprocal discourse with contemporaneous fiction. Landmark events in the movement were the trial of the publisher Henry Vizetelly in 1888, of Oscar Wilde in 1895, the publication of the English-language edition of Max Nordau's *Degeneration* in 1895, and international conferences on purity, featuring prominent English and American speakers, held at the Columbian Exposition in 1893 (organized by Anthony Comstock), at Baltimore in 1895, and The International Congress on the White Slave Trade held in London by the National Vigilance Association on June 21–22, 1899. In the welcoming address of the National Purity Congress held in Baltimore by the American Purity Alliance October 14–16, 1895, the speaker, Joshua Levering, observed "the purity question is one of great absorbing interest, equaled only by the legalized liquor traffic, and like it, occupying at the present time the mind and attention of humanitarians all over our country and in all lands."[46] As Amanda Claybaugh notes, the literary New Woman movement was the name for a debate rather than a set of coherent positions, and this was true of the Social Purity Movement as well.[47] At least two factions campaigned under the aegis of Social Purity: a more conservative branch focused on the amelioration of "impure" culture and a somewhat more liberal branch, which has been identified as feminist, centered around Josephine Butler's campaign for the repeal of the Contagious Diseases Act in Great Britain.[48] While one side of the movement focused on abolishing legal sex work and creating legislation to benefit women experiencing domestic violence, the other focused on removing any depictions of sexuality from popular media. The response to fin de siècle fiction generated by Social Purity reformers has been well documented, but the ways in which the rhetoric of the movement enters the fictions themselves has not.[49] The media-focused Social Purity reviewers whipped up a moral panic about art that depicted sexual themes. Kate Chopin responded with the creation of an art panic. Chopin's position represents a counter-reform discourse that sought to prevent popular literature from becoming mired in its own cultural and historical moment at the expense of artistic integrity.

One of Chopin's earliest stories, "Mrs. Mobry's Reason," concerns a family bent against marrying for secret reasons, reasons that become clear by the story's end when Mrs. Mobry's daughter Naomi experiences a mental breakdown and Mrs. Mobry must confess to her husband, "it has been in the blood that is mine for generations, John, and I knew it, and I married you."[50] Both Toth and Wolstenhome read this confession as Mrs. Mobry's understanding that she has inherited secondary syphilis. Elaine Showalter demonstrates the prevalence of syphiliphobia in fin de siècle Social Purity writings as well as in the British fiction of the same period and argues that the deformed or degenerate children resultant of unfortunate liaisons in these works are often depicted as syphilitic:

> Deformed or retarded, the syphilitic infant was a pitiful sight, described by one doctor as 'small, wisened, atrophied, weakly, sickly creature,' resembling a 'monkey or a little old man.' Suffering, apish, shriveled, and prematurely aged, these syphilitic children appeared to feminists as living symbols of the devolutionary force of male vice.[51]

The notion that these fictions depict—that children produced in lust would be degenerate—was widespread. American reformer and journalist Benjamin Orange Flower's 1895 polemic even argues against lustful sex *within* marriage, quoting a "scholarly physician," as saying "the taproot of immorality today is found in prostitution within the marriage relation, which for centuries has produced children of lust, and these children in turn have brought forth their kind until the moral fabric is weakened throughout civilization."[52] Flower goes beyond arguments common to activists who protested marital rape, which was a cause most frequently taken up within the temperance movement, to imply that *any* lustful intercourse within marriage—he does not even obliquely speak to issues of consent, as Elizabeth Cady Stanton would do directly—would have this weakening effect on society. The use of children as a rhetorical center of the argument against unchecked sexuality was common to both factions of the Social Purity movement.

In *Sex Panic and the Punitive State* (2011), Roger Lancaster outlines the social, cultural, and juridical power of sex panics from the late-nineteenth century to the present day. Echoing Lee Edelman's argument in *No Future* (2004), Lancaster asserts that "the constant element in successive waves of panic is the figure of the imperiled innocent child—a child whose innocence is defined in terms of his imagined sexlessness and whose protection from sex looms as an ever more urgent and exacting demand."[53] This effective rhetoric is the beating heart of Margaret Oliphant's widely read and cited review of *Jude the Obscure*, "The Anti-Marriage League." Oliphant writes, "to make [sex] the supreme incident, always in the foreground, to be discussed by young men and women, and held up before boys and girls . . . seems to me an outrage for which there is no justification." After harping upon the dangers to young people that *Jude* and Grant Allen's *The Woman Who Did* (1895) pose, she laments the extermination of Jude and Sue's children, who are murdered by Jude's son from a previous marriage after Sue unintentionally suggests to the boy that the children are the cause of the family's misfortunes. "Does Mr. Hardy think this is a good way of disposing of the progeny of such unfortunate connections? Does he recommend it for general adoption?"[54] She goes on to relate a true-life anecdote of a young woman who murdered the baby that was the consequence of her own out-of-wedlock affair. Sex outside of marriage, she seems to imply, will only be productive of children whose very lives are under constant threat. Novels about sexual "vice" like *Jude* and Sarah Grand's internationally bestselling *The Heavenly Twins* (1893) became the center of a scandal about "sex fiction" that would preoccupy the Victorian press throughout the decade for reasons both moral and financial.

By the 1890s, control of the literary market in England had shifted from monopolistic subscription libraries to reviewers, and while this gave readers more options in the marketplace and more agency over the selection of their reading material, it also created a fractious power vacuum.[55] Previously, Mudie's—the most successful of the circulating libraries—had been the de facto enforcer of moral standards in literature, well known for its promise to protect "The Young Person," the advertised audience for whom the library selected its books. As Paul Delany writes,

> Victorian reviewers sought to claim for themselves the moral authority of Victorian canonical fiction, by explicitly upholding those moral standards that had been silently enforced by Mudie. They mounted regular campaigns against unconventionality in fiction, from Hardy's *Jude the Obscure* (1895) to Lawrence's *The Rainbow* (1915). They found the causes of degeneracy either in infection from across the channel ("Zolaism"), or in a welling-up from below of the primal instincts of the dangerous classes.[56]

These moral debates, ostensibly over the control of the literary marketplace, also constituted a body of media highly profitable in its own right. Reviews, especially the hyperbolically condemnatory ones, sold magazines. Following the decline of Mudie's, a flurry of articles descended to protest or defend the sex fiction dominating the market.

Often these articles took the form of direct responses; for example, Charles Hamilton Aïdé's 1895 "The Modern Young Person," which appeared in *Belgravia* attributed pseudonymously to "Rita," bore the subtitle "A Response to 'The Tree of Knowledge.'" "The Tree of Knowledge," published in *The New Review* in 1894, is a collection of fourteen brief responses from authors, scientists, and social activists, as to whether young women should be given access to texts that contain references to sex. Almost all the contributors agree: there is no reason to protect young women from knowledge of any sort. Aïdé's "The Modern Young Person" is a satire of the kind of New Woman the authors of "The Tree of Knowledge" would create. This modern young person, like Chopin herself, reads novels by Zola and Grand. She arrogantly chuckles, thinking:

> there had been times not so very far back, when Mr. Mudie had catered for Her especially. When poor, tortured authors and authoresses had been compelled to write a sort of Bowdlerized literature, for fear her morals might sustain injury. But those days were also over, and the Young Person grinned delightedly as she thought of it, and thought, too, how easily she had, even in those days, circumvented Mr. Mudie and the watchful mamma.[57]

Of course, Aïdé's Young Person is punished at the story's end, marrying a man her father warns against who is sure to wreak disaster for her.

The debate in the House of Commons that subsequently led to the trial and sentencing of Henry Vizetelly, publisher of Zola's English editions, was printed and distributed, along with other NVA texts and newspaper contributions, as a pamphlet entitled "Pernicious Literature" by the NVA in 1889. This pamphlet makes many far-fetched suggestions such as that the purveyors of French realism were "in league with houses of the worst class," leading young women into sex work after poisoning their minds with salacious texts, and that "it would be impossible for any young man . . . to have read [Zola] without committing some form of outward sin within twenty-four hours after." The pamphlet's most curious anxiety, however, is not directed towards the purveyors and practitioners of impure texts and habits, but towards other, unsavory Social Purity activists, seeking only to profit from the movement's visibility:

> We must confess to looking with suspicion upon the many "vigilance" societies which have been started to look after our morals. The idea . . . has been very much abused by its connection with a vast array of irresponsible persons who have their own notoriety at stake first, and then the morals of the people.[58]

The anonymous contributor makes a clear distinction between those who enter into the field of reform with true aims for the realization of a higher moral purpose, and those who mimic the conventions of society speeches and tracts in order to profit from their popularity.

Though she stood on the other side of the moral debates from the reviewers who lobbied to protect the Young Person, Chopin would agree with their sentiments of disapproval for those who would feign moral outrage to garner publicity. She expressed her disapproval of the kind of attention generated by this practice of hyperbolic reviewing through her own review of *Jude*, published in the St. Louis *Criterion* in 1897. Here she expressed a very different concern with regards to the welfare of the Young Person. Instead of entering a debate about morality, Chopin expresses a sarcastic concern about artistic integrity.

The review begins with an anecdote about the shock her copy, left out on a visiting-room table, elicited from a polite guest. Outwardly, Chopin's review is damning—"the book is detestably bad"—and yet betrays certain admiration for, or perhaps merely uncomfortable identification with, the novel it purports to hate. When "one or two youngsters" ask her about the book, Chopin responds that it is "unutterably tiresome . . . but you might like it." Indeed, Chopin's primary objection to the novel, reformulated and repeated throughout the review, is that it's boring: "ponderous . . . formidable . . . nothing alluring . . . the outward appearance of a Congressional Record . . . colorless . . . unpardonably dull" etc., etc. She laments that no one was interested in the book prior to the controversy it stirred in the press, a controversy into which she, as yet another reviewer of the novel, has now entered; but under what terms?

> It seems rather irrelevant and late in the day to say all this about *Jude the Obscure*. It is only sympathy for the young person which moves me to do so. I hate to know that deceptions are being practiced upon him. He has been led to believe that the work is quite dangerous and alluring. . . . I feel very sorry to think that he should part with so many good silver quarters and receive nothing in return but disappointment and dissolution.[59]

This assertion of concern for "the young person" wasting his money on a boring novel in which he had hoped to find something satisfyingly lurid is Chopin's satirical response to the overzealous parade of reviewers that damned *Jude* in both the English and American presses out of fear for what it might do to impressionable minds. Her use of the phrase "the young person" clearly references the moral politics of Mudie's. Chopin enters the debate not to defend the portrayal of sexuality in *Jude*, but rather to lament that the young reader who goes to the book in search of it will find little to gratify his curiosity. The performance of her own aesthetic outrage at the dullness of Hardy's novel is less a gesture aimed at Hardy or *Jude* than it is a perverse counterstrike against reviewers who object to the immorality of novels that portray sexual desire. Kate Chopin counters their sex panic with an art panic of her own.

Moralistic criticism and imitative reform fiction posed dual threats to the popularity of substantive literary art: if the moralists crowded the marketplace, would the writers of art fiction without an explicit purpose be able to secure their audience? Chopin privileged innovative literary works over what she perceived of as cheap imitations. But she also viewed market victory as crucial to upholding high aesthetic standards for popular literature. As Barbara Ewell notes, the ledgers where Chopin recorded her periodical submissions, "reflect a woman who was keeping track of what worked and what didn't, how much she was paid, and . . . how much her writing had ultimately earned."[60] She wanted to avoid catering to the popular taste for cause-based fiction but knew she needed to follow its forms to get her work published and read. She found a solution by utilizing the venue of the popular periodical to publish satires about the conventions of such fictions, engaging in a mode of aesthetic-reform writing that opposes political-reform writing.

These stories adapt the formula of Social Purity rhetoric, wherein so-called legitimate sex—that is, sex within marriage for the purposes of reproduction—produces a pure child while any sex outside of those terms produces a degenerate child, to the production of texts. Just as social purists like Flower believed that lust would corrupt civilization, Chopin believed moralizing reform critics and imitative realist writers would corrupt literature. While Social Purity activists, popular writers, and sexologists filled periodicals with debates over morality, Chopin preferred to sidestep any active involvement in overtly political reform or "preaching," as she called it, in her fiction.[61] Instead, her quarrel with society took the form of satire. Chopin might be thought of as what Aaron Matz calls a satirical realist: "satirical realism does not dissent in order to correct: it judges existing reality against a standard that reality can never achieve, and so it relinquishes any hope of correction."[62] A good example of this mode of satirical double-speak is when

Chopin writes that the editor for *The Criterion*, who attempted to solicit an opinion piece from her on issues of the day, was mistaken

> in supposing that I had any opinions . . . I have sometimes thought of cultivating a few—a batch of sound, marketable opinions, in anticipation of just such an emergency, but I neglected to do so. Of course there are such a thing as transplanted opinions; then one may know them, even steal them; there are lots of ways; but what is the use?[63]

The joke about "stolen" or "transplanted" opinions is a dig at writers who would insert a popular purpose in their fiction to court support or controversy. Chopin portrayed artistic production and biological reproduction in fictional double-exposures to air a real grievance about how the debates occasioned by the Social Purity movement were preventing the proliferation of "real" art—that is to say, art that depends on literary rather than moral merit to stake a claim for its value.

Her fictions protest the hijacking of literature by the moral debates of reform in a manner that had to be indirect in order to avoid undermining its own message. "I did not tell all this to the editor of *The Criterion*," Chopin writes towards the end of her account, "because I might have lost the opportunity of telling it to the public."[64] Instead of editorializing, she speaks to the public through her fiction. Her 1891 short story "Miss Witherwell's Mistake" uses a series of sexual puns to equate Miss Witherwell's textual production with sexual reproduction—riffing on Social Purity rhetoric. Miss Witherwell is an unmarried writer for the *Boredomville Battery*, with a "lively and prolific pen;" she writes "with a promptness and precision that seldom miscarried," fostering in her readers the "growth of soft desire."[65] When Miss Witherwell falls ill, her niece is sent in as a literary replacement, "bewildering the small Cerberus, who mounted guard at the head of the editorial stairs, with the glaringly unbelievable announcement that she was 'Miss Witherwell.'"[66] The prolific, formulaic journalist has somehow managed to produce a copy of even herself. Her niece eventually asks for some writerly advice on devising an ending for the love story she claims to be writing. (The story is a ruse for her actual affair with a young man whom her parents forbade her to marry.) Her aunt exclaims "the poison of the realistic school has certainly tainted and withered your fancy in the bud, my dear, if you hesitate a moment. Marry them, most certainly, or let them die"—making Miss Witherwell's thoughts on extramarital sex and literary innovation equally clear.[67]

In Chopin's short story, the unimaginative journalist who champions conservative sexual values is associated with a decline in the quality of art. That Miss Witherwell should possess so formulaic a fictional strategy reflects a preoccupation with overly imitative styles, copies of copies easily produced and reproduced without the integrity of innovation. The fear of such enervated copies mirrors the conservative fear that sex outside of marriage would produce corrupt or debilitated citizens, weakening the moral fabric of civilization.

A FAILED REVOLT?

Chopin's critique of the bad aesthetic consequences of Social Purity rhetoric is not without its own innovative conclusions about the role of art and literature in social change. The revolt of Edna Pontellier ends in her death because she does not stake a large enough claim in the power of her imaginative faculties, nor does she enact her fantasies through a sufficiently innovative form. Edna's revolutionary politics are there—but her ability to effectively express those sentiments through art is not. Her personal revolt fails for aesthetic reasons. Edna's marriage to Léonce can be read as her first failed attempt at overthrowing existing structures of power:

> [Léonce] pleased her; his absolute devotion flattered her. She fancied there was a sympathy of thought and taste between them, in which fancy she was mistaken. Add to this the violent opposition of her father and her sister Margaret to her marriage with a Catholic, and we need seek no further for the motives which led her to accept Monsieur Pontellier for her husband.

In marrying Léonce, she believes herself to be acting rebelliously, because he is an unsatisfactory choice in the eyes of her dictatorial father and conformist sister. Her desire to overthrow the control of her father is well placed, but her mode of doing so is not. Worse still, she begins to believe in the virtue of a marriage we might think of as its own kind of coldness without poetry: "she grew fond of her husband, realizing with some unaccountable satisfaction that no trace of passion or excessive and fictitious warmth colored her affection, thereby threatening its dissolution."[68] She is satisfied with the image of a marriage rather than the real, embodied thing. A marriage is, for Edna, a thing to be had, a box to be ticked—an opinion her husband shares.

Edna's status as the property of her husband Léonce is solidified at the beginning of the novel in the oft-quoted moment wherein he looks at his sunburned wife "as one looks at a valuable piece of personal property which has suffered some damage."[69] Léonce comes to stand for both economic and sexual power; the two are entirely intermingled when, after Edna's receipt of a package of expensive *friandises* in his absence, Mr. Pontellier is declared "the best husband in the world," demonstrating that pecuniary strength and its ostentatious display are the most important criteria for an ideal masculine partner.[70] Understanding it as the seat of his power, Léonce takes great delight in his property—both human and inanimate: "He greatly valued his possessions, chiefly because they were his, and derived genuine pleasure from contemplating a painting, a statuette, a rare lace curtain—no matter what—after he had bought it and placed it among his household gods."[71] Many critics read Edna's generation of her own income, and appropriation of her own space, as her triumph over Léonce's all-consuming ownership, yet Ivy Schweitzer convincingly articulates an objection to this position: "By becoming a producer, rather than remaining a re-producer, Edna enters more deeply into the system of exchange in which she was considered 'goods' to be acquired and possessed," and, furthermore, when Edna asserts that she is her own "to keep or give away," that, as Schweitzer continues, "to conceive of the self as that which can be possessed, and thus given away, necessarily assumes the possibility of self-as-property."[72] Edna's rebellion is incomplete if it is anything less than an upheaval of the structure of ownership altogether.[73]

Edna's most successful revolt, in my estimation, occurs in acts of vandalism that can be read as an emergent—if not fully formed—radical aesthetic. Similar to how Davis's Hugh Wolfe uses a waste product to make art he then typically destroys, Edna's best works are her acts of destruction. She tears up a handkerchief and shatters a vase because "she wanted to destroy something. The crash and clatter were what she wanted to hear."[74] She not only wants to ruin things that, like herself, Léonce owns, she also wants to *make* something out of her demolition: "the crash and clatter." This sonic intervention punctures the silence of the bourgeois domestic sphere. John W. Crowley goes so far as to assert that, in Edna's deep appreciation of musical experimentation, Kate Chopin becomes "the only writer of her generation to anticipate jazz."[75] We see Edna's radical aesthetic again when she listens to Mademoiselle Reisz's music and gives the pieces her own titles. These small violences, along with her two affairs, destabilize the existent property relations and their attendant modes of identification. But without a commitment to originality, she cannot go far enough.

Critics who argue against reading Edna as a revolutionary figure often do so on the basis of the novel's reassertion of conventional social forms. Patricia Yaeger, for example, claims that because Edna's adultery is acknowledged and dismissed by her husband and the Weir-Mitchell-like Dr. Mandelet, it only more deeply inscribes her into the patriarchal system.[76] I read Edna's relationship with Robert as more of an alliance-in-oppression than a romantic intrigue. Together they dream of discovering pirate gold—stolen capital. Instead of spending it in the male-dominated, exchange economy, they would use it like Edna's vase and handkerchief, to engage in acts of creative destruction:

> "Pirate gold isn't a thing to be hoarded or utilized. It is something to squander and throw to the four winds, for the fun of seeing the golden specks fly."
>
> "We'd share it, and scatter it together," he said. His face flushed.[77]

Blushing as if sexually excited, Robert finds his *jouissance* in the thought of the class upheaval in which he can engage with Mrs. Pontellier, a woman who, unlike the many others who preceded her to whom Robert "had constituted himself the devoted attendant of some fair dame or damsel," takes him "seriously."[78] Early on in the novel, he becomes angry with Adèle Ratignolle, who urges him to accept that he and Edna can never consummate their flirtation:

> His face flushed with annoyance, and taking off his soft hat he began to beat it impatiently against his leg as he walked. "Why shouldn't she take me seriously?" he demanded sharply. "Am I a comedian, a clown, a jack-in-the-box? Why shouldn't she? You Creoles! I have no patience with you! Am I always to be regarded as a feature of an amusing programme?"[79]

Robert responds most vociferously to Adèle's euphemism: he wants to be taken "seriously." He wants to be seen as a man rather than as an aesthetic object—a comedian, a clown, or a jack-in-the-box—reprimanding Madame Pontellier for the suggestion: "you ought to feel that such things are not flattering to say to a fellow."[80] Eventually, Robert would rather have a non-aesthetic function. This is why he goes to Mexico to explore his options for a career in business, an abandonment of the revolutionary solidarity he may once have shared with Edna.

Robert's departure is made all the more regrettable for Edna by his failure to present her with a photographic token. Undiscouraged, Edna goes to Madame Lebrun's home and seizes upon the collection of his childhood photographs:

> She gazed around the room at the pictures and photographs hanging upon the wall, and discovered in some corner an old family album, which she examined with the keenest interest. . . . But there was no recent picture. . . . "Oh, Robert stopped having his pictures taken when he had to pay for them himself! He found wiser use for his money, he says," explained Madame Lebrun.[81]

The pictures of Robert contained in the family photograph album are for the edification of the Lebrun family, not for the benefit of Robert himself. As Pierre Bourdieu argues, family photographs are "nothing but the group's image of its own integration."[82] Robert's appearance in these images locates him as a part of a familial whole. His graduation into adulthood is marked here by his parents' discontinuance of the practice of photographically integrating him into a desexualized familial context. It now falls to Robert to pay to produce his own image because the never-produced images of Robert as an adult would have served a markedly different purpose than his mother's collection of baby pictures. His vision of "wiser use for his money" is now to enter the male, transactional economy, to produce desires that can be exchanged or acted upon in the physical world.

Once Robert is out of the picture, Edna moves on to Arobin. Arobin is described as a "conventional man of fashion," and is clearly meant to reference a familiar character in what Linda Dowling calls "the fin de siècle bestiary."[83] Ellen Moers observes of English literature of the period that "for the amusement and gratification of the New Woman, the best-selling novelists created a new kind of masculine foil which combined the aesthete, the decadent, and the dandy. . . . More playthings than heroes, these gentlemen are actually 'kept men,'" an apt description of Arobin's role in the novel and his position in relation to Edna.[84] But, as with Robert before him, Edna sees in the dandiacal Arobin the possibility of a revolutionary coconspirator.

Dowling traces the reception of the dandy at the fin de siècle, showing how the press associated the dandy with revolutionary politics by way of French decadence and often conflated paranoia about the dandy's weakened morals with paranoia about the anarcho-socialist "threat." She quotes Hugh E. M. Stutfield's June 1895 *Blackwood's Edinburgh Magazine* article

"Tommyrotics," which cautions readers, "the aesthetic sensualist and the communist are, in a sense, nearly related. Both have . . . a common parentage in exaggerated emotionalism. . . . In these days the unbridled licentiousness of your literary decadent has its counterpart in the violence of the political anarchist."[85] The real nature of the political threat promised by Arobin is suggested in this exchange with Edna, surrounding the party she plans for her twenty-ninth birthday:

> "What about the dinner?" he asked; "the grand event, the coup d'état?"
> "It will be the day after to-morrow. Why do you call it the 'coup d'état?' Oh! it will be very fine; all my best of everything—crystal, silver and gold, Sèvres, flowers, music, and champagne to swim in. I'll let Léonce pay the bills. I wonder what he'll say when he sees the bills."
> "And you ask me why I call it a coup d'état?"[86]

Arobin recognizes that the best way to overthrow "l'etat" is through an appropriation of its funds to one's own, wasteful end. Edna's luxuriant spending on an event unsanctioned by Léonce subverts her function as his vicarious, conspicuous consumer. She is now consuming for herself. Her fantasy of revolution with Robert—to scatter found capital rather than reinvest it in the market—is reimagined as a deliberate attack on "state" property.

The terms of the attack are once again aesthetic rather than sociopolitical. Her dinner party demonstrates the radical possibilities of a manipulation of forms. Edna attends several dinner parties in the novel which are, like one at the Highcamp's, "quiet and uninteresting." But the decisions she makes about her party, coupled with her eccentric guest list, reinvent the staid form as subversive. At Edna's party, "There was something extremely gorgeous about the appearance of the table, an effect of splendor conveyed by a cover of pale yellow satin under strips of lace-work. . . . The ordinary stiff dining chairs had been discarded for the occasion and replaced by the most commodious and luxurious which could be collected throughout the house." But it is Edna's self-presentation most of all that changes the meaning of the event: "There was something in her attitude, in her whole appearance when she leaned her head against the high-backed chair and spread her arms, which suggested the regal woman, the one who rules, who looks on, who stands alone."[87] Such victories are short-lived for Edna, who cannot maintain the brief spurts of abstraction and distortion that most clearly capture her revolutionary impulses.

It is often noted that *The Awakening* is itself a copy of Flaubert's 1856 *Madame Bovary*.[88] The distinction between these two works—besides the obvious differences of length and setting—is that in copying Flaubert, Chopin makes a kind of double-voiced argument about both realism and politicized literature. Flaubert's heroine is merely a mindless consumer of popular romantic ideas, but Edna possesses a desire to create. She may fall victim to the same social forces and poor aesthetic products that occasion Emma's downfall, but in giving Edna the will to make her own art—if not exactly the means— Chopin suggests that the proliferation of imitative realist literature overly bent on making a political argument dulls the liberatory potential of aesthetic products with more impressionistic styles. By giving us impressions rather than arguments, such works of fiction as Chopin prized encourage readers to become innovative writers and thinkers that challenge existing social orders. And this was precisely the impact her work had on many of the readers who would encounter it for the first time seventy years after her death.

Paradoxically, had Chopin's novel been more overtly linked to the feminist movements of her own time, like those of the American novelist Elizabeth Stuart Phelps or the British novelist Mona Caird—both of whom addressed specific topics of proposed reform in their fiction—it may not have had the kind of intense impact so many individual readers report experiencing. For example, the literary critic Mary E. Papke writes of her own first encounter with *The Awakening*:

> I had found the copy in what was then, I think, the only English-language feminist bookstore in Montreal. I stayed up all night, one arm hanging outside the bedcovers holding up the book, exposing as little of myself to the cold air as was possible. And when I got to the end, I was profoundly shocked. . . . I had never before read a novel that so assaulted my senses and left me so distraught as its end that I had to return to it again and again to determine why.[89]

Papke is distraught at the end because Edna's revolt fails—she swims out into the bay rather than starting a women's club to rescue sex workers, as the heroine of the Social Purity activist Ursula Newel Gestefeld's 1892 *The Woman Who Dares* does; or, fighting for suffrage, as the heroine of women's rights activist Mary Johnston's 1913 novel *Hagar* does. The novel with a purpose may ultimately not always be the best way to get that purpose met. In the 1884 essay "The Art of Fiction," Henry James writes,

> The essence of moral energy is to survey the whole field, and I should . . . not [say] that the English novel has a purpose, but that it has a diffidence. To what degree a purpose in a work of art is a source of corruption I shall

not attempt to inquire; the one that seems to me least dangerous is the purpose of making a perfect work. As for our novel, I may say, lastly, on this score, that, as we find it in England to-day, it strikes me as addressed in a large degree to "young people," and that this in itself constitutes a presumption that it will be rather shy. There are certain things which it is generally agreed not to discuss, not even to mention, before young people. That is very well, but the absence of discussion is not a symptom of the moral passion. The purpose of the English novel . . . strikes me, therefore, as rather negative.[90]

James's sardonic reference to "the young person" as a site for the unnecessary entanglement of literature and morality is there first, as in Chopin's review of *Jude*, to suggest a direct critique of those who would continue to uphold the Mudie's-like standards and rage against the texts that violate them. But it is also there to connote that the ideological letter obliquely addressed to just such a reader will eventually reach its destination. In stating that "the absence of discussion is not a symptom of the moral passion," he implies the truth will out. Just as Chopin later expressed sympathy for the young person who would mourn such an "absence of discussion" in *Jude the Obscure*, James here reasons that young people will find in aesthetically—rather than morally—good fiction the messages they need to hear and shape our collective futures by them. Edna is a case study in how to feel but what not to do about it. To paraphrase Chopin's own words, her story contains all of the poetry and none of the isms and ologies.

PART TWO
There Is No Opposition

CHAPTER THREE

POLITICAL INTIMACY IN HENRY JAMES

"I like opposition," Verena exclaimed, with a happy smile.

—Henry James, *The Bostonians*

While writers like Davis and Chopin saw moralistic criticism and fiction invested in overtly political agendas to be antithetical to the aims of art, the mid-career, realist work of Henry James looks to destabilize such binaristic oppositions altogether. In 1886, he published two realist novels: *The Princess Casamassima* and *The Bostonians*, which are often thought of as his only two "political novels" and therefore seen as distinct from, and often less accomplished than, the rest of his oeuvre. This chapter will argue that these novels offer a critique of a particular strategy of reform realism that I call demographic realism. As I'll demonstrate, demographic realism is both a political and an aesthetic style that relies on the flattening of individual subjects into representatives of larger groups or types. The Jamesian critique of demographic realism works by invoking the realist conventions of surface description and dialogue but, rather than engage directly in these established modes of depiction, James focuses on the individualized affective responses his characters have to their settings and conversations. Like Davis, he repeatedly disavows the realist claim to accuracy in narrative asides like the one he makes in *The Bostonians*: "no stranger situation can be imagined than that of these extraordinary young women at this juncture; it was so singular on Verena's part, in particular, that I despair of presenting it to the reader with the air of reality."[1] Rather than "daguerreotyping" scenes or exchanges for his reader, James focuses on how such scenes and exchanges make his characters feel.

The depiction of such affective responses foregrounds the problems of appropriation and erasure inherent to reform realism. The Jamesian aesthetic critique has both a literary and a political dimension and these novels demonstrate the similar ways in which social reform and other aesthetic modes, like aestheticism itself, traffic in forms of economic and social capital that abstract the affective exchanges constitutive of satisfying human relationships. In them, James begins to imagine his own vision of political intimacy that might more effectively bridge the gulfs between distinct political subjects than the sympathetic identification engendered by literary realism's usual forms of engagement.

REFORM AND AESTHETICISM

Hyacinth Robinson, the protagonist of *The Princess Casamassima*, is a poor bookbinder and the unacknowledged son of a criminal and an aristocrat; therefore, he is positioned at the center of the "social problem" of class that dominated much reform realism in both England and the United States in the second half of the century. A lover of art, Hyacinth is seemingly forced to choose between his allegiance to high culture and a new commitment to upending the social order he develops under the influence of a friendship with the titular anarchist-sympathizing Princess, Christina Casamassima, who is a crossover character that first appeared in James's 1875 *kunstleroman Roderick Hudson*. In that novel, Christina chooses to marry a prince over the impoverished artist Roderick, who dies in a storm at the novel's close after being betrayed by her. Hyacinth ends up, seemingly, another of Christina's victims. The Princess engages him in an anarchist plot to assassinate a duke, but rather than carry out the assassination, he ends his own life.

The Princess Casamassima is typically taken to be about the debate between the relative merits of art and social justice. As Joyce L. Jenkins writes most succinctly, "Some live in luxury, others in squalor. Whether or not this distribution is justified because of the art and high culture such disparity produces is the central question of *The Princess Casamassima*."[2] I would argue, instead, that it is the unnecessary opposition of these two realms that *The Princess Casamassima* dismantles. Hyacinth's destruction at the end of the novel, which Kent Puckett describes as "a spectacular collapse of character embodied at the level of content," is a result of the false opposition of the new demands of his awakened political consciousness with the beauty that had previously sustained him.[3] As Hyacinth himself observes, the world's "monuments and treasures of art" are the result of "all the despotisms, the cruelties, the exclusions, the monopolies and the rapacities of the past, but thanks to which, all the same, the world is less of a 'bloody sell' and life more of a lark."[4] Perhaps the deepest lesson of the novel is contained in this sentence's "all the same." Just as painful experiences can grant access to a self capable of giving and receiving pleasure, so too does the suffering of the world as a whole contribute to its ability to make us sentient beings capable of observation, thought, and feeling. Such feeling and beauty is not in spite of suffering, but a part of its legacy—"all the same." Nevertheless, these revelations almost always lead to guilty feelings. (How can we take pleasure where there has been suffering?) Hyacinth's guilt, according to Lionel Trilling, is at the root of his suicide. He suggests that Hyacinth takes on the guilt of "two ideals": the ideal of an end to suffering via a destructive act of social protest and the ideal of artistic beauty.[5] I think that, beyond the result of this doubled guilt, Hyacinth's death can be attributed to his own misunderstanding of the two ideals as engaged in a fundamental conflict. He kills himself not because he is faced with an impossible choice he must make, but because the choice is itself a false one. On the last night of his life, he walks through the city whose beauty has always moved him:

> The day was gray and damp, though no rain fell, and London had never appeared to him to wear more proudly and publicly the stamp of her imperial history. He passed slowly to and fro over Westminster bridge and watched the black barges drift on the great brown river, and looked up at the huge fretted palace that rose there as a fortress of the social order which he, like the young David, had been commissioned to attack with a sling and a pebble.[6]

He has become blinded to the virtue of being able to live inside of contradiction—"all the same"—by the Princess's empty revolutionary rhetoric, to appreciate the beauty of the imperial history as a tragedy whose traces move us to justice.

In the novel's pivotal scene, the Princess and Hyacinth engage in a well-worn debate: does society benefit enough from high art and culture to make it worth the conditions of economic inequity that allow for its production? The Princess suggests, "When thousands and tens of thousands haven't bread to put in their mouths, I can dispense with tapestry and old china," to which Hyacinth responds, "I think there can't be too many pictures and statues and works of art . . . more the better, whether people are hungry or not." But the terms of this debate are, in short order, revealed to be false. Though the opposition of social movements designed to resolve economic equality and art is often taken seriously in criticisms of the novel, one of the more famous passages that illustrates this problem is a letter from Hyacinth to the Princess wherein he recognizes the absurdity of such an opposition in describing the revolutionary leader Hoffendahl as one who "would cut up the ceilings of the Veronese into strips, so that every one might have a little piece."[7] The implication here is that the destruction of art and culture would do very little to practically aid the poor.

Nevertheless, throughout the Progressive Era, reformers would consistently see an opposition between art and political activism. In fact, as Tom Otten reminds us, "attacks on works of art became almost stereotypically associated with such activists at the time," citing Mary Wood's 1914 slashing of Sargent's portrait of James himself, among several other such incidents involving social activists including an axe attack against Sir Hubert von Herkomer's portrait of the Duke of Wellington and a meat chopper taken to the Rokeby Venus of Velázquez in the National Gallery that same year.[8]

In both *The Princess Casamassima* and *The Bostonians*, one of the ways James collapses the distinction between art and politics is by satirizing aesthete and reformist characters into sameness. Like *The Princess Casamassima*, *The Bostonians* centers on an unlikely dyad: Verena Tarrant, a popular women's rights lecturer; and Basil Ransom, a politically conservative lawyer and aspiring writer from the American South. The two meet through Basil's cousin Olive Chancellor, whose drawing room serves as a hub of the women's rights movement in Boston—such characters as Miss Birdseye, a first-wave feminist reformer of the midcentury old guard, frequent her drawing room with regularity. Basil and Olive, along with the aesthete Henry Burrage, engage in a competition for Verena's affections. Verena must choose between suitors who enflame her respective passions for social justice (Chancellor), sex (Ransom), and money (Burrage). This contest of suitors is also a contest of values that gets enacted in the novel through a series of represented interiors. By using the common trope of interior description in an uncharacteristic way, James is able to critique how each character's supposed "value" is—like Chopin's aesthete Arobin—all surface.

James's introduction of his characters through the description of their domestic spaces is a characteristic gesture of literary realism. As Peter

Brooks writes, "[y]ou cannot, the realist claims, represent people without taking account of the things that people use and acquire in order to define themselves—their tools, their furniture, their accessories. These things are indeed part of the very definition of character of who one is."[9] The interior descriptions that typically take up so much space in the nineteenth-century realist novel are there to tell us about the characters who inhabit them, to lay bare the interiority of the character through the depiction of the surfaces of the interior of their home. This is a theory of literary depiction voiced by James's own character Madame Merle in his 1881 novel *The Portrait of a Lady*:

> There's no such thing as an isolated man or woman; we're each of us made up of some cluster of appurtenances. What shall we call our "self"? Where does it begin? where does it end? It overflows into everything that belongs to us—and then it flows back again. I know a large part of myself is in the clothes I choose to wear. I've a great respect for *things*! One's self—for other people—is one's expression of one's self; and one's house, one's furniture, one's garments, the books one reads, the company one keeps—these things are all expressive.[10]

But in *The Bostonians* James upends this technique. Rather than revealing the characters' interiority, the interiors in *The Bostonians* merely replicate their surfaces.

Readers of the novel first encounter Olive's drawing room through Basil's eyes: "it seemed to [Basil] he had never seen an interior that was so much an interior as this queer corridor-shaped drawing-room of his new-found kinswoman." His tone here is sarcastic: "An interior . . . so much an interior" signals an interior that advertises its interiority so loudly it only asserts it has none. We don't even get a detailed description of the drawing room, just Basil's reaction to it: "he had never felt himself in the presence of so much organised privacy or of so many objects that spoke of habits and tastes."[11] Olive's drawing room tells us nothing concrete about her thoughts, desires, or history—it only demonstrates what she wants others to see about her.

James's description of Olive's drawing room also sets the stage for his critique of political reform as a kind of bad style. We later learn a bit more about her personal interior(ity) through free indirect discourse, when the narrator discloses that

> her most poignant suffering came from the injury of her taste. She had tried to kill that nerve, to persuade herself that taste was only frivolity in the disguise of knowledge; but her susceptibility was constantly

blooming afresh and making her wonder whether an absence of nice arrangements were a necessary part of the enthusiasm of humanity.

Her deliberate relinquishment of "nice arrangements" is an aesthetic decision to adhere to the conventional appearance of a reformist lifestyle. This reflection that she has somehow sacrificed her taste on the altar of morality belies the fact that she has merely substituted one set of tastes for another. Her political aspirations dictate both her behavior and her consumption habits, so her politics become a style. Olive's drawing room is explicitly compared to Miss Birdseye's parlor and, once again, the narrator deems the austerity of that august space to be an aesthetic choice made to reflect and advertise her abstract principles: "the bareness of [Miss Birdseye's] long, loose, empty parlour (it was shaped exactly like Miss Chancellor's) told that she had never had any needs but moral needs, and that all her history had been that of her sympathies." In describing Miss Birdseye's person, the narrator draws the same conclusions about the ways her aesthetic choices reflect her desired self-presentation:

> She always dressed in the same way: she wore a loose black jacket, with deep pockets, which were stuffed with papers, memoranda of a voluminous correspondence; and from beneath her jacket depended a short stuff dress. The brevity of this simple garment was the one device by which Miss Birdseye managed to suggest that she was a woman of business, that she wished to be free for action.[12]

Such a description communicates that there is really very little difference between an opulent aesthetic style of dress that is designed to advertise that its wearer is artistic or fashionable and a "short stuff dress" there to alert observers that its wearer is "free for action."

So while it would seem that characters such as Miss Birdseye and Olive, whose "only needs are moral needs," are in opposition to characters like Henry Burrage, whose life purpose seems to be the gratification of his every material desire, the relationship between their shallow consumption styles and their pretenses towards depth are effectively aligned by James's descriptive technique. The design of Henry Burrage's rooms in Cambridge is, like that of the Birdseye and Chancellor receiving rooms, calculated to produce a particular impression of their inhabitant's worldview on their visitors:

> The covered lamps made a glow here and there, and the cabinets and brackets produced brown shadows, out of which some precious object

gleamed. . . . Civilisation, under such an influence, in such a setting, appeared to have done its work; harmony ruled the scene; human life ceased to be a battle.[13]

While the moral sparseness of the Birdseye parlor makes visitors think only of the inequities she rails against, the curated opulence of the Burrage rooms performs a strategic erasure of these inequities—"human life ceased to be a battle."

Rather than establish a contrast between the moral posturing of reformers and the material posturing of wealthy aesthetes, *The Bostonians* illuminates the similarity between both sets of behaviors. Reform provides a profession for Olive and aestheticism a profession for Burrage. As Jonathan L. Freedman argues, the aesthetic movement,

> represent[ed] a process by which the newly emergent sphere of the "aesthetic"—a sphere hitherto defined for the Anglo-American audience by the likes of German idealist philosophers and romantic poets—got put into social play as a startlingly successful form of professionalism. For what is the aesthete but the consummate professional: the possessor of a "monopoly of knowledge" about the provenance and extent of this mysterious entity, "the aesthetic."[14]

Both reform and aestheticism are styles that mask the tyranny of Olive and Henry's social and financial power. By depicting both endeavors as professions—or as they are called in relation to Miss Birdseye, "occupations"—masquerading as disinterested pursuits, both the aesthetic and moral tastes of the aesthete and the reformer are transformed into consistent positions that ossify their power. Just as the aesthete possesses a monopoly of knowledge on what is aesthetic, the reformer possesses a monopoly of knowledge on what is moral. In this capacity, the reformer can offer promises of both edification and entertainment to paying audiences.

DEMOGRAPHIC REALISM

The ineffective political style that James most clearly criticizes in *The Bostonians* is one I'll call demographic realism. Just as many literary realists shared with sociologists the tendency to understand humanity as constituted by a limited variety of social types, demographic realism chooses an ideal subject who represents a particular issue or set of concerns for an imagined constituency. Using this subject, reformers or politicians attempt to relate to those they will save or govern. The roots of demographic realism can most clearly be traced to the abolition movement of the mid-century, though it persists well into the present day. Autumn Womack describes, for example, the historical example of the Bakers, an African American family who escaped a lynching only to become utilized in a series of performances by the white abolitionist and novelist Lillian Jewett. Jewett hired the Bakers to dramatically recreate their escape for paying white audiences. As Womack notes, "Jewett not only trafficked in a genre of domestic rhetoric that proved successful for a previous generation of white female activists, but she also tapped into the well-rehearsed project of offering black bodies as empirical evidence in the name of political reform; that is, black bodies as 'object lessons.'"[15]

In a very different context, the 2008 campaign of John McCain and Sarah Palin used a similar rhetorical strategy in its invocation of Samuel Wurzelbacher—an individual the campaign referred to as "Joe the Plumber." Like McTeague-the-dentist or Maggie-the-girl-of-the-streets, Joe represents a specific population reduced to a cartoonish character. The difference is that, like the Bakers, he is not a fictional character who represents a type of person—he is a person who is forced to represent a type of person. Representation and represented are collapsed in a single body. Rather than render an abstract demographic concrete, as such a gesture is likely intended, demographic realism turns both the person and the population they represent into fiction. No facts of Joe's individual life (such as, for example, that his first name is Samuel, not Joe, and he has never possessed a plumber's license) nor any beliefs of his own are so relevant as the identity he metonymically represents.[16] Demographic realism is a political style that promises perfect transparency but effectively functions through imaginary categories of identity possessed of imaginary desires. There are no substantive grounds for relation nor identification between the fictional identity Joe the Plumber, his fictional concerns, and Samuel Wurzelbacher or any real American citizen. After the campaign, Wurzelbacher publicly stated, "[McCain] really screwed my life up, is how I look at it. . . . He was trying to use me. I happened to be the face of middle Americans. It was a ploy."[17] Such sentiments reflect those of Hyacinth Robinson and the circumstance of Verena Tarrant.

Verena is not precisely the protagonist of *The Bostonians* but rather its fulcrum—and its Samuel Wurzelbacher. Rather than explore her interiority in depth, the novel guesses around it via the contest for her affections waged by her three suitors, who seek her love in the way politicians court demographics. Many brilliant arguments have been made for the depth of Olive's romantic desire for Verena.[18] The question of why, in the novel's final moments, Verena abandons both her promising career and her domestic union with Olive—not to mention the opportunity for a sybaritic existence on the arm of a passive and wealthy Mr. Burrage—for the professionally unsuccessful and controlling Basil with whom she disagrees on the topic she supposedly holds most dear, that of women's rights, has been widely debated. These debates have typically taken the form of an analysis of Olive's character. Alfred Habegger suggests that James is sympathetic with his father's views about the inferiority of women and, thus, Olive Chancellor is designed to be an unsympathetic character. But I think Olive sees Verena more or less in the light of demographic realism—what she loves is not Verena herself, but what Verena represents and how she stands to further the movement around which Olive has built her life. The narrator describes Olive's love for Verena in the same way political strategists describe the quest to secure white, working-class voters: "[Olive] had an immense desire to know intimately some *very* poor girl."[19] It is the idea of Verena's imaginary identity as a "*very* poor girl" that Olive romanticizes:

> She liked to think that Verena, in her childhood, had known almost the extremity of poverty, and there was a kind of ferocity in the joy with which she reflected that there had been moments when this delicate creature came near (if the pinch had only lasted a little longer) to literally going without food. These things added to her value for Olive.[20]

Verena makes a convincing figure for Olive's cause because of the imagined authenticity of her experience, and, transversely, like the working-class citizen duped into identification with a political candidate via their sympathy for an imaginary character affixed to a physical person, Verena comes to be attached to Olive for how Olive imagines her own (Verena's) representation of herself.

The way that Olive comes to imagine and design the figure of Verena is, like the working-class citizen in the televised debate or the escaped lynching victim on the theatrical stage, through removing her from one context and inserting her into another. As Philip Fisher has explored, the significance of any aesthetic object—an ancient implement placed in a museum or a preparatory sketch in a gallery—is only made apparent via a dramatic act of recontextualization with serious consequences: "the museum has effaced features of the objects of the past, giving them a newer, abstract minimal identity as objects in a museum with new features that suit the world in which they have now been socialized."[21] The same is true for the figure of demographic realism.

At their second meeting, Olive visits Verena in her home, where "she was so taken up with the consideration of Verena's interior. It was as bad as she could have desired; desired in order to feel that (to take her out of such a *milieu* as that) she should have a right to draw her altogether to herself." Olive immediately imagines a new context for Verena: not only as a political speaker on a figuratively and literally larger stage, but also as a fixture in her own (Olive's) milieu which is depicted as a relocation from the "bad" parlor of the Tarrants to the "good" parlor of Olive's home. After moving in with Olive, Verena tells her mother that Olive cares "only to have an elegant parlour. Well, she *has* got that; it's a regular dream-like place to sit. She's going to have a tree in, next week; she says she wants to see me sitting under a tree." Olive incorporates Verena as an element of her décor. And Verena, a natural performer, rises to the occasion of her new context:

> [Verena] had learned to breathe and move in a rarefied air, as she would have learned to speak Chinese if her success in life had depended upon it; but this dazzling trick, and all her artlessly artful facilities, were not a part of her essence, an expression of her innermost preferences. What *was* a part of her essence was the extraordinary generosity with which she could expose herself, give herself away, turn herself inside out, for the satisfaction of a person who made demands of her.[22]

Verena neither wants to see nor become a figure for her demographic, all surface—like the "interior so much an interior" it expresses no interiority at all—but to more deeply inhabit her own experience, her depth, to "turn herself inside out" and have that experience be affectively registered by someone outside of herself who will recognize and express their own power over her rather than attempt to disavow it: "a person who made demands of her." This is why she ultimately chooses Ransom, at least in part because he doesn't engage in the same authenticity games that characterize Chancellor and Burrage.

Ironically, it is Basil's sarcasm—which stands in contrast to Olive's earnestness—that gives Verena her only impression of depth. In the very first paragraph of the novel, Mrs. Luna declares "She is very honest, is Olive

Chancellor; she is full of rectitude." And Mr. Tarrant observes, "he had never met any one so much in earnest as this definite, literal young woman, who had taken such an unhoped-for fancy to his daughter." This baseline established, Ransom's style takes Verena by force: "Verena, who had always lived with people who took the world very earnestly, had never encountered such a power of disparagement or heard so much sarcasm levelled at the institutions of her country and the tendencies of the age." Through sarcasm, Basil makes the surface of his talk, and hence the space between them, visible. His style is a reversal of Olive's demographic realism, which turns Verena's body into a fiction about her. In his relationship with Verena, the abstract expressions of beliefs and identity are secondary to embodiment. When Verena asks Basil, "Why should you ever listen to me again, when you loathe my ideas?" He responds, "I don't listen to your ideas; I listen to your voice." Basil is interested in her voice, how her body sounds, not the content of what she says. Likewise, their intimacy is characterized by *how* what is said is said, which the narrator notes explicitly: "for the tone, even more than the words, indicated a large increase of intimacy." James more than once elides the words Ransom uses to describe, instead, the physical effect that his speech has on Verena.

> Her reflexions . . . softly battled with each other as she listened . . . to his deep, sweet, distinct voice, expressing monstrous opinions with exotic cadences and mild, familiar laughs, which, as he leaned towards her, almost tickled her cheek and ear . . . there was a spell upon her as she listened.[23]

This response relocates her in her own specific, embodied existence and lays bare the work of recontextualization and disembodiment that Olive has performed upon her.

The relationship Basil offers her is neither more progressive nor more equitable than those arrangements offered by Olive and Henry; its only merit is that it is conducted via a more convincing form of realism that acknowledges the imbalance of power both between them and between representations and what they represent. Rather than a realism that disavows inequity through false promises of a more perfect surface representation, Basil offers Verena a realism of depth, physicality, interiority—her insides turned out. His commitment to an ironic stance models the destabilization of a distinction between inside and outside, public and private, the political and the intimate. His discourse style achieves what Olive's cannot.

In her "Cyborg Manifesto," Donna Haraway writes that "irony is about contradictions that do not resolve into larger wholes, even dialectically, about the tension of holding incompatible things together because both or all are necessary and true. Irony is about humor and serious play. It is also a rhetorical strategy and a political method," a political method she ties to potentially more successful emergent forms of socialist feminism.[24] While Verena finds her political content in Olive, she finds her political style in Basil. And while Verena is not precisely a cyborg, she is a figure who uses the conditions of her instrumentality toward liberation, whose choices and very existence disavow the notion that domination is the opposite of empowerment.

BECOMING ALL EDGE

Across the body of his work, James champions the value of suffering under domination through the depiction of characters whose strength is rooted in their adversity. Like Isabel Archer, the heroine of *Portrait of a Lady* (1881) who remains in a marriage with the cold and manipulative aesthete Gilbert Osmond, Verena Tarrant is resigned to a union with a despot who promises to "grind" her—a peculiar turn of phrase that emerges frequently in the James oeuvre to denote a particularly Jamesian relationship to structures of power. Ralph Touchett tells Isabel, "You wanted to look at life for yourself—but you were not allowed; you were punished for your wish. You were ground in the very mill of the conventional," and of Verena, "as the wheel of her experience went round she had the sensation of being ground very small indeed."[25] While it could be—and indeed was long—argued that these endings rife with female suffering are a testament to James's misogyny, critics have since pointed out the fond prose lavished on James's female protagonists and the despicable descriptions of their male antagonist-lovers, which gives less credence to that earlier interpretation.[26] Furthermore, it is not only the female characters in James's novels who get "ground." Jamesian young women, poor men, and artists all fall victim to the force of circumstances beyond their control that determine the shape of their lives.

It is not coincidental that "grinding" also signifies repetitive work and sexual tension.[27] The struggling artist Nick Dormer in *The Tragic Muse* (1890) tells the more successful Miriam Rooth, "I see before me an eternity of grinding."[28] And in *Roderick Hudson*, Christina tells Roderick that the worst fate would be to be ground by someone merely ordinary: "I could interest myself in a man of extraordinary power who should wish to turn all his passions to account. But if the power should turn out to be, after all, rather ordinary? Fancy feeling one's self ground in the mill of a third-rate talent!"[29] In *The Princess Casamassima*, it is Christina who does the grinding. Hyacinth writes to her near the end of their friendship: "my demoralisation began from the moment I first approached you. Dear Princess, I may have done you good, but you haven't done me much."[30] The effects of power on those who don't have or understand it fascinate James in general. More specifically, he prefers to examine how these forces of power alter the self—this is the process of being ground. So while being ground is painted as an experience of pain, for James, it is also an experience of value associated with desire and personal growth. And those who are ground are by his own account his finest, most passionate characters.

Perhaps the character who ignited James's interest in the process of being ground is to be found in Dickens' *David Copperfield* (1850). In writing of his childhood, James shares that "there sprouted in those years no such other crop of ready references as the golden harvest of Copperfield," and one of *Copperfield*'s most memorable characters is Rosa Dartle, the angry, young, paid companion of Mrs. Steerforth.[31] Rosa bears a scar on her lip from a hammer once thrown at her by Mrs. Steerforth's son. Young Steerforth is a consummate grinder, unaware of how his social power oppresses others, who he sees as insensate to his abuses. Speaking of what he calls "that sort of people," he explains, "Why, there's a pretty wide separation between them and us. . . . They are not to be expected to be as sensitive as we are. Their delicacy is not to be shocked, or hurt easily . . . they may be thankful that, like their coarse rough skins, they are not easily wounded."[32] Steerforth is a prototype of the kind of character blind to the power they wield and the seriousness of its effects on others that James will so often depict. Like the Princess, Steerforth is unaware of his own agency in the destruction he witnesses. He says of Rosa: "she brings everything to a grindstone . . . and sharpens it, as she has sharpened her own face and figure these years past. She has worn herself away by constant sharpening. She is all edge."[33] He fails to acknowledge that *he* is the grindstone to which she brings herself. His hammer has literally shaped her face, and what wears her away more generally are the conditions of subordination under which she lives in his home, conditions that—like those of the characters James will invent later on—cause her to love the force that grinds her with a passionate intensity that is capable of flourishing right alongside her hatred. As she says after Steerforth chooses another woman, "I could have loved [Steerforth], and asked no return. If I had been his wife, I could have been the slave of his caprices for a word of love a year."[34] This is clearly not an ideal nor healthy personal relationship, but it does begin to establish a model for a powerful kind of intimacy that may be of use to a novelist or a politician. As Lauren Hoffer writes,

> Dickens establishes a rich, complex dynamic of sympathy and repulsion between his characters. Rosa's ambivalent relationship with the family allows her the ability to sympathize with her mistress and Steerforth, to understand their emotions and motivations, but it also simultaneously allows her to undo that sympathy in order to present the reader as well as David with a satire of the Steerforths' social pretension and familial dysfunction. Rosa warps sympathy so that it is useful to her and damaging to the recipient, rather than salutary.[35]

Rosa weaponizes her own sympathy for her abusers. (Her abuse has the metaphorical function of sharpening her into a blade.) I would argue this has the added effect of allowing for readerly empathy for her circumstance without pity for her person. Her anger and vituperative rhetoric prevent her reception as a passive object onto whom fantasies of individual suffering can be projected. Likewise, despite her tragic decision to remain with Gilbert Osmond, Isabel Archer is difficult to pity. James casts such personal suffering in the light of strength.

Rosa, Isabel, Hyacinth, Verena, and other James characters who are likewise ground tell us something revealing about how intimacy without pity and understanding without sympathy might be cultivated in a work of art that sets out to shape the minds of its audience by illuminating an experience outside of their own. As James writes in a review of Rebecca Harding Davis's 1867 novel *Waiting for the Verdict*, "spontaneous pity is an excellent emotion, but there is nothing so hardening as to have your pity for ever tickled and stimulated, and nothing so debasing as to become an agent between the supply and demand of the commodity."[36] Readerly exposure to the experience of suffering should allow readers to feel *with* others without necessarily have to feel *like* them. By eschewing categories of identification that would lead to either artificial comparison or distancing, the depiction of such grinding demonstrates how suffering may be universal but it is rarely shared.

James's model of depicting the reciprocal relationship between the ground and the grinder is offered as an antidote to the flattening effect of reform realist sympathy or sentimentality, which can artificially level experiences of suffering through comparisons drawn along the lines of sociocultural identity. As Lauren Berlant writes, "the humanization strategies of sentimentality always traffic in cliché," clichés that rely on the politics of identity; which is why, as Berlant goes on to claim, such texts "indulge in the confirmation of the marginal subject's embodiment of inhumanity on the way to providing the privileged with heroic occasions of recognition, rescue, and inclusion."[37] *The Bostonians* demonstrates a mode of intimacy that might replace the realist tendency to connect with the audience on the basis of sentimentality or aesthetics alone.

Olive represents the structure of sympathy that characterizes bourgeois reform movements themselves: she connects to people and ideas through how they relate to her. After Olive buys Verena away from her parents (she pays them "with the most extravagant orders on her bank" to allow Verena to move in with her and, most importantly, to give her and Verena a wide berth), the relationship between the two women revolves around the cause that brought them together and the pursuit of further fame and remuneration for it via Verena.[38] In this, their private relationship is indistinct from Verena's lecture career. To her own mind, Olive is motivated to champion the cause of women in order to alleviate their universal suffering, but it is clear that she universalizes her own experience of suffering in the shape of the women's movement:

> Yes, she would do something, Olive Chancellor said to herself; she would do something to brighten the darkness of that dreadful image that was always before her, and against which it seemed to her at times that she had been born to lead a crusade the image of the unhappiness of women. The unhappiness of women! The voice of their silent suffering was always in her ears, the ocean of tears that they had shed from the beginning of time seemed to pour through her own eyes. Ages of oppression had rolled over them; uncounted millions had lived only to be tortured, to be crucified. They were her sisters, they were her own, and the day of their delivery had dawned.[39]

The suffering in her ears and the tears in her eyes are not her own—her activism is marred by appropriation. While the suffering masses remain passive material, Olive channels their pain into a vocation for herself: "her only consolation was that she expected to suffer intensely; for the prospect of suffering was always, spiritually speaking, so much cash in her pocket."[40] James is quick to identify a tendency of demographic realism wherein those who "help" others within the context of humanitarian aid models are liable to use disenfranchised individuals instrumentally in order to achieve their aims with respect to the greater group. His savage lambasting of this tendency in the character of Miss Birdseye was deemed too harsh by many of his contemporary critics—especially insofar as the character of Miss Birdeye seems to have been modeled on the real-life activist Elizabeth Peabody.[41] Miss Birdseye is a hero to Olive—and in the elder reformer we see the tendencies Olive emulates. In one of the most damning passages to this effect, James writes,

> Since the Civil War much of [Miss Birdseye's] occupation was gone; for before that her best hours had been spent in fancying that she was helping some Southern slave to escape. It would have been a nice question whether, in her heart of hearts, for the sake of this excitement, she did not sometimes wish the blacks back in bondage.[42]

Both Miss Birdseye and Olive Chancellor, like Verena, enjoy their own experience of suffering so much they wish to magnify it through comparison to the suffering of others. A significant feature of James's portrait of Miss Birdseye is that, while she has devoted her life to speaking on behalf of the oppressed, her personal experience of being ground is secondhand. Consider the portrait James paints of Miss Birdseye in comparison to Dickens' portrait of Rosa Dartle:

> [Birdseye] had a sad, soft, pale face, which (and it was the effect of her whole head) looked as if it had been soaked, blurred, and made vague by exposure to some slow dissolvent. The long practice of philanthropy had not given accent to her features; it had rubbed out their transitions, their meanings. The waves of sympathy, of enthusiasm, had wrought upon them in the same way in which the waves of time finally modify the surface of old marble busts, gradually washing away their sharpness, their details.[43]

While Rosa has sharpened herself to the point of becoming "all edge," Miss Birdeye's face has lost all sharpness and become "blurred." This is because Rosa's self is defined by the passionate intimacy she experiences with the individuals in her private home while Miss Birdseye only experiences a dull sympathy for an undefined mass. Her name, indeed, implies her view—hovering above, seeing all below her indistinctly.

Miss Birdseye's personal removal from the causes that define her life leaves her own sense of self equally undefined. Eva-Lynn Jagoe writes that intimate self-expression requires "that there is a transparent, authentic, and real self that needs recognition and mirroring." The problem that emerges for intimacy after the advent of public-sphere modernity is that the self becomes "a product of the neoliberal economization of the self, in which human capital becomes another site of investment and entrepreneurial ventures."[44] The vagueness of self we see embodied in Miss Birdseye's blurred face and, by extension, Olive's publicly tainted desires for Verena—"a *very poor girl*"—is, James implies, a product of the reform industry that takes the experience of personal suffering and turns it into a consistent ideological position ready for packaging, advertisement, and public distribution.

Reform realism accomplishes much of this through the language of direct address that cultivates an identification between the reader and a character based on a shared sense of identity. This could be Henry Mayhew's insertion of the occasional gentleman fallen on hard times into a London slum; Harriet Beecher Stowe's inclusion of a just, Christian, Anglo-looking African American mother; or, as Laura Fisher has shown, an "undercover" narrator who is able to build sympathetic identifications between the classes on the basis of social identities in common and therefore shared sensibilities.[45]

Augusta Rohrbach contends that, in Rose Terry Cooke's story "Sally Parson's Duty," Cooke uses direct address out of fear that "the lack of frank and direct language might allow readers to be seduced by the romance of fiction and fail to act politically."[46] This kind of fear is directly at odds with James's idea of generating intimacy with a reader. The Jamesian mode of generating political feeling relies upon the affect rather than ideology. Marjorie Garber observes that while "much energy has been expended in trying to decide whether *The Bostonians* is a novel primarily about politics . . . or primarily about sexuality," when, "it is not just that the two terms are metaphors for one another; they are the same."[47] *The Bostonians* wants precisely for readers to be seduced, just as Verena is seduced, and to trust them to draw their own conclusions based on what they feel rather than lead them to a preordained political message. And the sexual metaphor is an apt one for this kind of relation as, unlike in sympathy, which relies on drawing axes of similarity, it is so often difference that generates sexual desire. Michael Kearns suggests *The Bostonians* is "designed to stimulate better feelings than are demonstrated by any of its personages, including the narrator."[48]

And it is once again by negative example that the Jamesian reader is led. A negative purpose entails that readers are led not to a moral, an argument, or even an identification, but rather a passionate feeling-for. He suggests in "The Art of Fiction" that what matters for readers is not that they are able to identify with characters (on the basis of such structures of identity) but with their experiences:

> I am quite at a loss to imagine anything (at any rate in this matter of fiction) that people *ought* to like or to dislike. Selection will be sure to take care of itself, for it has a constant motive behind it. That motive is simply experience. As people feel life, so they will feel the art that is most closely related to it.[49]

If Jamesian fiction has a purpose, it is this: to get people to feel life, to be attuned to the world around them and act accordingly. And realism is the implied mode for this purpose—the art most closely related to life. But Jamesian realist sympathy functions quite differently. If Stowe's model of fictional activism is to encourage the reader to "feel right" (with an attached qualitative judgement), James's model is not precisely to encourage the reader to feel wrong, but to stew in the discomfort of feeling accurately. As Joseph Conrad wrote in a 1916 appreciation of James in the *North American Review*, "one is never set at rest by James's novels. His books end as an episode in life ends."[50] James was, for Conrad, a paradigm of literary conduct—as Emerson was for James. In a pivotal scene in Conrad's *The Secret Agent* (1907), a text often read alongside James's *The Princess Casamassima* because of their mutual fascination with the relationship between liberal sentiment and reactionary politics, the boy Stevie witnesses a man beating his horse. It is in this moment that Stevie feels the full weight of the world's injustices and inequities of power:

> "Poor! Poor!" stammered out Stevie, pushing his hands deeper into his pockets with convulsive sympathy. He could say nothing; for the tenderness to all pain and all misery, the desire to make the horse happy and the cabman happy, had reached the point of a bizarre longing to take them to bed with him. And that, he knew, was impossible. For Stevie was not mad. It was, as it were, a symbolic longing; and at the same time it was very distinct, because springing from experience, the mother of wisdom. Thus when as a child he cowered in a dark corner scared, wretched, sore, and miserable with the black, black misery of the soul, his sister Winnie used to come along, and carry him off to bed with her, as into a heaven of consoling peace. Stevie, though apt to forget mere facts, such as his name and address for instance, had a faithful memory

> of sensations. To be taken into a bed of compassion was the supreme
> remedy, with the only one disadvantage of being difficult of application
> on a large scale. And looking at the cabman, Stevie perceived this clearly,
> because he was reasonable.[51]

Here Stevie feels deeply for both the cabman and the horse, not because he likewise works in transportation or associates himself with the equine, but because he has a "faithful memory of sensations" and, looking at their suffering, can momentarily feel what they feel. I think that this is a close approximation of James's political aim as a novelist: not to forge identifications between his characters or his narrator and his reader, but to encourage a process of mutuality via cultivating an intimacy that is supremely personal—to be taken into the bed of compassion with the reader, who can be as different from the author or their characters as a boy is from a horse.

In his preface to the New York Edition of *The Princess Casamassima*, James describes Hyacinth as the ideal moral/political subject. He is "finely aware and richly responsible." What James particularly seems to admire about his creation, and others like him, is how he "'get[s] most' out of all that happens to [him] and . . . in so doing enable[s] us, as readers of [his] record, as participators by a fond attention, also to get most."[52] Preordained worldviews and overt political messages, especially when used as pretexts for the novel, prevent us from "getting most" by providing a set of ready conclusions. When our sociability is dependent on representing a proscribed set of roles and social positions, inconsistency is inevitable and sometimes deadly. "There are some things I feel," Verena confesses to Basil, "it seems to me as if I had been born to feel them; they are in my ears in the stillness of the night and before my face in the visions of the darkness."[53] Whatever these feelings are, her flight to Basil at the end of the novel suggests, they are not assuaged or sated by the offerings of Olive's reform movement. (And, significantly, we are not to know what they are—lest we take their content as a suggestion that we ought to feel them, too.)

James goes on in his preface to *The Princess* to write, "if you haven't, for fiction, the root of the matter in you, haven't the sense of life and the penetrating imagination, you are a fool in the very presence of the revealed and assured; but that if you are so armed you are not really helpless, not without your resource, even before mysteries abysmal." This resource is the ability, like Hyacinth's and Verena's, to feel life with all of its unresolvable complexity. He notes, "it's in a degree an exclusion and a state of weakness to be without experience of the meaner conditions, the lower manners and types, the general sordid struggle, the weight of the burden of labour, the ignorance, the misery and the vice," suggesting that another method of survival is to embrace the grinding as productive of beauty and begin to appreciate the value of feeling.[54] Perhaps the problem is, in other words, not that the poor ought to suffer less, but that the rich ought to suffer more. That those who benefit from inequity would be better served by being forced to confront their feelings of guilt and anger, instead of being encouraged to appropriate the suffering of others. Only then might they be able to see others as equals.

THE OPPOSITES OF INTIMACY

The embattled, masochistic relationship Verena has with Basil is the only one in the novel where intimacy is experienced as private and individualized. With Henry and Olive, we only ever see Verena skating along the surface of interaction. Candace Vogler describes what she calls "depersonalizing intimacy": an intimate encounter that is not predicated on exchanges of self but instead characterized by moments of what Leo Bersani calls "impersonal intimacy," which he describes as "self-shattering and solipsistic jouissance."[55] Bersani takes the concept of "self-shattering" from Jean Laplanche, who associates it with the Freudian death-drive.[56]

The desire for self-annihilation has, since its earliest articulations, been connected to pleasure. As Freud writes, "the subject's destruction of himself cannot take place without libidinal satisfaction."[57] Subsequent theorists have, to varying degrees, suggested a queer embrace of the death drive along these lines—citing its associations with destruction (and hence rebellion and revolution) and the shaping of communitarian impulses.[58] My claim is that James had a similar idea in mind in establishing a model of the kind of intimacy he wanted to share with the audience of a work of art—especially a work of art designed to engage political feelings. Like Rosa Dartle's grinding, this kind of work would make us feel close but also pained. It would make its readers suffer pleasurably. Works of political art would not, as many novels of reform do, make us feel self-satisfied for reading them.

To illustrate what depersonalizing intimacy might look like in a conversation, Vogler close-reads the Adrienne Rich poem "Dialogue," paying careful attention to the dislocation of time and space in the poem and the past-tense way in which the conversation its characters engage in "for hours" is treated. But the poem does not represent this conversation directly; it describes the setting and tone of the dialogue—not its content. Vogler suggests that "in order to imagine [depersonalizing intimacy], we have to imagine a kind of intimacy that has nothing to do with tracking or expanding the borders of selfhood. We have to imagine . . . a style of verbal intercourse in which one can forget who one is." In general, it seems difficult for theorists of depersonalizing/impersonal intimacy to do this imaginary work. None that I have found convey a real or hypothetical transcript of such an exchange. This is not the case with the other kind of intimacy, which Vogler calls "self-conscious intimacy," after the term used by the therapist-author Michael Vincent Miller. She has no trouble imagining what the content of exchanges of self-conscious intimacy would be. Indeed, Vogler finds reams of examples in psychological case studies and summarizes them with a sense of exhaustion at just how mundane and familiar they would be to anyone: "'I'm like this' 'you're like that,' 'you never,' 'I always,' 'you always,' 'I never,' that sort of thing."[59] These kinds of exchanges are easy to find not only because of their ubiquity, but because the very definition of self-conscious intimacy is a matter of its content: these are exchanges that are about describing the self, the other, and the gulf between.

The reason it's difficult to assert an imagined content to depersonalizing intimacy is because the content is incidental. If exchanges of self-conscious intimacy are about the self and its relation to the other, exchanges of depersonalizing intimacy can be about practically anything else. This is because what is significant to self-conscious intimacy is the subject (*matter*); whereas, depersonalizing intimacy is a *manner* of relating rather than a specific content. These two different modes of intimacy are illustrated by the contrast between the dialogues in *The Bostonians* between Verena and her two primary suitors.

Verena's dialogues with Olive are characterized primarily by communications about themselves and their relationship. To give some examples, Olive begins their first dialogue, "I want to know you . . . I felt that I must last night, as soon as I heard you speak . . . I don't know what to make of you." Later, she declares, "You are so simple—so much like a child. . . . Will you be my friend, my friend of friends, beyond every one, everything, for ever and for ever?" Olive's great speech in which she attempts to keep Verena, later in the novel, amounts to a bird's-eye description of their circumstance:

> My dear child, you are so young—so strangely young. I am a thousand years old; I have lived through generations—through centuries. I know

what I know by experience; you know it by imagination. That is consistent with your being the fresh, bright creature that you are. I am constantly forgetting the difference between us—that you are a mere child as yet, though a child destined for great things. I forgot it the other night, but I have remembered it since. You must pass through a certain phase, and it would be very wrong in me to pretend to suppress it. That is all clear to me now; I see it was my jealousy that spoke—my restless, hungry jealousy. I have far too much of that.[60]

Olive describes their relationship and its problems by telling Verena what they each are like.

Basil and Verena's talk, on the other hand, consists of much verbal play with very little description of themselves or one another. Characteristic of depersonalizing intimacy, it's difficult to demonstrate what James is up to without quoting long stretches of conversation about other things (mainly their political disagreements) which read clearly as flirting. But perhaps more significant than their constant verbal sparring is the affective response such talks produce. In the silent spaces between their chatter, they begin to see one another as individuals rather than types:

She felt his eyes on her face—ever so close and fixed there—after he had chosen to reply to her question that way. She was beginning to blush; if he had kept them longer, and on the part of anyone else, she would have called such a stare impertinent. Verena had been commended of old by Olive for her serenity "while exposed to the gaze of hundreds"; but a change had taken place, and she was now unable to endure the contemplation of an individual. She wished to detach him, to lead him off again into the general; and for this purpose, at the end of a moment, she made another inquiry.[61]

It is this characteristic of their exchanges that is at the root of Basil's success in winning her to his side. She is not general to him, but specific. His love is not the abstract love of the crowd, but the targeted desire of an individual. The intensity of his desire for her is as unbearable as it is pleasurable. And much of this pleasure comes from the detours in their conversation. Their verbal play is markedly different from the straightforward political conversations she has with Olive and the other reformers. As Bersani observes of James more generally,

[James] admit[s] and enjoy[s] the play of [individual] needs along the surfaces of talk. Ideas by themselves are neither attractive nor powerful in conversation; the appeal of civilized speech comes from our recognizing those detours—of wit, of tone, of shifting rhythms and of ideas–which "being civilized" imposes on the expression of a desire.[62]

This intimacy produced by a manner, rather than a subject, is a mutual facet of Verena and Basil's relationship. As he claims to be attracted to her voice—not what she says—Verena is equally attracted to his, which produces in her a strong affective response. Her attraction to his voice is furthermore characterized as intensely private; its "deep, sweet, distinctness" is pitted against the "hum of the immense city." This opposition suggests comparison with the usual outlet from which adoration is issued to Verena: an indistinctly humming crowd.

Verena is the consummate object of a Miss-Birdseye-like gaze. She is accustomed to being "loved" by the masses of listeners who, like Olive, pity her as some "*very* poor girl." With Basil, for the first time, she experiences a feeling of passion dislodged from this limited and damaging sense of her worth:

> She loved, she was in love—she felt it in every throb of her being. Instead of being constituted by nature for entertaining that sentiment in an exceptionally small degree (which had been the implication of her whole crusade, the warrant for her offer of old to Olive to renounce), she was framed, apparently, to allow it the largest range, the highest intensity. It was always passion, in fact; but now the object was other.[63]

Verena's experience of this feeling is previously "exceptionally small" because of its abstraction through distance and the filter of an imposed identity. While others may love her because she is poor or because she is a celebrity, both she and Basil desire one another *in spite of* such conditions. In the context of her relationship with Basil, the object of her desire is "other"—something she cannot locate or understand, something outside of herself. This experience of desire as "other" would be, precisely, depersonalizing intimacy. And it is through depersonalizing intimacy, the novel implies, that the "transparent, authentic, and real self," to quote Jagoe—a self shaped by what it desires and feels rather than how it fits into a social system—can be found.[64]

POLITICAL INTIMACY

If the goal of most reform realist novels is to bridge the gap between the haves (the readers) and the have-nots (the subjects of the fiction), the goal of *The Bostonians* and *The Princess Casamassima* is to theorize how these bonds of sympathy might be more effectively imagined within the context of the novel form. James wrote *The Bostonians* and *The Princess Casamassima* instead of writing the second half of "The Art of Fiction"—first published in *Longman's Magazine* in 1884. Amanda Claybaugh convincingly interprets this fact to suggest that these mid-period realist novels are a continuation of the project of examining the form of the realist novel that he undertakes in the critical work. Claybaugh argues that these two mid-period novels "seek to be realist without being purposeful"—that though they depict political questions, they take no political stance. She claims *The Bostonians* is interested in the tendency of the realist novel to engage in typicality, drawing our attention to how both reform and realism are deeply engaged in the process of "the finding or creating of representative figures."[65] In this sense, the novel can be seen, like "The Art of Fiction," as a work of criticism.

James's work reminds us that a reform novel's primary task is to convince, and in *The Bostonians*, he takes up the question of how one most effectively convinces. This question, which is ostensibly carried out through the novel's plot, is nevertheless a formal one: How do we generate feeling in others through our words? James suggests a set of answers to these questions via the strategies, or forms, employed by different characters: Olive Chancellor, who reflects the aesthetic strategies of reform realism; Henry Burrage, who reflects the decadent aesthetics of an art-for-art's-sake aestheticism; and Basil Ransom, who reflects the anti-modern conservative retreat to the aesthetics of romance. All three are represented via, and traffic in, various forms of realism, but it is only Ransom who is able to generate an affective response in Verena, and it is for this reason that Verena chooses him among the three suitors at the novel's end.

Critics of Jamesian modernism have long identified style—specifically modernist style—to be the location of political or moral consciousness for James. The prehistory to this idea of style has, however, gone largely unnoticed. In James's mid-period realist works, as in his critical prefaces and essays, these ideas are present in a discourse about style that occurs at the level of content. *The Bostonians* underscores the importance of being able to feel with our ideological opponents through the depiction of the depersonalizing intimacy of Verena and Basil, two characters who are fundamentally ideological opposites. The novel explores the lack of a need to agree with someone ideologically in order to be able to experience passionate love for them. This is the first step towards an understanding of James's way of thinking politically via a realism that is based on the production of intimacy with the reader, rather than the production of sympathy for the subject.

That Basil's politics are in direct opposition to Verena's is wholly true on the level of content, but there is more to Basil's political associations than *what* he thinks. There is also the matter of *how* he thinks. The narrator gives the following account of Basil's political position:

> I shall not attempt a complete description of Ransom's ill-starred views. . . . I shall do them sufficient justice in saying that he was by natural disposition a good deal of a stoic, and that, as the result of a considerable intellectual experience, he was, in social and political matters, a reactionary. . . . He was an immense admirer of the late Thomas Carlyle, and was very suspicious of the encroachments of modern democracy. I know not exactly how these queer heresies had planted themselves.[66]

The tone of this passage alone ("ill-starred views," "queer heresies," etc.) should dispel any critical estimates that the politics of the narrator are aligned with those of Basil or that use the portrayal of Basil as a testament to James's own conservativeness. Habegger argues that "*The Bostonians* is a conservative novel gilded . . . with conservative guilt."[67] But I suggest that while James may have set out to write "a very *American* tale, a tale very characteristic of our social condition . . . [about] the most salient and peculiar point in our social life . . . the situation of women, the decline of the sentiment of sex, the agitation on their behalf," he ends up with a novel that considers the problematic style of reform discourse, which he reveals to be at the heart of his critique of liberal politics.[68] *The Bostonians is* a guilty novel in the sense that it exhibits an internal self-conflict with its own mode of representation rather than its ideology. As Adelais Mills has shown, "James's letters indicate that he was left vacillating between these modes of relating to [The Bostonians]—drawn to embrace it, compelled to turn from it."[69] The order of the human world it injures is neither liberal nor conservative politics but how such ideological positions are engaged by the materialist aesthetics of literary realism. Both *The Bostonians* and *The Princess Casamassima* are acutely aware of how the form they inhabit encourages the very sentimental creation of sympathy they criticize at the level of content—a tendency in conflict with what Habegger identifies as James's "strong aversion to the sentimentalizing of the downtrodden."[70]

Rather than see this "guilt" as a pejoratively self-contradictory quality, I'd like to suggest that James presents such internal conflict as a desirable alternative to the violence of capitulation to an externally imposed ideological consistency. James thematizes such unsolvable and desirable contradictions in many ways, such as the hybrid identity of Hyacinth Robinson, who is, by the logic of naturalist determinism, a member of both classes (son of both an aristocrat and a criminal). This pedigree is intimated to have contributed to his peculiar and laudable sensitivity and sets the stage for his inability to thrive within a mode of representation that insists on "resolving" social problems. And in the sexual desires of Verena Tarrant—which encompass both a women's rights activist and a conservative misogynist—*The Bostonians* illustrates how such openness to internal conflict offers the possibility of productive accord with ideological adversaries. In his alignment with Carlyle, a thinker with whose ideas both Henry James Sr. and Jr. disagreed almost entirely, Basil Ransom's character demonstrates how possible it is to be what we might call "politically intimate"—that is, intimate about politics, with someone with whom you share scant few beliefs. As Andrew Taylor reminds us, Carlyle "regularly proved a convenient opponent for James Senior" and long rehearsals of James Senior's complaints against "the dour Scott" were well known in the James household.[71] In a lecture given at the Cooper Institute in 1866, James Senior claimed Carlyle

> sees nothing hopeful; no way of dealing with feeble races except by enslaving them; no way of treating the wicked except exterminating them. . . . A real desire for reform he hates. The reason why he hates Americans is, that we believe in reform, and believe him to be such a reformer as some of his writings indicate; and no thing maddens him so much as to be reckoned a reformer.[72]

Here James Sr. clearly ideologically identifies against Carlyle, ("*He* hates . . . *we* believe"). For James Jr., Carlyle would be an easy reference point for this kind of deep, categorical anti-reformism. The anti-reform stance of *The Bostonians* is grounded in the tone of the discourse of reform rather than its social aims. As Bersani observes, "James treats the energetic projects of revolutionaries and social reformers with a distrust he reserves for all forms of direct pursuit."[73] James did not believe in direct forms of persuasion (preaching to) but preferred interactive modes of engagement (feeling with). He divides these modes between his characters, who come to represent not only two different styles of intimacy, but also the relative efficacies of discourses dependent on content and those dependent on form.

The Bostonians creates a split between an intimacy based on the subject matter of ideas (Olive's), and an intimacy based on a mode of interaction (Basil's). This split itself is present in James's own assessment of Carlyle. In 1883, during the composition of The Bostonians, he published a review of Charles Eliot Norton's edition of the correspondence between Emerson and Carlyle in The Century, in which he writes, "Altogether the charm of the book is that as one reads it one is in excellent company. Two men of rare and beautiful genius converse with each other."[74] While he, like his father, disdained the conservative philosopher's staunch political opinions, James admires Carlyle's repartee with his friend. In his assessment of the relationship between the New England transcendentalist and the conservative Scottish philosopher, we see James's high regard for the ability to foster intimacy between individuals with polarized viewpoints but an equal respect for dialogue and inquiry:

> Both were men of the poetic quality, men of imagination . . . both of them set above everything else the importance of conduct—of what Carlyle called veracity and Emerson called harmony with the universe . . . but their variations of feeling were of the widest, and the temperament of the one was absolutely opposed to the temperament of the other. . . . Their correspondence is to an extraordinary degree the record, on either side, of a career with which nothing base, nothing interested, no worldly avidity, no vulgar vanity or personal error was ever mingled—a career of public distinction and private honor.[75]

This is a tender portrait of intellectual reciprocity—a practice that does not rely upon its interlocutors to necessarily share the same views or "temperament." (James notes that Emerson was entirely an optimist and Carlyle "the pessimist of pessimists" but that this difference did not prevent them from enjoying a deeply intimate friendship.)[76] Verena's decision to choose Basil, the suitor with the "monstrous opinions," amounts to a privileging of one mode of intimacy, one manner of conduct, over another, rather than one political position over another. And this, I think, should inspire rather than repel. Though she disagrees with him—though we may disagree with him—he can still be loved.

The perverseness of Verena choosing to share her life with someone whose ideas are in conflict with her own also demonstrates the powerful connection between desire and being ground. To be intimate with someone with whom one disagrees so wholly is to lose one's self in an affective relationship that offers the experience of jouissance. As Julia Obert notes, "[u]ltimately, what we talk about when we talk about intimacy is less stability than it is ecstasy, both the orienting elation and the vertiginous sense of *ekstasisd*—of being 'beside oneself' or out of place—that accompany the proximity of Self to Other."[77] James's use of the form of the realist novel to portray a politicized romance built on exchanges of depersonalizing intimacy suggests that it is in highly partial, seductive, and private modes that the political issues the intentionally removed or impartial style of reform realist writing attempts to take up are more effectively addressed.

Demographic realism pushes Verena away from a movement that might actually stand to benefit her and into the arms of a man who "was, in social and political matters, a reactionary." The opacity that marks late Jamesian style is anticipated here by a series of plots that demonstrate the importance of dismantling oppositions that render the sociopolitical landscape with a false clarity. In so doing, these aesthetic realist novels call attention to the contradictions inherent to reform realism itself as a mode that many of its practitioners purport to be flawlessly verisimilitudinous. Such a mode presents an oversimplified and potentially dangerous view of the world it portrays. He demonstrates that our experience of public social and intellectual life cannot be flattened into ideological positions instrumentalized for action. Such calls to action need to be addressed through the recesses of private feeling in such a way that our desire to understand the other does not require that we purport to be the same as they are and that our love of beauty is not made out to be in conflict with an urge for justice.

PART THREE

Art in an Emergency

CHAPTER FOUR

JAMES WELDON JOHNSON'S POLITICAL FORMALISM

> This subject is not wholly cultural, by extension it becomes social and political. It has a direct bearing on the American interracial situation, and, in a wider sense, a direct bearing on the question of American democracy.
>
> —"Contributions of the Negro to American Culture," undated address by James Weldon Johnson

WHOSE PROBLEM?

Like Henry James, whose work he studied and admired, James Weldon Johnson ultimately came to understand his own conservative view toward the preservation and creation of artistic culture as a form of radical politics. The home at 187 West 135th St. in New York that Johnson shared with his wife, Grace Nail, from 1925 until his death in 1938 served as a nexus for Black writers to network with artistic power brokers both Black and white. As his close friend and NAACP assistant Walter White observed, "The color line was never drawn at Jim's. It was there that many who were later to do much in wiping out the color line learned to know each other as fellow human beings and fellow artists without consciousness of race."[1] Zora Neale Hurston was among the many Harlem Renaissance authors whose careers Johnson fostered. Hurston recognized his status not only in the African American community at Harlem, but in the greater worlds of early twentieth-century print culture and the emergent field of cultural ethnography. When she jokingly addresses her November 5, 1937 letter to Johnson and his wife "TO THEIR ROYAL HIGHNESSES KING JAMES AND QUEEN GRACE," she refers to their inarguable position as cultural elites.

123

She goes on to invite them to "a program of Negro folk music" and assures them that she would never "start nothing like that without consulting you, because it wouldn't be done right, you knowing all that you do about folk things."[2] Hurston's lighthearted sentiment that such an event had to be passed by the Johnsons signals their real power as cultural legitimators, a role that is central to what I will refer to as Johnson's project—consisting of his own writings; his encouragement of Black artists and writers; and his work as a cultural historian, anthologizer, and ethnographer. To this end, he emphasized the importance of creating a recognized and respected African American artistic culture and cementing the legacy of Black contributions to American culture at large as well as an irreducible dialectic between art and politics. Johnson's creative and professional emphasis on the primacy of forms artistic, political, and social makes any analysis that draws a distinction between "artistic" and "political" work inapplicable to the scope and aims of his career.

Caroline Levine argues that distinctions between new historical readings that emphasize the political context of a work and formalist readings that are often taken to be apolitical neglect to consider how formalism as a mode of critical analysis can be applicable to both aesthetic and social forms.[3] In this light, Johnson was a formalist through and through, revising artistic forms alongside political structures and engaging in formal debates with cultural historians as well as United States senators. Johnson often acted in a supervisory role, both politically and artistically, connecting promising young Black writers and artists to cultural and political leaders. Through this project, which was motivated by both political and aesthetic aims, Johnson ultimately came to view African American literature's commitment to the race problem novel to be misguided.

Though often treated separately in literary critical histories, the tradition of the African American protest novel is central to the transatlantic reform realist tradition. Richard Wright's 1940 *Native Son* is perhaps the most famous entrant into this category, but such texts as William Wells Brown's *Clotel* (1853), Frances Harper's *Iola Leroy* (1892), Pauline Elizabeth Hopkins' *Contending Forces* (1900), Paul Laurence Dunbar's *The Sport of the Gods* (1902), and Jessie Redmond Fauset's *There is Confusion* (1924) were all well known in their time and read by both Black and white audiences. While problem novels throughout the period took up issues great and small, by far the greatest social problem Americans faced in the early twentieth century was the political problem these works addressed—commonly referred to as "the race problem," or even more problematically, "the negro problem." As many have pointed out in different ways, "the race problem" is not itself a Black-authored problem, but an enforced response to the circumstance of violence and inequality created by the group James Baldwin referred to as "the people who think of themselves as White."[4] W. E. B. Du Bois famously declared that "the problem of the twentieth century is the problem of the color-line" in his 1903 *The Souls of Black Folk*, a sentiment Johnson amplified and made explicit his address to the Hampton Institute twenty years later, which explored "the problem which is commonly called the Negro Problem but which is, in fact, the American Problem."[5] The history of African American culture was for Johnson, like the history of the American race problem itself, synonymous with the history of America and all Americans.

Convincing the nation that the histories—political and cultural—of Black and white Americans were one and the same would be the primary aim of Johnson's career, undertaken through various modes. Over the course of his adult life, Johnson worked as a novelist, poet, songwriter, professional speaker, lawyer, schoolteacher, high school principal, university professor, and diplomat. His professional involvement in politics dominated the largest part of his time during his most active decades, most notably in his turns at diplomacy as U.S. consul in Venezuela and Nicaragua between 1906 and 1913, and his extensive involvement with the NAACP (he served as field secretary and executive secretary from 1915 to 1930 and remained as vice president and board member for the duration of his life.) During his time abroad in Central America, when he felt more removed from the problem of race than he would at any point during his time in the States, he wrote and anonymously published a novel—the 1912 *The Autobiography of an Ex-Colored Man*—as well as a number of essays, poems, and edited collections. Just as significantly, he served as a cultural ambassador and liaison between up-and-coming writers and editors, becoming one of the three men frequently cited as the architects of the Harlem Renaissance.[6]

In some ways, the two endeavors for which he was best known—his political work for the NAACP and his literary career—were overtly linked. Johnson, who was appointed field secretary to the NAACP in 1916 and executive secretary in 1920, took charge of the organization's cultural arm with the help of Walter White. The early cultural missions were twofold. The first was to protest negative portrayals of African Americans in literature, drama, and film. The second was to support the creation of cultural products (plastic art, music, films, literature, etc.) that disseminated positive images of African Americans. As to the guiding ideology behind these missions, Johnson fostered subtle but important disagreements with organization cofounder Du Bois. Though Du Bois, like Johnson, believed that the African American vernacular tradition was the beating heart of American culture as a whole, Johnson would devote his career to furthering not only the recognition of that contribution, but encouraging the production of almost any and all innovative new works that would highlight that past tradition through the creative adoption of its forms. Du Bois took a less catholic view, arguing that all portrayals of African Americans should stress their positive attributes and, in his 1926 call for entries for the Amy Spingarn prize, stated that he did not "believe in art for art's sake"—it must have some other purpose. In a 1926 address to the NAACP, later published in *The Crisis*, entitled "Criteria of Negro Art," Du Bois outlines what Gene Andrew Jarrett calls his "political warrior" mentality towards art, suggesting that the primary goal of African American art is to respond to the white editors who "want Uncle Toms, Topsies, good 'darkies' and clowns" with a literature that spreads the gospel of racial equality; Du Bois famously concludes the essay by asserting that "all Art is propaganda and ever must be, despite the wailing of the purists . . . I do not care a damn for any art that is not used for propaganda."[7] The claim mirrors Upton Sinclair's, in *Mammonart* (1925), that "All art is propaganda. It is universally and inescapably propaganda; sometimes unconsciously, but often deliberately, propaganda."[8]

Johnson, certainly closer to one of Du Bois's "purists," though he may not have "wailed" as loudly as others, would neither use art exclusively as a political tool nor place restrictions on Black or white art that Du Bois might consider unflattering, offensive, or appropriationist.[9] Johnson advised against "[suggesting] racial limits for Negro artists; any such bounds would be strangling"; instead, he would prefer to "resta[te] what is axiomatic; that the artist produces his best when working at his best with the materials he knows best."[10]

An example of how seriously Johnson took this position is his stance on Carl Van Vechten's highly controversial 1926 novel *N——Heaven*, a work Du Bois called "a blow in the face" and "an affront to the hospitality of Black folk and the intelligence of white."[11] While the NAACP roundly condemned the white author and photographer, Johnson rose to his defense, highlighting Van Vechten's worthy prose, his evocative portrayals of what Johnson called "High Harlem," and citing artistic license to dismiss criticisms of the novel's descriptions of licentious behavior. Johnson admired Van Vechten's commitment to highlighting artistic achievement and felt that because the novel offered a white audience a more complete sense of African American artistry, it was celebratory and valuable rather than appropriative and worthy of dismissal.

Johnson was also an ardent proponent of ragtime, despite Du Bois's opinion that it was a musical genre that rose out of undesirable venues and valorized low themes. While Du Bois saw art as valuable in so far as it served a political agenda, Johnson saw art, especially African American artistic production, as a necessary space that would encourage cultural change through improving the minds of those who consumed it while creating a new cultural narrative that would ultimately serve the cause.

Several critics have called attention to the debate over aesthetics and politics among Black writers in the early twentieth century, often framing the debate as a clash of personalities between individual figures such as Du Bois and Alain Locke (for Jarrett) or Sutton Griggs and Claude McKay (for Kenneth Warren).[12] Warren notes that "McKay, despite his political activities, was more inclined to view writing as an end in itself than was Griggs, for whom social and moral ends were always paramount," labeling these positions the "indexical" and the "instrumental."[13] In *What Was African American Literature?* (2011) and elsewhere, Warren claims that African American literature only properly describes works produced by Black Americans during a discrete historical period and in response to a specific set of political concerns—more specifically, that African American literature was a "Jim Crow phenomenon."[14] Jarrett argues for a much broader view of this literary category, suggesting that we include such considerations as "African American Literature beyond race"—works by Black writers who choose not to address the race issue.[15] The terms of this debate define African American literature exclusively via the politics of identity: work written by African Americans. While Johnson would most likely agree with the importance of an identity-based aspect to this category, in his broader conception, African American literature and art are instead a set of forms that come out of African American culture itself. Johnson did not purposefully avoid the direct treatment of race in his own work, but his commitment lay elsewhere: to forge a lasting tradition of African American literature whose existence was not contingent on the pertinence of political circumstance or specific themes.

What mattered to Johnson was that artistic products by or about African Americans be exemplary in terms of *how* they depicted, not *what* they depicted. Like James and his close friend and colleague Edith Wharton, Johnson believed that political strategies were effective only in so far as they adopted aesthetically successful forms. He admired Wharton and James's novels for this reason. In his lecture notes for the American Literature course he taught at Fisk in 1933, he writes,

> James and Wharton—exponents of the "well made novel." The novel made in accordance with the approved pattern—with what became the continental pattern. The novel in which life is dealt with—no matter what phase of it—in accordance with the standards of good taste. In the "well made novel" the social and economic orders may be criticized, but they are at the same time taken for granted—they are not *questioned*—as to right to continue.[16]

The value of these works, to his mind, was their mastery of form. That they are well made is, for Johnson, not only more significant than their failure to question "social and economic orders," but this failure is even a part of their "good taste"—an epithet that recurs throughout Johnson's writings to signal the greatest respect, as in "people of intelligence and good taste."[17] He goes on to declare Wharton's *Ethan Frome* (1911) the highest work by either writer in his lecture notes, as that novel "comprehend[s] a richer, deeper sweep of emotions than any of James's novels or than any other by her" and has "the best chance of survival out of all the work done by these two writers," concluding that James and Wharton "will always be considered a valuable social record of life in the period they cover."[18] Johnson's concern with a work's ability to survive the test of time speaks to his preference for deep historical traditions over of-the-moment political writing. He frames the realist commitment to documentation and the formally masterful novels of writers like Wharton and James as its own kind of political strategy. In an undated note to himself, he observes that "ideas of good form are more binding than ideas of good morals. Make lynching 'bad form,' show that it is perpetrated only by ignorant; low-brow . . . persons."[19] His guiding belief in the power of aesthetic forms to transcend political struggles motivates both his work rehabilitating the African American past and imagining the African American future.

This view has led to many dismissals of Johnson as politically tepid at best or, at worst, an accomodationist. Brian Russell Roberts writes that Johnson's "oblique aesthetic methods might be seen as emblematic of the indirection that [Richard] Wright criticized," referencing Wright's 1937 essay "Blueprint for Negro Writing," in which he claims that often "technically brilliant" writing was rarely "addressed to the Negro himself, his needs, his suffering, his aspirations."[20] Brent Edwards notes the ubiquity of dismals of Johnson's political significance, describing how "Johnson is usually portrayed as [a] stilted aesthetic aristocrat."[21] Of his contemporaries, Johnson's views were the most sympathetic to those of the Jamaican poet Claude McKay. Their correspondence expresses frustrations with the increasing politicization of the African American arts community in the late thirties, during which time McKay proposed the organization of a literary group that would eschew direct political action:

> I find myself rather averse to the various literary groups springing up in the present era of political confusion and whose complexion is generally more political than literary. From my social and political experience, I think that among writers the literary quality should take precedence over the political attitudes of the times. Take our group for example (I mean the older). Fifteen years ago we were all individually different in our political outlook. Some of us were Socialists, some Communists, some Republicans, some Democrats, and some Pan-African, some nationalist and some internationalist. Yet what remains significant about our work today is not the political angle, but the literary quality.[22]

McKay understands politics to be intimately connected with the current moment, whereas a literature of the kind he identifies himself and Johnson to be producing holds the possibility of transcending these often-shifting allegiances.

For McKay and Johnson, continued cultural work was the milieu in which African Americans could set the discourse, whereas political action was the necessary answer to the short-term situation on the ground created by white America and inevitably confronted on white America's terms. Johnson's influence on the younger generation of writers and artists associated with the Harlem Renaissance, (Larsen, Hurston, Fauset, Hughes, Cullen, etc.) many of whose careers he helped facilitate, was largely due to this belief in the primacy of arts advocacy for social change.

Several scholars, including Nathan Irvin Huggins and David Levering Lewis, and more recently Lawrence P. Jackson and Kenneth Warren, have argued that the arts-based politics of the Harlem Renaissance were ultimately unsuccessful insofar as they failed to achieve advances for the race movement.[23] On the other side of such debates, Jarrett describes "reciprocal connections between literary aesthetics and political action" that do not exclusively rely on "public expressions of protest, rebellion, and revolution," suggesting that "more 'quiet' or 'interior' expressions of pensiveness, intimacy, spirituality, solemnity, love and even vulnerability belong on the continuum of political action."[24] Beyond these quieter victories, Johnson had his own reasons for why cultural achievements stood to effect the greatest impact on the status of Black people in America.

As Johnson identifies the wrongs to African Americans as primarily perpetuated by cultural products, he reasons they can only be undone by cultural products. Despite Jim Crow, despite lynching, Johnson saw the deepest wound to Black America as occurring in the aesthetic regime of the arts, blaming the former atrocities on attitudes that

> have, for the greater part, been molded by what may be termed literary and artistic processes. Some of the most persistent of them were formed on the minstrel stage. For nearly three-quarters of a century Black-faced minstrelsy was the chief and most popular form of American entertainment. Hardly a hamlet in the country was too small to be visited by a minstrel show. And it was from the minstrel show that millions of white Americans got their conception of Negro character. . . . Now, just as these stereotypes were molded and circulated and perpetuated by literary and artistic processes, they must be broken up and replaced through similar means. No other means can be as fully effective. Some of this work has already been done, but the greater portion remains to be done—and by Negro writers and artists.[25]

He locates the germ of the persistence of racial oppression in the United States in the form of white minstrelsy and is determined to emphasize previous forms significant to the Black cultural tradition that might supplant it as the primary cultural depiction of Black Americans.

His call to action is articulated in an essay called "Race Prejudice and the Negro Artist" (1928), wherein he argues that a shift must be made from a united folk culture, such as is represented by the spirituals, to a canon of *individual* Black artists who can be celebrated for their discreet achievements. He writes,

> A number of approaches to the heart of the race problem have been tried: religious, educational, political, industrial, ethical, economic,

sociological. Along several of these approaches considerable progress has been made. To-day a newer approach is being tried, an approach which discards most of the older methods. It requires a minimum of please, or propaganda, or philanthropy. It depends more upon what the Negro himself does than upon what someone does for him. It is the approach along the lines of intellectual and artistic achievement by Negroes, and may be called the art approach to the Negro problem. This method of approaching a solution of the race question has the advantage of affording great and rapid progress with least friction and of providing a common platform upon which most people are willing to stand. The results of this method seem to carry a high degree of finality, to be the thing itself that was to be demonstrated.[26]

Whereas critics of such aesthetic approaches to liberation within African American literature and its criticism argue that the race problem must be dealt with head-on, Johnson positions such overtly political projects as representational rather than actual. In his formulation, the creation of art is "the thing itself that was to be demonstrated"—a sense of art as *doing* that goes beyond even contemporary notions of the subtle import of the aesthetic such as Jarrett's concept of the quiet or the interior. For Johnson, cultivating the public's aesthetic sensibilities reclaims the Black literary and cultural past, while the continued work of producing and historicizing a Black artistic tradition stakes out territory in the cultural and political landscapes of the future.

Many critics have explored the subversive ways in which African American writers have utilized Anglo aesthetics towards a political agenda. In the 1970s, Addison Gayle Jr. influentially argued that "Black artists of the past expropriated and remodeled the forms of white America to fit the needs of Black people. Nowhere is this more evident than in the letters, speeches, and essays of David Walker, Henry Highland Garnet, Charles Redmond, and Frederick Douglass."[27] Maggie Sale writes that Douglass's turn to Anglo-political rhetoric redefined it by using the "language that was shared with those . . . [he was] trying to persuade" and allowed him to "enter into a discourse used by dominant groups and reinscribe it with a different meaning."[28] Carla L. Peterson and Shelley Fisher Fishkin argue that Douglass used such borrowed rhetoric to create a counter discourse and Ivy Wilson suggests that writers ranging from Fredrick Douglass to William Wells Brown create a "shadow discourse" by "remixing" dominant Anglo-American rhetorical tropes to insert the African American into the narrative of democracy.[29] This was a popular and successful strategy, especially in the first half of the nineteenth century, that Johnson reverses.

The aim of Johnson's project—one he undertook throughout the three most active decades of his professional career in various methods and guises—was to demonstrate the ways in which popular American aesthetic forms are always already African American. While Du Bois posed the rhetorical question, "Would America have been America without her Negro People?" and stated that "there is no true American music but the wild sweet melodies of the Negro slave," Johnson set out to definitively *prove* the centrality of African American culture to American culture as a whole and reengineer existing cultural narratives that would suggest otherwise.[30] The primary tool of this task was literary and artistic formalism. To properly identify and understand the African American foundations of American literary and cultural traditions, Johnson's corpus suggests, the reading and viewing public must be able to parse and identify these forms in all their various iterations.

FORMS NOT GENRES

Throughout many of Johnson's writings, a single argument emerges again and again: that American culture *is* African American culture. In multiple essays and public addresses given throughout the 1920s and 1930s as well as in *The Autobiography*, he cites the Uncle Remus stories, the cakewalk, ragtime, and the spirituals, as being the most quintessentially and originally American forms. In his 1926 preface to *The Second Book of Negro Spirituals*, he writes "the Negro is the possessor of a wealth of natural endowments; that he has long been a generous giver to America; that he has helped to shape and mold it; that he has put an indelible imprint upon it; that America is the exact America it is today because of his influence." Here, in Johnson's enthusiasm, we see a strain of almost essentialist race rhetoric extoling the gifts of the African American artist. This is not an isolated phenomenon in his *oeuvre*. Elsewhere, for example, he writes in an editorial for *The New York Age* in 1915 that "white musicians can play ragtime as well as Negro musicians; that is, white musicians can play exactly what is put down on the paper. But negro musicians are able to put into the music something that can't be put on the paper; a certain abandon which seems to enter in the blood of the dancers; and that is . . . why Negro musicians are preferred."[31] He reverses the stereotype of African Americans as mere "mimics" or automatons, attributing this quality to Anglo-Americans and highlighting that ragtime is, in its origins, a Black form.

His goal to illuminate the African American roots of American culture via the study of a history of forms is predicated on a vision of the reversal of white supremacist power structures in the sociopolitical culture at large. In his autobiography *Along This Way*, he writes,

> the part [African American] music plays in American life and its acceptance by the world at large cannot be ignored. It is to this music that America in general gives over its leisure hours . . . at these times, the Negro drags his captors captive. On occasions, I have been amazed and amused watching white people dancing to a negro band in a Harlem cabaret; striving to yield to the feel and experience of abandon . . . in a word, doing their best to pass for colored.[32]

His return to the idea of "abandon" that he associates with African American music speaks to an ineffable quality Johnson finds in many works of African American art, a quality that perhaps, with its references to blood, might read like biological race rhetoric when viewed in the context of the racist ideology of the period. Yet this rhetoric is deployed only in the service of addressing the white audience to whom it belongs. Because elsewhere Johnson knowingly, directly, and critically confronts this essentialist logic. In a section of his preface to the 1921 Edition of *The Book of American Negro Poetry* that praises the artistic merit of the work of Paul Laurence Dunbar, he writes:

> It has a bearing on this entire subject to note that Dunbar was of unmixed negro blood; so, as the greatest figure in literature which the colored race in the United States has produced, he stands as an example at once refuting and confounding those who wish to believe that whatever extraordinary ability an Aframerican [*sic*] shows is due to an admixture of white blood.[33]

This is an example of a rhetorical move that Johnson makes again and again, one I'd classify as a Black answer to a white question. The race rhetoric is not Johnson's own, but is instead a necessary rejoinder to a preexisting racist discourse. It is essential for Johnson that such questions be answered, but they are asymptotic to the discourse of culture that Johnson sees as the invention—and the potential salvation—of non-white peoples.

Johnson's reasoning behind the superiority of the artistic accomplishments of the African race is more akin to a Hegelian assertion of the superior competence of the oppressed to the oppressor than to the eugenicist thinking about hereditary traits that was popular in his own time. In a 1919 editorial responding to racist attempts to curtail Japanese immigration and employment in California, Johnson succinctly explains why white businesses are less successful than Japanese businesses: "The white man does not want to work that hard. He wants some time to ride around in his Ford and to socialize." And so while white people have dominated in the arts of domination, they stagnate everywhere else. The white discourse may employ biological rhetoric to claim superiority, but Johnson raises the specter of history to suggest otherwise:

> as soon as anything is recognized as great, [the white race] sets about to claim credit for it. In this manner they have attempted to rob the Negro of the credit of originating the plantation stories and songs. . . . By this method, the white race has gathered to itself credit for originating nearly all the great and good things in the world. It has taken credit for what has been accomplished by the ancient Egyptians, the East Indians and the Arabs, by the simple process of declaring those Black people to be white . . . the pure white race did not originate even the religion it uses.[34]

His explanation for the unoriginality of the white race is the very fact of its political dominance. It was Johnson's belief that it was only a matter of time before this phenomenon was brought fully to light, and he worked to speed that process by scrupulously tracing cultural forms taken to be purely American—which is to say, Anglo-American—back to their African American antecedents. This was a project of historiography, but one that had to rely on historical nodes beyond famous figures or events.

It was among Johnson's chief complaints that the average citizen was not more well versed in history. In a *New York Age* editorial he laments, "let anyone with common sense read history, and . . . he will absolutely agree with Bernard Shaw in saying that Hegel was right when he said that we learn from history that men never learn anything from history."[35] His solution to this sweeping problem of ignorance was to educate in the conventional ways (via the public lecture hall and the university classroom) but also to incorporate historical forms into new cultural productions. He classifies it as "a startling truth . . . that America would not be precisely the America it is except for the silent power the Negro has exerted upon it."[36] His reference to the "silent power" is a curious one, because it addresses both a hope ("power") and a pessimism ("silent") regarding the future understanding of Black cultural production in white America. As Brent Edwards argues, "Johnson worries not that U.S. culture will absorb or consume African American culture, but in fact that the latter has so fully defined the national culture that its origins have gone unrecognized."[37] Noelle Morrisette articulates the double-edge of this position by suggesting it "could be taken as an assimilationist argument—Black culture was American culture, American culture was Black culture," but she importantly notes that "Johnson wished for some of the distinction to remain."[38] Situated within the larger body of his work, it becomes clear that Johnson's ethnographic project is motivated by a desire to highlight this distinction.

The creation of the concept of African American literature is a significant example of how Johnson sought to bring African American cultural achievements to the fore in such a manner that presented them *as* African American cultural achievements. In an undated note, written to himself some time during the early 1930s while he was planning *Along This Way*, he writes that he is "not primarily interested in showing how the Negro can imitate the white man—even the white man's best qualities—I am more interested in showing that what the Negro *has* and *had done* . . . is of equal value."[39] Johnson worked tirelessly to prove this assertion, engaging in projects ranging from ethnographic recordings to reimagining how American literature would be taught in his role as professor of English at Fisk University. Chris Mustazza argues that Johnson's dialect poetry attempts to produce an ethnographic record of the cadences and rhythms of nineteenth-century African American sermons.[40] Johnson also worked with Columbia Professor of Speech George W. Hibbitt and Barnard colleague Professor W. Cabell Greet to create recordings of these poems and others in the context of an oral history project that would lay the groundwork for the field of sociolinguistics. As Johnson's poetry performs this important historical work, it simultaneously perpetuates and expands the African American cultural tradition. This strategy has the dual purpose of creating an accurate formal record of African American cultural contributions while inventing new works that keep that history vital. Warren describes how Johnson saw "figures such as Phillis Wheatley or Frederick Douglass [as] simply Negroes who were writers" whereas writers of his own moment—such as Langston Hughes and Claude McKay—"were writers of Negro (African American) literature."[41] And while it is true that he felt the need to transition from a folk culture to a culture of fine artists celebrated for their individual visions, within the scope of Johnson's full recovery project, this latter kind of literature would, through formal allusion, strengthen both the historical import and make more apparent the artistry of the earlier works.

Johnson's ultimate goal was the edification and education of the American public—both Black and white. In his syllabus for a course on the "Negro in American Literature," he includes a small section under a heading that reads "Fiction: White Authors" that includes Julia Peterkin, DuBose Heyward, Howard W. Odum, Carl Van Vechten, Roark Bradford, Paul Green, and Ridgeley Torrence. Beyond featuring African American protagonists, the works by these white authors are based on African American vernacular forms and utilize African American colloquial dialect. Arranging the syllabus in this way, Johnson invites his students to read white writers as the ones inserting themselves into an existent discourse by focusing on the formal aspects of the texts.[42] In the notes for a class titled "Lecture 6," on slave narratives, Johnson writes "Slave narratives—became a popular auto-biographical form and an effective weapon in the anti-slavery cause. Became also a popular fictional form—a form that was exploited by ghost writers," going on to claim "Booker T. Washington Up From Slavery—best of the slave narratives—why? Style effects work." For Johnson, political argument or content were secondary to stylistic effects.[43]

Johnson's attention to form is born out of his interest in the *longue durée* of culture. In the context of his project, form more importantly serves as the trail of evidence that allows him to legitimize his claim for Black originality and innovation. By tracing formal patterns back through various genres to their original Black authors, he is able to "prove" his case for the primacy of Black culture. For example, in *Along This Way*, he describes the act his brother Rosamund performed with his partner Bob Cole in great detail, claiming that Rosamund "was among the first musicians in America to go beyond one-two-three and one-two-three-four styles of arrangements and to adapt counterpoint to the arrangements of popular songs," suggesting that "a comparison of the arrangements . . . with other songs of the period will substantiate this statement."[44] Noting and historicizing these formal details *is* political content for Johnson.

He concludes his description of Johnson and Cole's act by asserting that it was "the act that started a vogue of acts consisting of two men in dress suits and a piano"—a form that then became known as a "class act."[45] This is a claim that music historian Brenda Ellis confirms, noting how by "interject[ing] classical themes and art songs into their syncopated dance tunes, [Rosamond] Johnson and Cole gradually overcame the image of the Black minstrel entertainer and created a new image for future Black performers," becoming "the hottest duo on Broadway" by 1903.[46] The work James Weldon Johnson did in his capacity as a composer, poet, novelist, and anthologizer was connected to the work undertaken by Johnson and Cole in their performances. He later joined their duo as a composer, and subsequently partnered with his brother to provide the historical and musicological background to accompany Rosamond's original compositions, based on African American vernacular classics, in *The Book of American Spirituals* (1925) and *The Second Book of American Spirituals* (1926).

James Weldon Johnson's claim about Johnson and Cole's innovation of the "class act" has considerable historical consequences when considered with formal sensitivity. We can see these consequences as a case study for Johnson's greater argument for African American culture as the foundation of American culture. Johnson and Cole's "class act" emerges out of the late-nineteenth-century vaudeville stage protocol known as the "two-colored rule," which stated that a negro performer could not appear alone on the stage, as such an act would lend too much attention and subsequently grant too much power to the performer.[47] Black artists like Johnson and Cole responded with acts where dancers dressed identically would perform side-by-side in complete synchrony.

Early practitioners of the "class act" after Johnson and Cole include the acts "Buck and Bubbles" and "The Nichols Brothers." This form had evolved into countless iterations in dominant white spaces such as Hollywood cinema by the time Johnson was writing his autobiography, most notably in the films of Fred Astaire such as *Top Hat* (1935) and the *Ziegfield Follies* (1936). The reach of the class act form continues to be long and wide; the choreographer of the synchronized dance sequence in the music video for Michael Jackson's *Thriller* (1982) was Michael Peters, who was educated by Bernice Johnson, the proprietor of a well-known dance school in Queens from 1949–2000 and one of the original dancers at the Cotton Club, where Bill Robinson and The Nichols Brothers headlined.[48]

If you look closely at the *Thriller* zombie dancers, you can see that the male dancers wear shredded suits. The form can also be seen today in popular music videos by (to name just a few) Justin Timberlake, Janelle Monáe, and the Nigerian-American artists P-Square.[49]

In addition to his claims about Johnson and Cole's innovation, Johnson points out in several addresses on Black contributions to American culture and in his NYU teaching notes that Bill Robinson, the first Black vaudeville performer to break the "two-colored rule," was the teacher of the Roxy dancing girls—the precursor to the Radio City Rockettes.[50] What Johnson does not discuss is Robinson's later film career as Bojangles, the persona in which he appeared, most famously, alongside Shirley Temple in class-act-inspired routines. Though Robinson would not appear onscreen with Temple until 1935, after the publication of *Along This Way*, Johnson would continue to give addresses on this material that included discussions of Robinson's influence without a mention of the Shirley Temple films. This omission reinforces his narrative of Bill Robinson as a choreographer and cultural influencer who is the genius behind an entire aesthetic movement.[51] When we see Bill Robinson in a Shirley Temple film, we are more apt to perceive him as such a delimited Black performer entering a white-authored creative production. Johnson's goal in stressing Robinson's career as a choreographer and educator privileges the dance pioneer Bill Robinson over the Bojangles character. With Robinson refigured as a point of origin, a stage show at Radio City Music Hall, featuring fifty white women dancing in synchrony or a studio film with an all-white cast like *Top Hat* are now re-coded as Black formal inventions into which white performers have inserted themselves, as opposed to white-authored works to which Blacks are either denied entry or, like vaudeville dancers, allowed to enter only on delimited bases.

By consistently drawing his readers' attention to aesthetic forms—from the class act to the cake walk to ragtime—Johnson works to create an aesthetically literate public who will be able to identify the formal roots of contemporary works. Their ability to do so would ensure that Black cultural forms will be recognized as such, no matter who adopts them. As Levine argues, "more stable than genre, configurations and arrangements organize materials in distinct and iterable ways no matter their context or audience. Forms thus migrate across contexts in a way genres cannot."[52] Johnson's definition of African American art is a body of work connected through its formal interventions rather than exclusively by the theme of racial oppression or the identity of its producers. Presciently, Johnson also saw in aesthetic forms an exportability that would give their expert practitioners power and voice in many different contexts. Because of this, Johnson has a remarkably optimistic take on the issue of cultural appropriation, so long as the concomitant work of tracing the origins of those forms is also done. As Noelle Morrisette observes of the afterlives of Johnson's reworkings of African American spirituals—which were interpolated into works ranging from political campaign songs to T. S. Eliot's *Sweeney Agonistes*, "[Johnson] was proud of the appropriative measures that such borrowing facilitated, for not only were the spirituals and work songs given new voice by their compositions, they were sung enthusiastically by white as well as Black people."[53] This pride and optimism is a mark of his belief in the political power of art to erode the color line. His critical writings and practices as a writer of poetry and fiction suggest that, rather than curtailing appropriative works, Black critics and activists ought to be working on the project of arts education and cultural historiography.

REFRAMING *THE AUTOBIOGRAPHY OF AN EX-COLORED MAN* AS CULTURAL PARABLE

Creating and fostering such connections between past African American forms and new ones was at the heart of all of Johnson's creative endeavors. Just as Johnson's dialect poems refined and reinvigorated the tradition of the African American sermon, *The Autobiography* set out to rework and repoliticize the literary tradition of the African American life narrative. Before Johnson's creative intervention, the genre of African American life writing had been marked by racist framing techniques that denied Black authors the literary recognition they deserved. John Sekora describes this phenomenon in his 1987 essay "Black Message/White Envelope," which calls on critics to create "a new literary history [that would] jettison the preemptive metaphor of the Black author as literary child" by revisiting early American slave narratives.[54] Sekora outlines the problem of creating a literary history that positions the slave narrative as the ur-text of African American literature. Such narratives were often edited and preceded with a preface by a prominent white editor or writers. Both at the time of their publication and in their afterlives as historical documents, readers and critics have struggled to identify who, precisely, should be credited with their authorship. Sekora notes the prevailing nineteenth-century ideas that prevented the recognition of Black writers as the creators of an original literature, quoting James Clarke's 1842 sermon: "The colored man has not so much invention as the white, but more imitation. He has not so much of the reflective, but more of the perceptive powers," the same widely reproduced prejudicial sentiment Rebecca Harding Davis critiques in her story, "Blind Tom," discussed in chapter 1.[55]

Because of this deep-seated popular stereotype and the circumstances under which such narratives were generated and published, many contemporary readers understood slave narratives to be a white literary product composed of the raw material of African American lives. Johnson sought to reclaim the Black literary past by reimaging the slave narrative with significant formal changes that collapse the white editor and the Black author into a single figure in *The Autobiography*. Johnson's only novel is typically read as a "passing" tale—the story of a Black man who inserts himself into the dominant white culture.[56] But if we understand his goal to be the reversal of the paradigm that establishes white culture as dominant, the notion of "passing" too is reversed; *The Autobiography* shows how such life narratives are Black texts that "pass" as white, and the significance of the novel becomes not its confessions about crossing the color line, but its formal status as a parable about African American aesthetic culture.

The narrator of *The Autobiography* is mixed race and able to experience the world as both a Black man and a white man. Throughout the course of the novel, he is forced to decide whether he should assume his white privilege for personal and financial gain or openly identify as Black. He is a gifted musician who plays to great acclaim for both Black and white audiences and, like Johnson himself, an ethnomusicologist who dreams of inscribing African American spirituals into the canon of world classical music. The narrator's racial heritage (he does not, in fact, know that he is Black according to what Mark Twain calls the "fiction of law and custom," until an incident at school in middle childhood) is like that of the nation itself: a shared background of two cultures that are, no matter how historically opposed, inseparable from one another.[57] Through the device of the mixed-race artist/narrator, who is what Werner Sollors has called "neither Black nor white yet both," and trained in both African American and classical European music, Johnson is able to assert an argument that American culture is itself like this narrator—a mix of African and Anglo American heritage.[58] Just as the unnamed ex-colored man is positioned as the quintessential American, Black culture is relocated from the margins to the center of the American cultural and historical tradition.

Johnson dramatizes the creation of American forms out of the mixing of Anglo and African American cultures in a section of the novel that deals with the narrator's trip to Europe as the paid companion of an eccentric white millionaire. In one scene, the narrator is tasked with an exhibition performance that produces surprising results:

> My "millionaire" planned, in the midst of the discussion on music, to have me play the "new American music" and astonish everybody present. The result was that I was more astonished than anyone else. I went to the piano and played the most intricate ragtime piece I knew. Before there was time for anybody to express an opinion on what I had done, a big be-spectacled, bushy-headed man rushed over, and, shoving me out of the chair, exclaimed, "Get up! Get up!" He seated himself at the piano, and taking the theme of my ragtime, played it through first in straight chords; then varied and developed it through every known musical form. I sat amazed. I had been turning classic music into ragtime, a comparatively easy task; and this man had taken ragtime and made it classic. The thought came across me like a flash.—It can be done, why can't I do it? From that moment my mind was made up. I clearly saw the way of carrying out the ambition I had formed when a boy.[59]

Bruce Barnhart reads this scene as one of problematic appropriation, asserting that the bushy-headed man "treats the narrator's ragtime as a kind of raw material, a material that can be contained in classical forms and utilized to further the ends of these forms. In taking the narrator's place at the piano, he usurps the prerogative of the narrator to determine the fate of his piece's theme."[60] But in light of Johnson's larger cultural project, and the narrator's unabashed enthusiasm for the German musician's performance and the revelation it yields, we might instead read this scene as a testament to the genius of ragtime compositions and Johnson's endorsement of the power of such forms to transcend cultural divisions. After all, the scene is an origin story for what would become Johnson's own project: the task of placing the African American tradition as the original rather than the imitation in relation to white culture. Earlier in the novel, the narrator asserts,

> One thing cannot be denied; [ragtime] is music which possesses at least one strong element of greatness; it appeals universally; not only the American, but the English, the French, and even the German people, find delight in it. In fact, there is not a corner of the civilized world in which it is not known, and this proves its originality; for if it were an imitation, the people of Europe, anyhow, would not have found it a novelty.[61]

According to Johnson, by inventing a new form that arises from their own cultural past and encouraging its subsequent adoption and remixing into Anglo traditions, African Americans secure a position of cultural dominance. The ex-colored man's dream is to spread the gospel of African American music, furthering its popularity and renown around the world.

Towards the end of the novel, The ex-colored man is present at a lynching, the sight of which horrifies him into abandoning his ties to the race and with it his cultural mission. He chooses to let the world assume that he is white, and he goes on to lead a successful career in business, amassing wealth and enjoying a life of ease. In the closing lines of the novel, he looks back on his forsaken musical career and his former dream of fostering racial uplift through artistic expression:

> I sometimes open a little box in which I still keep my fast yellowing manuscripts, the only tangible remnants of a vanished dream, a dead ambition, a sacrificed talent, I cannot repress the thought that, after all, I have chosen the lesser part, that I have sold my birthright for a mess of pottage.[62]

In this reference to the biblical story of Jacob and Esau, Johnson casts privilege (racial, economic, political) as the mess of pottage—the foolish, exigent choice made in a moment of desperation—and the inheritance of a rich culture as the birthright. Lisa Hinrichsen writes that it is the narrator's adoption of the terms of white culture and white success which amounts to what the novel calls a cruel joke: "in contrast to the slave narratives upon which *The Autobiography* draws, the Ex-colored man ends up not in freedom but in a position of being rhetorically and psychologically imprisoned within modes of normative or 'ordinarily successful' whiteness that offer him little in the way of choice and mobility."[63] Womack argues that Johnson's narrator's near lynching leads him to realize "that to be black in America is perhaps to always be narrowly avoiding a lynching, a revelation that leads to confinement in his own kind of permanent racial purgatory."[64] If the ex-colored man represents the hybrid nature of American culture itself, how he chooses to investigate and articulate his own personal and historical past is the largest determinate of how he—and hence America writ large—will come to understand its direction.[65]

The narrator's tragic choice to deny the Black cultural tradition is in some ways the inverse of the choices Johnson makes in writing the novel—a negative purpose. Johnson's adoption and revision of the life-narrative genre changes the way we view the works of the past through his strategy of authorship. By writing the *Autobiography* anonymously, Johnson muddies the question of its genesis and veracity. *Is this a real account or a fiction?* This is the central question that was asked of popular slave narratives published in the nineteenth century. As Augusta Rohrbach writes, "Prefaces and reviews of the narratives, as well as the narrators themselves, always provided verifiable details to satisfy the demand, not just for verisimilitude, but for true experience."[66] Rohrbach goes on to describe how a part of the case often made for the veracity of such accounts was the white editor's insistence on the Black author's "artlessness." To verify the authenticity of the slave narrative, it was deemed necessary to discredit him or her as an artist. Johnson addresses this racist convention by establishing himself as both the inventor of the "raw material" and his own "envelope" (to borrow Sekora's term)—composing the preface to the original edition only attributed to the equally anonymous "publishers" himself.

Whereas the white-authored preface of the slave narrative typically served a legitimizing function, assuring the reader that the following account is indeed true and, in the most desirable circumstances, told in the subject's own words, the purpose of Johnson's preface to *The Autobiography* seems to be to create a sense of racial instability that exceeds the boundaries of its pages:

> These pages also reveal the unsuspected fact that prejudice against the Negro is exerting a pressure, which, in New York and other large cities where the opportunity is open, is actually and constantly forcing an unascertainable number of fair-complexioned colored people over into the white race.[67]

Rather than authenticating the narrator's singular experience, the preface universalizes it to suggest that anyone could be "colored"—destabilizing racial divisions both sociopolitical and literary. As Edwards argues, Johnson reimagines both the white-authored prefaces of slave narratives and the Black author's preface of Du Bois's *The Souls of Black Folk* to suggest the racial indeterminacy of such texts themselves. In this new imagining, the preface becomes "not a door or frontier, but a kind of parodic 'hinge' both opening and closing an 'impossible text.'"[68] To maintain this sense of artistic and political destabilization, Johnson chose to withhold his own identity as author for fifteen years, later writing: "I am not, today, exactly sure of what my reasons were for publishing the book anonymously. I guess the main reason was that then I thought it would have a greater effect by being taken as a human document. If my name were signed to it, that would make it impossible."[69] Johnson perpetuated and legitimized Black cultural products on Black terms—eliminating the perception that African Americans did not or could not produce compelling and innovative works on their own. Jacqueline Goldsby notes that to call a work about a Black life an "autobiography"—rather than a "narrative of the life"—at this time was itself "a heretical act."[70] *The Autobiography* not only validates the Black experience through the production of a fictional literary product called an "autobiography," it sets out to prove that many cultural products Americans collectively thought of as "white" were originated by Black artists. What is significant in the cultural projects that Johnson created and facilitated is thus not the authenticity of their historical truths, but the authenticity of their forms and their connection to the African American cultural tradition he reinscribed.

When he decided to reveal his identity and reissue the novel in 1927, at the height of NAACP debates on the role of art in the race movement, Johnson selected none other than the controversial Van Vechten to write the new introduction. While this move could be interpreted as reopening the problem of white authorization, Van Vechten's introduction furthers Johnson's aims by seizing the opportunity, as Johnson himself does in his preface to *The Book of Negro Spirituals*, to act as an historian of African American culture in a place where the convention up to that point had been to act as an historian of the African American experience. Giving a brief overview of the canon of African American literature, ranging from Chesnutt to Washington to Du Bois and many others, Van Vechten solidifies *The Autobiography*'s centrality to the important work of producing and recognizing such a canon. By the time of the reissue, enough recovery work and new developments had transpired to more solidly position the novel within the context of a linear tradition.

Part of the praise Van Vechten sings is the novel's lack of a didactic tone, which marked other more explicitly reformist texts: "Dr. Du Bois's important work, *The Souls of Black Folk* (1903) does, certainly, explore a wide territory, but these essays lack the insinuating influence of Mr. Johnson's calm, dispassionate tone."[71] What Van Vechten praises here is Johnson's art—his ability to write a novel that transcends any political agenda and allows its reader to become entirely absorbed in the world it creates. As the attorney Clarence Darrow wrote of the novel, "it is an exquisite work. It is simple and plain and delightfully easy to read. It would melt the heart of a stone or a white man—if only stones or white people had hearts."[72] But the availability of an apolitical reading is the note on which Van Vechten concludes, claiming that "new readers . . . will examine this book with interest: some to acquire through its mellow pages a new conception of how a coloured man lives and feels, others to simply follow the course of its fascinating story."[73] The crucial work, in Van Vechten's estimation, that *The Autobiography* performs is its broad cultural anthropology and documentation of African American cultural history, most notably in its prescient "singing" of "hosanas to ragtime."[74] Van Vechten and Johnson shared the sense that the novel's import lay, beyond its engrossing depiction of Jim Crow America, in its proposition that further work be undertaken to create a thorough history of African American artistic forms.

POLITICAL FORMS

Johnson's work revealing and recoding African American cultural forms would take on an explicitly political valence in his capacity as a servant of the NAACP. Perhaps his most enduring contribution to American culture is one of his least known: his orchestration of the NAACP's 1917 Silent Protest Parade in New York. Following the gruesome riots that took place in East St. Louis after a group of white men marched in the streets to protest Black non-union strikebreakers in the packing industry, resulting in the death of at least forty African Americans and the destruction of at least $400,000 worth of Black property, the NAACP became determined to stage a response.[75] Johnson suggested the parade, which was likely the most elaborately staged and formally coherent event of political activism that had yet occurred in the United States.[76] Harper Barnes would call the parade "America's first major civil rights march."[77]

Including between eight and ten thousand African American participants, the parade exhibited an unusual attention to formal detail so sophisticated and ahead of its time it would easily be considered political performance art today. All participants were carefully arranged in even rows as they marched. Women and children wore all white, men wore Black suits. Children were placed in front, followed by women and then men. Protestors wielded plain, black-and-white uniform posters with slogans ranging from the biblical—"Thou Shalt Not Kill"—to the political—"President Wilson, Make Our Country Safe for Democracy"—to the statistical—"We own 250,000 farms with 20,000,000 acres of land worth $500,000,000." The childrens' placards were particularly affecting, bearing slogans such as "Mother, Do Lynchers Go to Heaven?" and "Treat Us That We May Love Our Country." The parade ended with a giant American flag and a banner that read "Your Hands are Full of Blood."[78] The strictly imposed silence of the parade was itself a form of dramatic effect.

Comprised of well-dressed, Black bodies silently moving forward through city streets, the parade reversed both the manic spectacle of lynching and the chaos and violence of the East St. Louis Riots. Like the class act, the parade is a Black-authored response to a white-authored problem. Both the dance form and the silent protest form emphasize the equality of the performer through dress—nothing signals respectable male citizenship and "good taste" so much as a suit—and the significance and solidarity of the population through coordinated movements and identical costume. Soyica Diggs Colbert has described how the respectability of the parade's aesthetic decisions (the suits, the silence) were an effective backdrop for the contrast between both the violence of the riots they responded to and the strong language of many of the placards: "the variety of signs, many of which protested physical violence, disrupted the well-designed and pristine presentation of respectability. Although the marchers displayed reservation, respect, and quiet in their comportment and dress, their sign system emphasized anger, outrage, patriotism, and revolution."[79] Through his experience as a scholar of form, Johnson saw that political movements needed—perhaps above all—to rely on innovative formal strategies.

In *Along This Way*, he celebrates how the formal accomplishments of the parade produced a profound emotional reaction in its viewers, noting with satisfaction that "among the watchers were those with tears in their eyes."[80] The Silent Protest Parade set the terms of non-violent resistance and forever changed what political demonstrations across the globe would look like. Just as the class act has become a form widely employed by Americans of all races and backgrounds, so too has this kind of silent, theatrical protest in America become a form that transcends race (although its connections to the Black Lives Matter movement have been noted) that has been utilized by movements like Anonymous, Occupy, and #MeToo in response to acts of domestic terrorism across the world.[81]

In some ways, however, the Silent Protest Parade was nothing new. Benjamin Fagan describes how, by the middle of the nineteenth century, "parades had been an integral part of Black life in New York City for generations."[82] Fagan goes on to document how Black communities in New York had been regularly staging peaceful parades for anniversaries, funerals, and the formation of new societies since the eighteenth century. By reframing the tradition of the African American parade as both a mode of protest and a formally coherent aesthetic spectacle, Johnson's response to the murderous violence of white Americans was largely to reinscribe the importance of African American cultural history and innovation. One of the uniform placards Johnson designed read, "Our Music Is the Only American Music," a message that must have been devastating to encounter amidst a massive, silent crowd marching to monotonous drum beats.[83] In addition to protesting violence, the parade asked viewers to consider, in light of the murderous attempts at the erasure of the Black population nationwide, what it would it be like to live in an America where this entire population truly were silenced. This is a question Ralph Ellison would later take up seriously in his 1970 essay "What America Would Be Without Blacks," a work that builds heavily on Johnson's political essays and ethnographic work. The parade also features prominently in Toni Morrison's 1992 novel, *Jazz*, where the protagonist, Dorcas, "marvel [s] at the cold Black faces and listen[s] to drums saying what the graceful men and the marching women could not."[84] Johnson's formal aesthetic strategy gave the parade a cultural significance beyond political demonstration—its tentacles reach both backward and forward in time.

The attention garnered by the parade propelled Johnson into the most overtly political project of his career. Throughout the majority of 1916 and 1917, he had traveled across the American South investigating lynchings for an NAACP report preparatory to the campaign to support a proposed anti-lynching bill. As he had done previously as a diplomat, Johnson trained his eye to collect as much evidence as possible surrounding the activities of lynch mobs and the purported crimes of their victims. The facts he gathered with his colleagues were later published by the NAACP as *Thirty Years of Lynching in the United States, 1889–1918*, an impressive compendium of statistics that prove not only the widespread prevalence of lynchings during the years it treats but also how the vast majority of the victims of lynching were not guilty of their supposed crimes.

The prose style of the "Foreword" and the "First Appendix" to *Thirty Years of Lynching*, "Summation of the facts disclosed in tables," is flat and frequently punctuated by numbers. The only other prose section of the publication is a chapter called, "The Story of One Hundred Lynchings," which reluctantly acknowledges the need for prose renderings of the crimes it describes. This need is met by supplying newspaper copy with the following justification:

> To give concreteness and to make vivid the facts of lynching in the United States, we give below in chronological order an account of one hundred lynchings which have occurred in the period from 1894 to 1918. These "stories" as they are technically described in newspaper parlance, have been taken from press accounts and, in a few cases, from the reports of investigations made by the National Association for the Advancement of Colored People . . . these accounts serve to present a characteristic picture of the lynching sport, as it was picturesquely defined by Henry Watterson.[85]

By using scare quotes to repeatedly refer to the accounts as "stories," and deriding Watterson's description of such activities as "sport" and "picturesque," *Thirty Years of Lynching* objects to the aesthetic power lynchings wield and the pleasure derived not only from lynching acts, but lynching descriptions, which it circumspectly reproduces in the context of these newspaper accounts.[86] For example, one such account, titled "Investigation of the Burning of Ell Person at Memphis," quotes this report from the Memphis *Press*:

> Fifteen thousand of them—men, women, even little children . . . fought and screamed and crowed to get a glimpse of him, and the mob closed in and struggled about the fire as the flames flared high and the smoke rolled about their heads. Two of them hacked his ears off as he burned; another tried to cut off a toe but they stopped him. . . . The negro lay in the flames, his hands crossed on his chest. If he spoke no one ever heard him over the shouts of the crowd. He died quickly, though fifteen minutes later excitable persons still shouted that he lived when they saw the charred remains move as does meat on a hot frying pan.[87]

Dramatic and elaborate descriptions culled from newspapers like this one take up nearly twenty pages in the eighty-page publication, the remainder of which is filled with lists, charts, graphs, and a map. The newspaper accounts are stylistically at odds with the brief prose descriptions that introduce them. Consider that the above account is prefaced by this text written by Johnson:

> On April 30, Antoinette Rapal, a sixteen-year-old white girl, living on the outskirts of Memphis, disappeared on her way to school. On May third her body was found in a river, her head severed from it. On May 6 a Negro woodchopper, Ell Person, was arrested on suspicion. Under third degree methods he confessed to the crime of murder. . . . It was known that he would be brought back for trial to Memphis. Each incoming train was searched, and arrangements were made for a lynching.[88]

Though this passage also represents violence and dramatic circumstance, it refrains from sensory detail or any manner of rhetorical embellishment. The contrast between this prose style and that of the newspaper account is stark. The tension between the editorial resistance to the aestheticization of such brutal violence and its inclusion of the yellow newspaper accounts betrays the editors' understandable compulsion to witness the "stories" in all their vivid and horrifying detail—and their desperation to produce a report that would be politically effective.

At the 1924 Conference on Inter-Racial Justice, James Weldon Johnson described the aim of the research study that produced *Thirty Years of Lynching* as follows: "The raw, naked, brutal facts about lynching had to be held up before the eyes of the people until the conscience of the nation was sickened and a reaction of concern and humiliation set in."[89] But Johnson's initial belief in the power of "raw facts" would soon waver. Leigh Raiford outlines Johnson's sensitivity to the aesthetic minimalism of the 1922 advertisement "The Shame of America," which Walter White designed and had placed in ten major white-owned newspapers across the country. "The Shame of America" further condensed the findings of *Thirty Years* into a single-page ad reminiscent of an eighteenth-century broadside.

Black and white and including no images, the ad represents the starkest imaginable presentation of the facts Johnson and his team had uncovered alongside the most basic information about the Dyer Anti-Lynching Bill. While Johnson admired the ad's design and aim, he eventually conceded that, like *Thirty Years*, this ad with its simple presentation of facts would prove sensational but ineffective: "the facts, Johnson seemed to think, no matter how volatile or visceral their presentation, fell short in the quest to gain Black subjectivity within the law."[90] He might, furthermore, have recognized the dilemma that Womack describes Ida B. Wells encountering

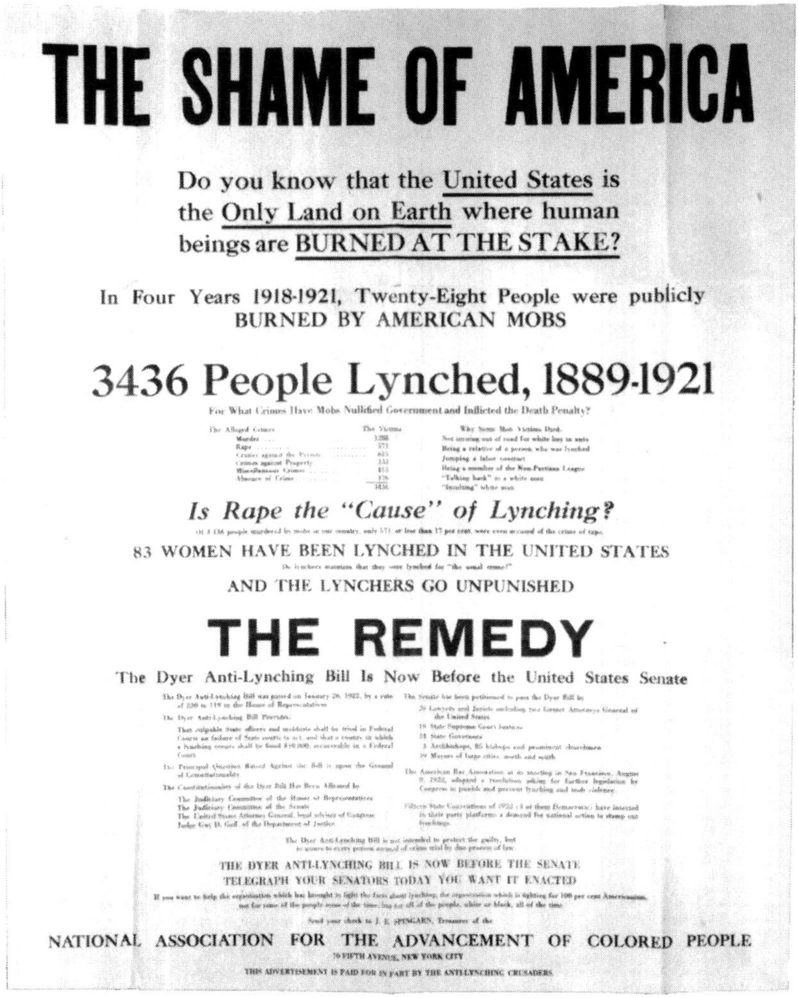

THE SHAME OF AMERICA

Do you know that the United States is the Only Land on Earth where human beings are BURNED AT THE STAKE?

In Four Years 1918-1921, Twenty-Eight People were publicly BURNED BY AMERICAN MOBS

3436 People Lynched, 1889-1921

For What Crimes Have Mobs Nullified Government and Inflicted the Death Penalty?

The Alleged Crimes	The Victims	Why Some Mob Victims Died
Murder	1288	Not getting out of road for white boy in auto
Rape	571	Being a relative of a person who was lynched
Crimes against the Person	615	Jumping a labor contract
Crimes against Property	333	Being a member of the Non-Partisan League
Miscellaneous Crimes	451	"Talking back" to a white man
Absence of Crime	178	Insulting white man
	3436	

Is Rape the "Cause" of Lynching?

Of 3436 people murdered by mobs in this country, only 571, or less than 17 per cent, were even accused of this crime of rape.

83 WOMEN HAVE BEEN LYNCHED IN THE UNITED STATES

Do lynchers maintain that they were lynched for "the usual crime?"

AND THE LYNCHERS GO UNPUNISHED

THE REMEDY

The Dyer Anti-Lynching Bill Is Now Before the United States Senate

[fine-print columns, largely illegible]

THE DYER ANTI-LYNCHING BILL IS NOW BEFORE THE SENATE
TELEGRAPH YOUR SENATORS TODAY YOU WANT IT ENACTED

NATIONAL ASSOCIATION FOR THE ADVANCEMENT OF COLORED PEOPLE

70 FIFTH AVENUE, NEW YORK CITY

THIS ADVERTISEMENT IS PAID FOR IN PART BY THE ANTI-LYNCHING CRUSADERS.

FIGURE 4. *New York Times*, November 23, 1922—American Social History Project.

in the production of her own documentary reports of lynching: that "lynching's data—whether expressed visually or numerically . . . risks a violent erasure of lynching survivors [like Johnson and his narrator] and consolidating the temporal and spatial boundaries of lynching as a geographically coherent event that unfolds in a linear fashion."[91] *Thirty Years* and "The Shame of America" represent the limits of a transparent, documentary style of representing a political problem—a style that Johnson would associate with the false impartiality of American democracy itself.

Johnson went on to wage a comprehensive campaign to pass the Dyer Bill, which would designate lynching as a federal crime. In addition to the extensive research undertaken for *Thirty Years*, he wrote hundreds of letters to friends in positions of political power, took meetings, cultivated his connections in the Republican party, and made repeated visits to Washington.[92] In *Along this Way* he writes, "I tramped the corridors of the Capitol and the two office buildings so constantly that toward the end, I could, I think, have been able to find my way about blindfolded."[93] More candidly, in a January 6, 1922 letter to White, Johnson reported "I used my time today in seeing and talking with the men who are to support the bill on the floor. I am pouring into them as much of our dope as they will hold."[94] Johnson felt confident his efforts would lead to law. One argument against the bill among the members of the Judiciary Committee was that the federal government could not impose laws regarding the punishment of murder at the state level. Johnson's statement to the Committee in response to this claim undertakes a formal analysis of the nature of the crime:

> The analogy between lynching and murder is not a true one. . . . In murder, one or more individuals take life. . . . In lynching, a mob sets itself up in place of the state and acts in place of due processes of law to mete out death as a punishment to a person accused of a crime. . . . In murder, the murderer merely violates the law of the state. In lynching, the mob arrogates to itself the powers of the state and the functions of government.[95]

Despite Johnson's recourse to strategies demonstrative, political, sensational, and formal, in the end, a Republican caucus voted to abandon the bill. Johnson wrote of his reaction to the news, "I think disgust was the dominant emotion."[96] The US Senate only formally apologized for the refusal to pass such a bill in 2005, and even then, the vote to issue the apology came in with twenty non-sponsors. It was not until 2018 that the Senate passed the anti-lynching legislation Justice for Victims of Lynching Act, on which the House of Representatives took no action. On February 26, 2020, the House passed a revised version, the Emmett Till Antilynching Act, by a vote of 410–4.[97]

The thirties had Johnson seeking answers for this unthinkable outcome among his many contacts in the Republican party. He simply could not understand why Republicans wouldn't work harder to mobilize against the Wilsonian Democrats and began to recognize the emergent Southern

Strategy of the party. In a 1938 letter to John D. Hamilton, Chairman of the Republican National Committee, he writes "placing a mere technical and political expedient above Americans as citizens will serve to strengthen the doubt which has for a number of years been in the minds of so many Negro Americans that the Republican Party has any sincere interest in their rights as citizens."[98] By the end of his life, Johnson's profound disillusionment with the political system he had invested so much time in leveraging was apparent. As McKay had suggested the year before, political alliances had shifted, and this shift reinforced Johnson's growing view that the usual channels of political power were not the most effective means at hand for promoting an agenda of racial equality.

While Johnson was very politically active, and viewed cultural work and politics as dialectically engaged, it is crucial to note the separation between the occupations of politics and literature he tried to enforce within the context of his own career. As Goldsby argues, "Ever a pragmatist but an imaginative thinker of the highest order, Johnson . . . understood that social change had to occur (if it was going to happen at all) both in the 'real' time of literature and the 'now-time' of history."[99] While these two different endeavors exert their influence on different planes of temporality, they both demand significant time within the context of an individual life and therefore sometimes threaten to eclipse one another. In *Along This Way*, Johnson writes, "my own literary efforts and what part I played in creating the new literary Harlem were . . . mere excursions; my main activity all the while was the work of the association. But my doubled activities began to tell on me, and my doctor began to give warning."[100] Johnson implies that the cultural work he did in the first two decades of the twentieth century was sidelined by the urgency of his NAACP duties. His reference to these two endeavors as "doubled activities" bespeaks not only the demanding nature of what were ostensibly two more-than-full-time occupations, but also the Du Boisian "double consciousness" of which Johnson was so acutely aware, or what he would call in the title of one of his essays "The Dilemma of the Negro Author."

In that essay, Johnson explains that the African American author is not only himself a divided consciousness—both Black and American—he also addresses a divided audience; furthermore, he acts on a doubled desire to express an artistic vision and an answer to "the negro problem." Johnson struggled throughout his life to negotiate these competing needs in the sense of how to divide his time and where to direct his energies. Facing ill health as a result of overwork, he resigned from NAACP leadership in December of 1930. In his resignation letter he writes simply: "It is my wish to devote my time more fully to writing than the administration of the office of Executive Secretary of the Association allows."[101] Given a choice between the political work and the creative work, he picked the latter—a reflection of his increasing sense that his writing would, in the end, be more effective. In a diary entry of June 27 of 1929, he more fully explains:

> There have been vital points at which my life has taken a decide change of direction. . . . Now, perhaps another vital point of departure has been reached. I have been with the NAACP thirteen years, nine years as its secretary. It has become a greater part of my life than anything else I have ever engaged in. Moreover, I feel that I am becoming limited and circumscribed by it. . . . And now I am leaving the NAACP for a year—at least a year—to do the only other work more in accord with my heart's desire—to write![102]

The political work his circumstances demanded he undertake also drew him away from the form of artistic expression that he felt was his calling. A secondary—but nonetheless significant—tragedy of the senate's failure to pass the Dyer Bill was the amount of time and energy Johnson took from his literary career to support it; he writes that during that time he "struggled constantly not to permit that part of me which was artist to become entirely submerged."[103] The part of Johnson that was artist—and art historian—ultimately became the author of his political successes to his own mind as well.

For Johnson, the aesthetic power of artistic forms to be found in well-wrought novels, performance genres, or poetry stood to offer a more enduring revision to the racist cultural narratives behind the oppression of Black Americans. In addition to this, Johnson came to realize that the halls of American politics were too dominated by white interests to be an effective site for the fight for Black rights. On meeting President Coolidge, Johnson writes

> I was expecting that he would make, at least, an inquiry or two about the state of mind and condition of the twelve million Negro citizens of the United States. I judged that curiosity, if not interest would make for that much conversation . . . but it was clear that Mr. Coolidge knew absolutely nothing about the colored people.[104]

Johnson's dejection at this interview is symptomatic of his greater realization that it was unlikely African Americans would be able to influence political discourse in Washington for some time. The present-day sociologist Elijah Anderson explains how contemporary American culture is divided into white space and Black space—describing how white people remain within their own spaces (white neighborhoods and establishments, workplaces, centers of government and education) avoiding Black spaces that they fear as ghettos, while Black people must by necessity negotiate white spaces, where they face cultural conflicts, fear, discrimination, and criminalization: "when judging a setting as too white, [Black people] can feel uneasy and consider it to be informally 'off limits.' For whites, however, the same settings are generally regarded as unremarkable, or as normal, taken-for-granted reflections of civil society."[105] We might think of Johnson's preferred strategy as one that operates by expanding and protecting Black spaces in culture (where Black people have proven and demonstrable authority) rather than waging change via reform politics which relied upon accessing the spaces of governmental power that were, in Johnson's adulthood, almost entirely white. By the end of his life, Johnson had become more convinced that governmental politics would not be an efficacious route to ending racial violence.

Johnson became acquainted with electoral politics early on through his brother Rosamund's commission to write a campaign song for Teddy Roosevelt, a man who later became a friend to both Johnson brothers. Nevertheless, he understood from Roosevelt that the American political system was essentially a closed one: "They control the political machinery and, so far as its manipulation is concerned, no one else really counts. In fact, nobody else is really interested in politics. The contrary premise leads to a great many errors and futile efforts."[106] To engage in the political arena, Johnson would always need to address a largely white audience in terms set by white people; even if he adopted their forms and methods, his appeals would, more often than not, go unheard. Instead, he created a new history of African American literature and culture apart from reform and its antecedents in white abolitionism.

CHAPTER FIVE

EDITH WHARTON AT WAR IN THE LAND OF LETTERS

I felt like some homeless waif who, after trying for years to take out
naturalization papers, and being rejected by every country, has finally
acquired a nationality. The Land of Letters was henceforth to be my
country, and I gloried in my new citizenship.

—Edith Wharton, *Backward Glance*

Citizens cannot relate well to the complex world around them by fac-
tual knowledge and logic alone. The third ability of the citizen, closely
related to the first two, is what we call the narrative imagination.

—Martha Nussbaum, *Not for Profit: Why Democracy Needs the
Humanities*

In 1927, Edith Wharton wrote a scathing letter to Upton Sinclair regarding his problem novel of the same year, *Oil*, which she called a "political
pamphlet."[1] Wharton was careful to communicate to Sinclair that what she
objected to was his novelistic treatment of the issue (the oil industry), not
(primarily) his views: "I make this criticism without regard to the views
which you teach, and which are detestable to me. Had you written in
favour of those in which I believe, my judgement would have been exactly
the same. I have never known a novel that was good enough to be good in
spite of its being adapted to the author's political views."[2] Though Wharton
would express much derision for the problem novel throughout her career,
she also—once—wrote one.

The Fruit of the Tree (1907) addresses two social issues most centrally:
euthanasia and workers' rights. It is also a problem*atic* novel in the sense

155

that it wrestles with its own generic identity and, like Eliot's *Daniel Deronda* (1876), uncomfortably navigates between one plot largely concerned with romantic intrigue and another that wants to say big things about social issues.[3] It's clear that Wharton is more drawn to writing the former plot— and saying big things about social issues indirectly rather than depicting them head-on. This tension both animates and confuses the novel itself. Her close friend Robert Grant wrote to Wharton after reading the manuscript,

> I am still doubting whether your theme was ethically worthy of your wonderful art—ethically in a deep, broad sense of course. You wish us to sympathize with Justine and most of us do. But through the irony of her suffering you have scarcely proved that her example should be imitated. One is thrilled by a dramatic, terrible situation; but after one cools off may one not challenge the purpose of your tragedy on the score of a lack of definitiveness?[4]

Writing a novel of purpose set in an industrial mill town was clearly not the task for Edith Wharton. Several critics have noted that somehow, despite the fact that she took a research trip to a mill in North Adams, Massachusetts, many of the details of factory life featured in the novel are incorrect.[5] This is highly atypical for Wharton, who had previously written an entire novel centered on a political plot in eighteenth-century Italy, for example, and therefore such missteps suggest a difficulty in portrayal, not research or acumen. Henry James would complain to Mary Cadwallader Jones that the novel suffered from "infirm composition and construction"[6] Dale Bauer writes that Wharton "fails to weave together the complicated issues of reform, scientific engineering, and medicine and the effects of these on the inner lives of the main characters."[7]

The Fruit of the Tree represents an early attempt on Wharton's behalf to translate into fiction her desire to understand and help to repair the fractures of the social world. Wharton is far more well known for her psychologically realistic depictions of the Gilded Age elite than for political sentiment or analysis. Her refusal to capitulate to contemporary trends in fiction both stylistic and thematic (e.g., modernism and social reform) has led to two significant dismissals of Wharton that continue to inform her present-day reputation. One such line of thinking about Wharton began with the Wharton biography produced by Percy Lubbock in 1947, ten years after her death. Despite the fact that Lubbock and Wharton had not spoken since 1927, he was still appointed to the task by Gaillard Lapsley, Wharton's close friend and literary executor.[8] Nothing could have been more antithetical to Wharton's beliefs than Lubbock's decision to omit the consideration of her literature from the story of her life. The portrait that Lubbock paints is of a stuffy relic of Gilded Age society. References to her work are tainted by a deep sexism. He refers to her "her pretty little literary talent" and her "clever little fictions" and even goes so far as to imply that she did not really read all of the books she claimed to have read.[9] This dismissal of the seriousness of her fiction built on previous—and equally damning—dismissals of her politics. As Jennie Kasanoff notes, "Since 1921, when Vernon L. Parrington dismissed Wharton as a 'literary aristocrat' who was preoccupied with 'rich nobodies,' Wharton's conservative politics have been treated as an obstacle to literary analysis."[10] These two dismissals are deeply interrelated in the sense that Wharton's reading program and the literature she produced are themselves the deepest indicators of her political philosophy.

Wharton's politics in the conventional sense—her views on government and the state—are notoriously difficult to identify. Lapsley recounts how Wharton disdained casual political conversation on the basis of its typically shallow contents: "She ruled out politics because, as she said, she did not like to hear people repeat what she, or they or both, had just read in the press."[11] Dale Bauer's excellent book-length study on Wharton's politics "resist[s] looking for a consistent logic in Wharton's reactions to social issues and in the political interest of her fictions since her ambivalence makes her difficult, if not impossible, to pin down"; ultimately, Bauer concludes that "while her views on race regrettably never altered . . . her celebration of gender and class privilege did change, bravely."[12] Robin Peel defines Wharton's stance as "aristocratic Toryism" and argues that while Wharton certainly "rejected what she saw as the cultural solipsism of modernism . . . it [is] not easy to decide whether this was for either progressive or conservative reasons."[13] While I agree that Wharton's political views change over the course of her career and at times seem to be self-conflicting, I believe that her understanding of the set of concerns we might generally call politics is mediated through her assessment of the value of short-term vs. long-term cultural development.

To examine Wharton's fiction for clues to a political ideology external to the text may perhaps be fruitless because the text itself is comprised of the aesthetic values shaped first by her own diverse scholarship and consumption of art and literature. Inevitably, Wharton's literary aesthetic sensibility was a product of her adoption of the values of one aspect (the literary) of the European culture that likewise shaped the tastes of Old New York. In both her literary endeavors and the establishment of her own network of charitable agencies during the First World War, Wharton's career would be an endlessly productive struggle to reconcile what she at times perceived to be the competing demands of a social consciousness and a devotion to tradition and beauty.[14]

In this chapter, I demonstrate Wharton's rejection of reform realist aesthetics, visible in her problem novel *The Fruit of the Tree* and her unflattering—at times even bitter—fictional and non-fictional portrayals of reformers. Instead of reading this rejection as Wharton's removal from political engagement, I show how Wharton's own political activism during the First World War tells a different story, one that insists on social projects that benefit only those they seek to aid. Finally, I describe how the anthology she produced to fund the charitable organizations she herself founded during the war stands as a model of literary engagement with the political that opposes the superficial concern with the betterment of the social world expressed by the reform realist novel.

WHARTON'S REFORMERS

The tension between beauty and political struggle is nowhere more present in *The Fruit of the Tree* than in the competing styles of representation it employs to describe its two settings. The novel alternates between the North Adams–based Hanaford, the location of the Westmore mills, and Lynbrook House, the mill owner's estate. Early on in the novel, Wharton struggles with sentimental, picturesque descriptions of the working-class squalor of the mills. The narration depicts Hanaford through the eyes of the idealist reformer John Amherst: "the rare street-lamps shone on cracked pavements, crooked telegraph-poles, hoardings tapestried with patent-medicine posters, and all the mean desolation of an American industrial suburb."[15] Such a description devolves into what is practically an acknowledgement of its own generalized, clichéd nature: "and all the mean desolation of an American industrial suburb," which is attributed to Amherst's inattention to detail: "the scene was so familiar to Amherst . . . and his absorption in the moral and material needs of the workers sometimes made him forget the outward setting of their lives."[16] Amherst would make a terrible realist novelist.

As it turns out, Amherst's point of view renders some of the most ineffective passages in the novel. It is as if Wharton's association between the problem novel and low literary art manifests itself in the moments of free indirect discourse that offer us a window into his mind. Consider the description of Hanaford quoted above in contrast with the novel's first glimpse of Lynbrook House through the eyes of Mrs. Eustace Ansell, a family friend who is always on hand to advise on topics like household decoration and the appropriate season for the consumption of terrapin:

> It might have been thought that the actual scene out-spread below her— the descending gardens, the tennis-courts, the farm-lands sloping away to the blue sea-like shimmer of the Hempstead plains—offered, at the moment, little material for her purpose; but that was to view them with a superficial eye. Mrs. Ansell's trained gaze was, for example, greatly enlightened by the fact that the tennis-courts were fringed by a group of people indolently watchful of the figures agitating themselves about the nets; and that, as she turned her head toward the entrance avenue, the receding view of a station omnibus, followed by a luggage-cart, announced that more guests were to be added to those who had almost taxed to its limits the expansibility of the luncheon-table. All this, to the initiated eye, was full of suggestion.

Though the description of the scene is presented likewise in list form, the language here is suffused with an obvious pleasure, and the superficiality of the scenery is subsequently dissected and explained by an expert observer. The arch socialite Mrs. Ansell has the "initiated" eye of the realist novelist, one that renders with specificity and draws inferences from detail. While the reformer Amherst dismisses the "outward setting" as subordinate to "moral and material needs," Mrs. Ansell understands that the best way to determine the moral and material needs of people is precisely to carefully inspect their outward setting. It's telling that Mrs. Ansell will not go to Hanaford: "though it had become a matter of habit to include her in the family pilgrimages to the mills she had firmly maintained the plea of more urgent engagements."[17] As the novel proceeds, the narrator too lingers considerably more on Lynbrook House than Hanaford. It's as though the novel itself wants to depict the problems of the mill without having to go there.

A recurring theme throughout *The Fruit of the Tree* is the financial inability of the Westmore family to support both the lavish lifestyle at Lynbrook and the progressive reforms needed at the mills. In a conversation between the two characters who speak the novel's truths most baldly, Mrs. Ansell and Mr. Langhope, the former asks "'There again—with this *train de vie*, how on earth are both ends to meet?' Mr. Langhope grown suddenly grave, struck his cane resoundingly on the terrace. 'Westmore and Lynbrook? I don't want them to—I want them to get farther and farther apart!'" This desire is ultimately shared by Bessy Westmore, the young owner of the mill who likes the romantic idea of social progress but, when given the opportunity to aid in its advancement, is unwilling to make any personal sacrifices. Her growing desire for Westmore and Lynbrook House to "get farther and farther apart" foments the dissolution of her marriage to Amherst. After he requests that Bessy curb her spending habits to support improvements to the mill that will benefit the workers but not increase profits, the couple separates, and Bessy begins planning the addition of an opulent and expensive athletics facility to Lynbrook House to spite him:

> As the scheme developed, various advisers suggested that it was a pity not to add a bowling-alley, a swimming-tank and a gymnasium; a fashionable architect was summoned from town, measurements were taken, sites discussed, sketches compared, and engineers consulted as to the cost of artesian wells and the best system for heating the tank. Bessy seemed filled with a feverish desire to carry out the plan as quickly as possible, and on as large a scale as even the architect's invention soared to.[18]

The symbolism of this gesture is clear: rather than protect the bodies of the mill workers (the novel begins with Bessy and John bonding over the plight of a worker who is maimed in a workplace accident), Bessy comes to value the preservation and perfection of the bodies of the wealthy elite. Through the device of the gymnasium, Wharton drives home the central theme of the novel: the parasitic relationship between Lynbrook House and the mills, and, therefore, between the wealthy elite and the workers who produce both their own incomes and the goods they consume.

Before construction on the Lynbrook House addition begins, Bessy suffers a fall from a horse that leaves her near death. Justine serves as her dutiful nurse, keeping her on a regimen of powerful anesthetics that make her existence tolerable. As Cynthia Davis argues, "[Justine's] capacity to aestheticize [Bessy's] pain, in short, makes her the gifted nurse every character in the novel avows her to be." Justine eventually gives Bessy an intentional overdose in a gesture of mercy—a fact which, when later revealed after John and Justine wed, leads Bessy's family and their circle to suspect the two reformers of conspiracy to gain control of the mills. In an attempt to temper these insinuations and honor his previous wife's memory, John dedicates the improvements he does eventually make to the mill to Bessy. At the dedication ceremony of the buildings, he brings up the plans for the Lynbrook gymnasium, which he recasts (knowingly or not—it is never revealed) as meant to be facilities for the mill workers at Hanford. The irony of this misrepresentation is too much for Justine to bear:

> Justine had listened with deepening amazement. She was seated so close to [Amherst] that she had recognized the blue-print the moment he unrolled it. There was no mistaking its origin—it was simply the plan of the gymnasium which Bessy had intended to build at Lynbrook, and which she had been constrained to abandon owing to her husband's increased expenditure at the mills. But how was it possible that Amherst knew nothing of the original purpose of the plans, and by what mocking turn of events had a project devised in deliberate defiance of his wishes, and intended to declare his wife's open contempt for them, been transformed into a Utopian vision for the betterment of the Westmore operatives? A wave of anger swept over Justine at this last derisive stroke of fate. It was grotesque and pitiable that a man like Amherst should create out of his regrets a being who had never existed, and then ascribe to her feelings and actions of which the real woman had again and again proved herself incapable! Ah, no, Justine had suffered enough—but to have this imaginary Bessy called from the grave, dressed in a semblance of self-devotion and idealism, to see her petty impulses of vindictiveness disguised as the motions of a lofty spirit—it was as though her small malicious ghost had devised this way of punishing the wife who had taken her place![19]

The selfless reformer Justine is ultimately and against all odds defeated in the game of moral goodness by her selfish, materialistic rival Bessy. Though the improvements to the mill are eventually made despite Bessy's original misgivings, the attribution of these improvements to Bessy's influence is the novelistic triumph of Lynbrookism over Hanafordism. In a bizarre irony that mirrors Wharton's ideas about the hypocrisy of the mild social reform sympathies of the wealthy elite, progressive change at the mills is ultimately (and unwittingly) effected through the selfish pursuit of beauty (in the form of Bessy's plans), not the brute force of moralistic righteousness. This is true in *The Fruit of the Tree* both thematically and stylistically. It is the romance plot, not the reform plot, that more convincingly illuminates the injustices of industrial capitalism—it's a far greater cause for sadness, within the novel, that the plight of the operatives ruins not one but two marriages. Though Justine is a far more likable character than Bessy, the cruelty of the latter's posthumous triumph is undoubtedly the greatest pleasure to be afforded by the novel.

The gymnasium incident in *The Fruit of the Tree* is a dramatic representation of a theme that Wharton, like other aesthetic realists, would turn to again and again in her later fiction: the hypocrisy of philanthropy and reform work. In Wharton's fiction, this commentary is more frequently carried out through humor than it is through drama or polemic. Sophy Viner in *The Reef* (1912) is subjected to life with the thoroughly bourgeois Farlows, whose associations with "a lady from Wichita, Kansas, who advocated free love and the abolition of the corset" and an anarchistic Russian are part and parcel of Mrs. Farlow's ineptitude as a writer and a consumer of culture.[20] Her endorsement of these beliefs is based on an attraction to that which she perceives as novel or fashionable and therefore able to grant her authenticity as a bohemian expatriate. This is precisely the kind of sham political interest that Wharton finds so aesthetically appalling.

Pauline Manford of the 1927 novel *Twilight Sleep* is likewise indiscriminately drawn to every brand of reform, a set of activities deemed stuffy by her daughter, Nona, who rejects "the audience of bright elderly women, with snowy hair" who strike her not only as stodgy rather than politically avant-garde, but also hypocritical:

> Whatever the question dealt with, these ladies always seemed to be the same, and always advocated with equal zeal Birth Control and unlimited maternity, free love or the return to the traditions of the American home; and neither they nor Mrs. Manford seemed aware that there was anything contradictory in these doctrines. All they knew was that they were determined to force certain persons to do things that those persons preferred not to do.[21]

Pauline is as faddish as they come—always a sin for Wharton, who respects judgments grounded in tradition and historical precedent. Their reformist zeal is a way of bringing the modernizing world around to their own ends and maintaining the superiority of their inherited positions.

In *Hudson River Bracketed* (1929), both of the central families in the text, who are otherwise opposed in a classic Whartonian East-coast, old-money/Middle-West, new-money split, have their own brand of reformist agenda. The New York–based Lorburn–Spears are of the Manford variety.

Creating gatherings of "dowdy middle-aged conformists whom Mrs. Spear still called revolutionaries." Mr. Spear,

> still wrote to the papers to denounce what he called crying evils, such as the fact that the consumption of whole wheat bread was not made compulsory ("If I may cite my own humble experience," that kind of letter always said), or that no method had been devised for automatically disinfecting the tin cups attached to public fountains. ("An instance of this criminal negligence may actually be found within a hundred feet of my own door," was the formula in such cases—thus revealing to his readers that Mr. Spear had a New York door.)[22]

For this decaying member of the American upper class, the reminder that he owns property in New York is the crucial message—not the cause of sanitation. Once again, such leanings toward social improvement are revealed to be merely vehicles for established elites to confirm their own status.

Reform work is the ground on which the novel's protagonists, the up-and-coming Westerner Vance Weston and the New York heiress Halo Tarrant's families come together. Vance's grandmother Scrimser "wanted to reform everything—it didn't particularly matter what: cooking, marriage, religion (of course religion), dentistry, saloons, corsets—even Grandpa." What differentiates Mrs. Scrimser from Mr. Spear is that she monetizes her reformist zeal rather than leveraging it for cultural authority. Her "literary" career rises quietly (within the context of the novel) in parallel to that of her grandson Vance's, the writer/protagonist of the novel. As he struggles to have stories placed in the fashionable little magazine "The Hour," she begins regularly contributing to a widely distributed popular religious journal, "Spirit Light." As he becomes a minor figure among the literati of bohemian New York, she becomes a savior to a cult-like group called "The Seekers," who are fervent readers of her publications. Finally, she signs what amounts to a corporate deal with Storecraft, a catch-all corporation in the business of commodifying art. Her "Storecraft" offer is "for a three months' tour . . . tell[ing] the world about her New Religion."[23] Grandma Scrimser's religion—worked up for a profit, invented, and wholly new—is a bad version of the aesthetic doctrine to which Wharton herself subscribed. It has no rich past standing behind it.

So, it is to Vance's great astonishment when Grandma Scrimser—the doyenne of the new—is invited to speak in the Spear drawing room. When Vance discovers this collision of his two worlds, he reflects "the idea of any connection between the Spear milieu and his grandmother was so unexpected that he began to wonder if, all unconsciously, he had spent his youth with an illustrious woman. Mrs. Spear was in touch with the newest that New York was thinking and saying."[24] The embrace of Mrs. Scrimser by a family with an old library full of the best of literature is deeply troubling for Wharton. It suggests that reform work and problem novels lend contemporary literature a false gravity that robs it of its antecedents. This plot asks us, how can an author like Lorraine Scrimser, who knows nothing of the literary past, come to be so celebrated by the people who do?

Wharton's objection to the reform work of these characters and especially its intersection with literature is an aesthetic one; it's not that the particular causes she satirizes are wrong—in fact, like Mr. Spear with his tin cups, Wharton wrote to her niece in 1935 that she was considering writing a letter to the *New York Times* about the lack of public drinking fountains for dogs.[25] And more broadly, like Grandma Scrimser and Pauline Manford, Wharton cared deeply about motherhood and birth control, as previous scholarship has shown.[26] What she objects to is rather the tastelessness— the bad form—of using the platform of political issues to further a different agenda, whether that be writing a bestseller on the basis of its connection to free thought or perpetuating one's visibility in papers and social circles through charitable activities.

In her own life, Wharton strongly turned her back on any political engagement she saw in this light. She worked to remove John Peter Haines (A Mr. Spear-like figure) from the presidency of the Society for the Prevention of Cruelty to Animals, a cause of great importance to her, because, as Mrs. Gordon K. Bell recalls, he was "more interested in asserting his authority than in helping animals."[27] Wharton wrote to George Dorr in 1906, "I have become involved in two arduous tasks—the dramatization of my novel, and the far more thrilling and important work of trying to reform our Society for the Prevention of Cruelty to Animals."[28] Wharton saw herself as a reformer of reform and this is only one example of many where Wharton grew frustrated with the shallow dealings of those who engaged in reform politics in the service of their own social or financial ambitions. During the war, she wrote, "There is so little choice, in all these war charities, between carrying the whole load and just pottering around and waiting to run errands"; and a 1933 letter declining an offer to speak at a convention of the National Council of Women of the United States declares that "she has made it a rule for many years past not to accept any nomination on a Committee in which she did not take a personal share, and she therefore hopes you will excuse her from membership"; this seems to be Wharton's general position as regards the many attempts to involve her in reform causes: if she isn't in charge, she won't participate.[29] While we may interpret this as a function of Wharton's domineering nature, I think it more likely that this was her way of ensuring that her work towards social change would be just that—effective and discrete—rather than tied up in attempts to achieve literary success or social status.

The kaleidoscopic reformism of the first and third decades of the twentieth century would inspire many of Wharton's more flippantly critical portrayals of reformers but it was her distaste for the fashionable relief work that consumed the nation (and, most particularly, its women) during the First World War wherein she found a subject of even deeper derision. In her war novella *The Marne* (1918), Wharton's anti-reformist humor is at its darkest:

> "It makes us so happy to help," beaming young women declared with a kind of ghoulish glee, doing up parcels, planning war tableaux and charity dances, rushing to "propaganda" lectures given by handsome French officers, and keeping up a kind of continuous picnic on the ruins of civilization.

She saw such war relief work as primarily in the service of generating social capital and attention for its practitioners, using the language of performance to drive home her point:

> In time Mrs. Belknap, finding herself hopelessly outstoried, outcharitied, outadventured, began insensibly to take a calmer and more distant view of the war. What was the use of trying to keep up her own enthusiasm when that of her *audience* had flagged?

Such opportunism, the protagonist Troy Belknap notes, began to be more openly noted and derided as the war progressed: "the funds collected were no longer raised by dancing and fancy balls. People who used the war as an opportunity to have fun were beginning to be treated almost as coldly as the pacifists."[30] Those who resist the United States' intervention for reasons of pacifism are lumped with the opportunists into a category that denotes nothing so much as the American tendency towards anti-intellectualism for which Wharton had such profound disdain.

PATRIOTISM IN THE LAND OF LETTERS

Wharton prided herself on her broad reading program, which was both classical and contemporary and took up a range of disciplines from science to philosophy to history to design to medicine.[31] Her work as a literary realist allowed her to express a particular world view informed by both her experience in and study of the world in which she lived. For Wharton, literary realism was not merely instrumental—a mode of depicting the world that would stir those within it to action—it was an intrinsic part of the world it sought to shape. Her characters are constantly reading or conspicuously not reading, leaving texts around their interiors and attempting to write them with a fury and passion that outrivals their desires even for love, sex, family, or belonging.

This transitive relationship between literature and the world it depicts emerges in an anecdote Wharton relates about her first experience of literary criticism: the subjection of a short story, written when she was eleven, to the judgement of her mother, Lucretia Rhinelander Jones. A line of the story's dialogue reads, "If only I had known you were going to call I should have tidied up the drawing room."[32] Lucretia's only response to the story, according to Wharton, was corrective: "Drawing rooms are always tidy."[33] This incident was clearly significant to the writer herself, as she chose to include it as a part of her literary origin story in the autobiography she wrote sixty years later. Critics and biographers like Cynthia Griffin Woolf have turned to it as an example of how Wharton's "lifelong love of words . . . sprang from her early emotional impoverishment," which may well be the case.[34] But we can also read this moment as an expression of Wharton's unique relationship to literary realism. Her mother's critique is one that not only insists upon a realist mode of representation (one should depict drawing rooms as they actually are) but also on literary realism as an expression of aesthetic judgements about the world itself. Of course, drawing rooms aren't always tidy, but we should nonetheless write as though they are because—according to Mrs. Jones at least—they *should* be.

The implied "should" of literary realism is the heart of Wharton's version of an aesthetic morality. Her review of *The Architecture of Humanism* by Geoffrey Scott, published in the *Times Literary Supplement* in 1914, quotes the following passage, which she deems "commendable"—high Whartonian praise:

> Great art will be distinguished from that which is merely aesthetically clever by a nobility that, in its final analysis, is moral; or, rather, the nobility which in life we call "moral" is itself aesthetic. But since it interests us in life as well as in art, we cannot—or should not—meet it in art without a sense of its imaginative reaches in life.[35]

Here Scott's reversal offers a profound key to the Whartonian imagination: what we think of as moral is really aesthetic—the implied "should" in the description of tidy drawing rooms. This crossing over of aesthetic/moral judgement from the fictional to the real is what Scott calls "the imaginative reaches of art in life." Such imaginative reaches constructed a worldview for Wharton that was at odds with the relationship between literature and the world to be found both in literary modernism and in the works of reform realism.

Wharton spent her childhood among the neglected volumes of her father's gentleman's library, preferring the practice of an art she called "making up," which consisted of pacing while holding a book and inventing stories irrelevant to the book's contents, to the company of other children. "I had to obey the furious Muse," she writes, "and there are deplorable tales of my abandoning the 'nice' playmates who had been invited to 'spend the day' and rushing to my mother with the desperate cry: 'Mamma, you must go and entertain that little girl for me. *I've got to make up*."[36] An outsider all her early life, Wharton finally felt acceptance and pride of association within the context of her first real literary success, the publication of *The House of Mirth* (1905), which Charles Scribner reported as having "the most rapid sale of any book ever published by Scribners."[37] In the quotation from her autobiography that begins this chapter, written about the period immediately following the success of *The House of Mirth*, Wharton employs a thoroughly nationalistic metaphor to express the solution to her personal problem of identification. Rather than assert something along the lines of "I discovered I really was a writer," she invokes the terms of a political territory to which she elaborately grants herself legal acceptance. Having lived in the United States and France and traveled throughout Europe and North Africa, Wharton only considered herself a true "citizen" of "the Land of Letters," a chosen nationality I suggest we might take seriously as a political orientation. Wharton's Land of Letters is a conservative place in the sense that it fosters a conservation of the past and its traditions, but progressive in the sense that there is a long history of subversive thought in the vast canon of art and literature that Wharton consumed. Accusations of Wharton's imperialism and racial prejudice are accurate when they avoid totalizing, and though it may make these tendencies no less difficult to swallow, it is important to note that her preference for Anglo European forms grows out her library.

The reading of her childhood that she describes in *A Backward Glance* remained important to her throughout her life: Milton, Carlyle, Hugo, Racine, Cowper, Lamb, Byron, Wordsworth, and Ruskin. This initiation into a set of aesthetic and moral judgments had an indelible impact on Wharton and the way she saw her world.[38] That these judgments were for the most part shaped by authors male, European, Christian, wealthy, and white is perhaps more responsible for the moments in her life and fiction that express bigotry or classism than any other factor. But by no means can we identify the orientations of these authors as wholly conservative in the political sense. So that when we label Wharton's views of marriage as "progressive" we might consider the genesis of those ideas in Milton more so than in connection to the woman movement of her own time. At any rate, the concept of the "New" Woman could not have seemed wholly "new" to Wharton.

Wharton's prejudices could be quite real when examined along sociopolitical lines; Irene Goldman Price writes of how, "she and her friends found Jews at best distasteful . . . with their foreign ways, their natural bad taste, and their incorrect usage."[39] Yet, within a literary context, Wharton was indifferent to race or religion, writing, for example, long praises of Jewish writers like Proust, who she counts among "the writers who have what one may call mass," adding that "Fortune had perhaps endowed him more lavishly with natural gifts than any French writer of fiction since Balzac."[40] In this formulation, Proust is French and counted among French writers because he writes in French—and the ability to express oneself in a given language is a more significant marker of nationhood for Wharton than any position rooted in the categories of identity. Within her fiction, Jewishness can become a kind of shorthand for crass mercantilism and boorish tastelessness because of her association between Jewish American businessmen and a lack of exposure to the Anglo European reading program she quite literally worshipped.

This association is ironic, or perhaps deeply significant in the Whartonian unconscious, as Wharton's relationship to politics traditionally defined is like the Victorian Jew's, who, as Karl Marx observes, "can behave towards the state only in a Jewish way—that is, by treating it as something alien to him, by counterposing his imaginary nationality to the real nationality, by counterposing his illusory law to the real law, by deeming himself justified in separating himself from mankind, by abstaining on principle from taking part in the historical movement."[41] Wharton's allegiance to her own "imaginary nationality" led to her resistance to the considerable historical shifts she experienced over the course of her career. Throughout her career, she retained a stubborn insistence on taking the long view of the Land of Letters rather than capitulating to political or literary fashions.

Her rigorous set of guiding aesthetic principles informed a totalized ideology by which she wrote and lived. According to her close friend Robert Grant:

> To say that she belonged to no group or movement is true in the narrow sense, but faulty from the point of view of her own attitude. Groups or eccentric expression counted for nothing in her own conception of literature. For her there was only one great current of the art of fiction which had its own universal laws from which there could be no deviation.[42]

As with dogmatic followers of any set of beliefs, Wharton could be subject to extreme prejudices against anything that violated her aesthetic order of morality. The direct political actions of others often fell into this category—not because of the progressivism of their motives, but because of the bad style in which they were enacted. These actions not only produce an ugliness that is moral, aesthetic, and social, but they are also, in Wharton's view, insincere, a form of social performance premised not on a deep belief but rather on a desire to belong to a movement, to identify as a bohemian, or to court undeserved respect from a targeted community.

Wharton understood herself as entirely separate from the oppressive conservatism of the Old New York of her youth. Not only did she permanently expatriate in 1907, but she continued to try to sever any associations between herself and that world outside of her fiction. In 1914, she wrote to her sister-in-law about her struggles to remove her name from the social register : "I have twice requested them to remove my name from their list, and they have refused, and it seems I have no legal redress!—so they can go to the devil."[43] And yet, it seems that, to some extent, Wharton adopted the fervent devotion to custom from the world she turned her back on only to critique and satirize it in her fiction and then apply it to her own set of Land-of-Letters beliefs.

LITERARY INVADERS

Alongside the writers with whom she competed for a readership, Wharton undoubtedly seems misplaced.[44] Often regarded as the most notable novelistic documentarian of nineteenth-century New York, Wharton never published a novel in the nineteenth century. Her Pulitzer Prize–winning *The Age of Innocence* came out in the same year (1920) as F. Scott Fitzgerald's *This Side of Paradise. Hudson River Bracketed* was published contemporaneously with Faulkner's *The Sound and the Fury* in 1929. Both novels' sales suffered from their release immediately on the heels of the stock market crash, yet only Faulkner's went on to achieve wide recognition. In a letter to F. Scott Fitzgerald, written after her reading of *The Great Gatsby* (1925) Wharton muses, "To your generation, which has taken such a flying leap into the future, I must represent the literary equivalent of tufted furniture and gas chandeliers."[45] This uncharacteristically self-effacing remark was likely meant as a gesture of kindness to a new writer she saw as her inferior. After his visit to her home the Pavillion Colombe outside of Paris, she wrote in her daybook "to Tea, Teddy Chanler & Scott Fitzgerald, the novelist (awful)."[46]

Elsewhere she dismissed many of the stalwarts of Fitzgerald's generation of writers, expressing her distaste for modernist writing. To her close friend Bernard Berenson she wrote, in 1923, "I know it's not because I'm getting old that I'm unresponsive. The trouble with all this new stuff [she previously names Joyce and Eliot, specifically] is that it's à these: the theory comes first, & dominates it. And it will go the way of 'unanimisme' & all the other isms."[47] Like James Weldon Johnson and Claude McKay, Wharton felt that the literary fashion of the time was disposable when it arrived so bound to its contemporary ideological positions.

Wharton's writing career bracketed considerable developments in both history and literature. Her oeuvre, however, is a testament to a remarkable restraint from capitalizing on these developments. As critics have shown, in both her life and her fiction, Wharton was at times an enthusiastic adopter of the new.[48] Yet, on the whole, while the twentieth century created in most a desire to embrace progress in all things, Wharton remained deeply committed to a long view of art, history, and literature that informed most every aspect of her life. Wharton's objection to direct authorial advances into politics was a consequence of her sense of literature as a discourse primarily in conversation with itself, operating on a timeline that dwarfs the political currents of the present moment. To her mind, all great art is deeply embedded in history. In *The Writing of Fiction*, she worries:

> The novelist of the present day is in danger of being caught in a vicious circle, for the insatiable demand for quick production tends to keep him in a state of perpetual immaturity, and the ready acceptance of his wares encourages him to think that no time need be wasted in studying the past history of his art, or in speculating on its principles.[49]

She was perhaps perplexed by the political aims of of-the-moment writing because, like György Lukács after her, she recognized that the historical novel—not the problem novel—was the quintessential novel of political protest.

Iterations of the historical novel marked two significant moments in Wharton's career and suggest her deep investment in making literary political interventions on her own terms. Wharton's first novel, *The Valley of Decision* (1902), is set in eighteenth-century Italy, a milieu she rigorously researched prior to the novel's composition. The novel is concerned with the naïve idealism of revolutionary thinking and the unsatisfying compromises of political reform. Using the historical setting as both a distancing technique and a way of creating a sense of the historical precedents—both social and psychological—for the challenges of reform politics, Wharton was able to express complex ideas about current political trends without venturing to write a popular novel of purpose.[50]

The Age of Innocence (1920), arguably her most famous novel and the one for which she became the first female Pulitzer Prize winner, uses its 1870s setting to perform the cultural work of contextualizing the pre-war era for her postwar readers. Betsy Klimasmith argues that in *The Age of Innocence*, Wharton reinvents the historical novel form to account for new theories of memory and time recently introduced by philosopher Henri Bergson and physicist Albert Einstein.[51] In Klimasmith's account, Wharton's formal response to the disorientation of the war is dissimilar to the modernist abstraction of her contemporaries and not, as others have suggested, an uncritical return to an outmoded genre. When Wharton writes to Berenson immediately following the war that "the historical novel with all its vices [would] be the only possible form for fiction," she expresses her investment in responding to the current political situation from her own land-of-letters vantage point.[52]

As a chronicler of Old New York, Wharton has already come to be heavily associated with the values of the "old," despite the fact that her most beloved depictions of that tradition-mired society, such as *The House of Mirth* (1905) and *The Age of Innocence* (1920), are largely critical.[53] While Wharton disdained the stodgy aesthetics and suffocating cultural practices of the faux-aristocratic coterie of her youth, she nevertheless developed her own appreciation for the value of custom and the maintenance of a sense of history through her devotion to aesthetic, rather than social or class tradition.

Wharton mocks the Old New York distrust of the new in *The Age of Innocence* when the socially conservative Sophy Jackson remarks that, in her youth,

> it was considered vulgar to dress in the newest fashions; and Amy Sillerton has always told me that in Boston the rule was to put away one's Paris dresses for two years. Old Mrs. Baxter Pennilow, who did everything handsomely, used to import twelve a year. . . . It was a standing order, and as she was ill for two years before she died they found forty-eight Worth dresses that had never been taken out of tissue paper; and when the girls left off their mourning they were able to wear the first lot at the Symphony concerts without looking in advance of the fashion.[54]

Such customs constitute the strict observances of Old New York, and while Wharton may consider it ridiculous to store forty-eight unworn dresses for fear of looking outré, she does export a similar logic to the tenets of her adopted ideology. Her bildungsromane, *Hudson River Bracketed* and *The Gods Arrive* (1932), struggle with the divide between old and new literary forms. It is often remarked that the divide between old and new money is a theme that is pervasive throughout her oeuvre; Amy Kaplan notes how Wharton "has long been seen to chronicle the rapid succession of New York's established elite by successive waves of parvenus, who supplanted inherited wealth with industrial fortunes and traditional values with conspicuous consumption."[55] In Wharton's own terminology, these parvenus are "invaders." *The Custom of the Country* (1913)'s Ralph Marvell "had early mingled with the Invaders, and curiously observed their rites and customs . . . they spoke the same language as his, though on their lips it had often so different a meaning."[56] As Stephanie Foote observes, "the parvenu is the figure who reveals to the individual members of a given group that they will remain loyal to its values even when they secretly feel apart from them"; for Foote, the parvenu reveals that class is a culture.[57] Even, as in the case of Wharton, if one wishes to distance oneself from their class and its culture, it will nevertheless inform their behaviors and cause them, if they deem it necessary, to patrol its borders. Wharton exports this same conflict to a consideration of literature.

The central tensions in *Hudson River Bracketed* stem from the divide between the invader culture of the Scrimsers and the old New York culture of the Lorburn-Spears. When Vance first comes to the Lorburn family seat in the Hudson River Valley, he learns what it means to have a rich past, complete with old houses, old connections, and most significantly for him, old books. He encounters great works for the first time at the Willows, the Lorburn family estate where he reads Coleridge and becomes enthralled with the past; "a past so remote, so full of elusive mystery, that Vance's first thought was: 'Why wasn't I ever told about the Past before?'"[58] Vance's initiation into the world of "the Past," comprised of the best—in Wharton's estimation—literature, is an intellectual awakening. In "The Vice of Reading," Wharton cautions against the idea of becoming well read as a moral imperative: "It is only natural that the reader who looks on reading as a moral obligation should confound moral and intellectual judgment."[59] Though there is a "should" implied everywhere in Wharton's discussions of reading good literature, as dogmatically as the "should" is implied in her mother's commentary on drawing rooms, her refusal to lend this suggestion a moral cast can be attributed to her belief that such thorough reading is not for everyone: "to read is not a virtue; but to read well is an art, and an art that only the born reader can acquire."[60] The idea of the "born reader" is consonant with the nationalistic rhetoric with which she views the Land of Letters. To read well and artfully is akin to a form of patriotism. As she wrote to Barrett Wendell in 1919, "How much longer are we going to think it necessary to be 'American' before (or in contradistinction to) being cultivated, being enlightened, being humane & having the same intellectual discipline as other civilized countries? It is really too easy a disguise for our short-comings to dress them up as a form of patriotism!"[61] She rejects the patriotism of her own nation of birth, which she sees as tied to anti-intellectualism, substituting instead a patriotic devotion to the Land of Letters.

Vance Weston is a character who has been compared to Wharton in this respect.[62] An invader hailing from the "New World" of the western states, he receives his intellectual awakening from his exposure to "Old World" (New York) characters. While Wharton manages to summon both nostalgia and disdain for these established elite, she definitively celebrates the aesthetic awareness of many Old New York characters because of their connection to the past. Ralph Marvell is another descendent of Old New York who chafes against its more socially restrictive conventions but nevertheless upholds its respect for tradition in his own patriotic devotion to literature.

Ralph is not only a born reader of the best works, he is also a struggling writer. Beverly Hume calls him a "Poesque Romantic," but his love of nature and his ontological musings speak, too, of a debt to Whitman, who, along with Emerson, Wharton called "the best we have" from nineteenth-century literature.[63] Ralph also has a past as a Whitman scholar, and early intentions to publish an essay on the poet's "rhythmical structures."[64] It sounds quite a bit like an essay Wharton herself would sketch out in 1908, which Susan Goodman describes as having being imagined in four parts, the last of which would, "analyze [Whitman's] use of 'vowel-colour,' melody, rhythm, and repetition."[65] Lastly, Ralph's surname, Marvell, recalls an even earlier tradition of metaphysical poetry. He may descend from Old New York, but Ralph is also a part of a literary genealogy—both characteristics he shares with Wharton herself. Undine, Ralph's fervently capitalistic, modern, and Western new bride, is an invader who has trouble adapting to his romantic/metaphysical aesthetic: while he is composing verses between the lines of the boughs on their picturesque Italian honeymoon, "[Undine] leaned against a gnarled tree with the slightly constrained air of a person unused to sylvan abandonments."[66] Named after a curling iron that was her father's invention, she is the modern commodity anthropomorphized. She is also a veritable consumption machine.

In order to keep up with his wife's increasing financial demands, Ralph must, for the first time, work for profit. Such labor represents a violation of the Old New York code of leisure class conduct and also constitutes a threat to his literary integrity. His conception of his book project goes from being an ideal expression of his inner life to a practical concern: "These questions would fling him back on the thought of his projected book, which was, after all, to be what the masterpieces of literature had mostly been—a pot-boiler. Well! Why not?"[67] Even Undine becomes momentarily seduced by the idea of Ralph as a successful writer, but she imagines this new role as an extension of her social brand: "She perceived for the first time that literature was becoming fashionable, and . . . saw herself as the wife of a celebrated author, wearing 'artistic' dresses and doing the drawing-room over with Gothic tapestries and dim lights in altar candle-sticks."[68] Our own historical moment saw the full arrival of this concern in the phenomenon of the witchy/literary "dark academia" aesthetic popular on social media of which Ana Quiring writes,

> With its eclectic reading lists and aspirational images of pleated plaid skirts, dark academia demonstrates how online communities collaboratively build aesthetic categories. More soberingly, this particular aesthetic category offers a kind of grassroots postmortem on the pursuit of humanistic study, reduced by the ever-economizing university to a professionalization tool, that students then repurpose as a fashion trend.[69]

This is to Wharton the ultimate nightmare outcome for the fate of literature: that a vague, baseless association with literature would acquire social cachet, especially after years of her own authentic literariness devaluing her social capital. In her autobiography, she writes of her family's rush to "debut" her in society out of fear she was growing too "bookish" to be considered marriageable.

The great cause of *The Custom of the Country*—among many other Wharton works—is that of literature itself, a point lost to most if not all of its contemporary reviewers, who were primed to search for the social purpose to be found in the popular novels of the day. The reviewer for the *New York Times* seems genuinely puzzled: "With hardly a hint of the propagandist in her literary makeup and no disposition to deal with so-called 'problems' in a sociological way, she arouses a large amount of comment and discussion with each new novel"; while the reviewer for *The Evening Standard* November 24, 1913 relies on vagueness: "If not a novel with a purpose, [*The Custom of the Country*] is one with a very social theme." This confusion and ambiguity is typical of the majority of the reviews, which, in general, seem hard-pressed to describe the novel's political intent. Wharton herself noted that "Reading most reviews of my books—the kindest as well as the most disapproving—is like watching somebody in boxing gloves trying to dissect a flower"—a bon mot that neatly asserts the frustration of responding to a reading audience increasingly trained to be spoon-fed moralistic political rhetoric.[70]

All of the contemporary reviewers seemed to agree that the negative portrayal of Undine Spragg was a critique of *something*; within the novel's critical history, several suggestions have been offered as to *what*, divorce primary among them.[71] Here I suggest that Undine's violations of the doctrines of the Land of Letters are her primary offense. Undine's bad literary taste is a recurring theme of the novel. The only book she has read that is mentioned by name is *"When the Kissing Had to Stop,"* presumably a sentimental melodrama.[72] Its title is taken from Browning's "A Tocatta of Galupi's," a poem with which Undine would certainly not be familiar. *When the Kissing Had to Stop* is a cheap American appropriation of an English work, stripped entirely of the value of allusion. Undine's destruction of Ralph's moral universe is twofold. Her repeated divorces, for which the novel is most infamous, threaten Old New York's codes of conduct. Her disregard for literary antecedents threatens the aesthetic codes of the Land of Letters. Ignorance of literature in general is, in Wharton's works, a reliable indicator of reprehensible philistinism. In *The Age of Innocence*, for example, May Welland is "amused" to tell Newland Archer "that Kate Merry had never even heard of a poet called Robert Browning."[73] May and Newland, two characters who are dealt with somewhat harshly by a novel that looks back on a bygone era weighed down by tradition, are made sympathetic by their mutually sound literary judgments.

Wharton novels also heap scorn upon characters who buy books they don't read. Percy Gryce, *The House of Mirth*'s collector of Americana and the protagonist Lily's failed suitor, spends his fortune buying rare volumes he never opens. As Lily remarks, "It seems so odd to want to pay a lot for an ugly badly-printed book that one is never going to read!"[74] These gestures shut the gates of the Land of Letters on their most enthusiastic would-be citizens. The pathetic ending of *The Custom of the Country* depicts Ralph's literary young son, Paul, in a library full of his father-in-law's valuable books, which Paul is not permitted to read.[75] If Wharton's novels uniformly lament any single social problem, it is the problem of unequal access to the Land of Letters. Barbara Hochman characterizes the relationship between Lily and another suitor, Lawrence Selden, as one between writer (Lily) and reader (Selden). The "Republic of the Spirit" that Selden describes to Lily and that subsequently becomes her ideal place of residence bears a striking resemblance to the Land of Letters:

> "My idea of success," he said, "is personal freedom."
> "Freedom? Freedom from worries?"
> "From everything—from money, from poverty, from ease and anxiety, from all the material accidents. To keep a kind of republic of the spirit—that's what I call success . . . it's a country one has to find the way to one's self."[76]

The Republic of the Spirit is an artistic and intellectual nation for the self-selected few where creativity and ideas are rewarded above the crass mercenary concerns that underlie the dealings of the physical world.[77] Within the utopic description of such a place is contained a criticism of its idealism. Lily immediately observes to Selden, "you are as bad as the other sectarians . . . why do you call your republic a republic? It is a closed corporation, and you create arbitrary objections in order to keep people out."[78] Despite the feelings of many young readers, Selden is hardly an ideal partner (especially given that he leaves Lily alone to die by the end of the novel) and the Republic of the Spirit is as accessible to Lily, given her social and economic circumstances, as a yachting trip along the French coast would be to the charwoman who cleans Selden's rooms.

Just as "The Republic of the Spirit" is an ideal held up to the light only to demonstrate its flaws, the problematic aspects of Lily's virtues are made everywhere apparent. Wharton always folds within her praises for Lily's advanced aesthetics an awareness of their social costs. Selden, "ha[s] a confused sense that [Lily] must have cost a great deal to make, that a great many dull and ugly people must, in some mysterious way, have been sacrificed to produce her."[79] This is another way of articulating the central concern of the great socialist novelists of the period: the many who are sacrificed to enable the extravagant lifestyles of the privileged few.

The foil to Lily's graceful beauty is Gerty Farish, Selden's homely cousin who is more concerned with her philanthropic work aiding the "dull and ugly people" than she is with the beautification and preservation of her own existence. To Lily, Gerty is "dull and ugly" herself. Lily expresses the difference between herself and Gerty succinctly: "she has a horrid little place, and no maid, and such queer things to eat. . . . We're so different, you know: she likes being good, and I like being happy."[80] But the dichotomy is a false one.

To be happy *is* to be good for Wharton.[81] The choice to be a Gerty or a Lily is no choice at all, as Lily muses:

> What choice had she? To be herself, or a Gerty Farish. As she entered her bedroom, with its softly-shaded lights, her lace dressing-gown lying across the silken bedspread, her little embroidered slippers before the fire, a vase of carnations filling the air with perfume, and the last novels and magazines lying uncut on a table beside the reading-lamp, she had a vision of Miss Farish's cramped flat, with its cheap conveniences and hideous wall-papers. No; she was not made for mean and shabby surroundings, for the squalid compromises of poverty.[82]

And it is ugliness—including the ugliness of poverty and its descriptions—that Wharton's fiction can't abide.

THE BOOK OF THE HOMELESS

Wharton's love of beauty and culture led to her permanent relocation to France in 1909. Her association between French culture and her own system of values made the destruction of France during the war years all the more painful to her. In her war chronicle, *Fighting France* (1915), she writes,

> In great trials a race is tested by its values; and the war has shown the world what are the real values of France. Never for an instant has this people, so expert in the great art of living, imagined that life consisted in being alive. Enamored of pleasure and beauty, dwelling freely and frankly in the present, they have yet kept their sense of larger meanings, have understood life to be made up of many things past and to come, of renunciation as well as satisfaction, of traditions as well as experiments, of dying as much as living. Never have they considered life as a thing to be cherished in itself, apart from its reactions and its relations.[83]

Her decision to undertake war relief work is motivated by a desire to preserve these dialectical values: of a life lived in the present but suffused with an awe for the past. Of a profound respect for art and beauty that is for Wharton, as for Chopin, above even life itself. The war death Wharton fights against through her relief work is the same death she understands the French army to be combatting: "the only death that Frenchmen fear is not death in the trenches but death by extinction of their national ideal . . . it is the reasoned recognition of their peril which, at this moment, is making the most intelligent people in the world the most sublime."[84] Sharon Kehl Califano asserts that Wharton came to her relief work "reluctantly, against her own sense of desire or self-preservation" for reasons of "deep personal conviction, a powerful moral obligation that overrode any kind of self-interested impulse."[85] Wharton does seem to have been motivated by the sense that something ought to be done and that those who were currently engaged in doing it were, unfortunately, not doing a very good job. In her letters to her closest friends at the time, she expresses her frustration at the inadequacy of the empty gestures made by Americans in France, and at home. To Bernard Berenson, she writes of American women in France: "The silly idiot women who have turned their drawing-rooms into hospitals (at great expense), & are now making shirts for the wounded, are robbing the poor stranded ouvrières of their only means of living."[86] She complains of American tourists who have become war voyeurs ("I don't know anything ghastlier & more idiotic than 'doing' hospitals en touriste, like museums!") and to Minnie Cadwallader Jones, she writes of well-meaning but uninformed Americans and unfeeling French bureaucrats:

> I was really heartbroken over the sending of all these useless blankets, when a three word cable to me before sending would have saved the waste, and perhaps given us the money we need so desperately. . . . When I think of the money those blankets represent I can only "curse and swear" . . . But I am also discouraged by the American attitude. All my friends knew I was working here as hard as I could, yet thousands have been poured into France-Amérique and the Securs National, both of the abysses of French inertia . . . the incompetence and callousness of the French charitable operations is notorious among French people, I wish you would do what you can to make it known. The petite bourgeoisie and the people are admirable, but all their funds are administered by the "gros bonnets", social and political, who are so hide-bound, timid, and unpractical that they spend most of their time inventing ways how not to give.[87]

It is Wharton's growing sense that any aid projects mediated by or invested in governmental nationalism will not succeed.

When Wharton did eventually develop her own charitable organizations as a part of the war relief effort in France, she mobilized her literary and artistic skill sets as well as her connections in the art world and in the New York social elite. Access to both networks—monied New Yorkers and talented artists—allowed her to exert absolute control over seemingly every aspect of the operations of her charities. In 1914, she established the American Hostels for Refugees, which, in its first year, provided housing to 9,300 displaced persons.[88] The following year, she expanded this effort to include the Children of Flanders Rescue Committee, which housed 750 children and 150 elderly persons and nuns. These were in addition to her organization of a tubercular hospital for soldiers and her volunteerism across the continent for the Red Cross.[89]

Bauer argues that Wharton saw herself as "fighting alone and figuratively in the dark" in her efforts to offer relief to war refugees in France.[90] Yet, in order to fund her charities and produce her the 1916 anthology *The Book of the Homeless*, Wharton had to leverage her connections in both the world of New York society from which she came and the world of arts and culture in which she successfully established herself as an adult. The list of donors to her "American Hostels" organization up to October 8, 1915 includes such names as Mrs. Andrew Carnegie, Mrs. Henry Clay Frick, Mr. L. Gordon Hamersley, Mrs. Vanderbilt, Mrs. Willard Straight, Mrs. George Whitney, etc.—all of whom appear in the issue of the social register that Wharton lobbied to be removed from herself.[91] While she attempted to disengage herself from the prestige game New York society played, she also utilized these relationships to achieve her own desired charitable ends—a process that is not dissimilar from her work in organizing *The Book of the Homeless* in an entirely different milieu. An anthology of poems, essays, stories, drawings, and even music about the war featuring illustrious contributors ranging from Pierre-Auguste Renoir to Joseph Conrad to Igor Stravinsky, *The Book of the Homeless* stands as a testament to Wharton's powerful position in the artistic elite of her day.

It is also a document explicitly of its own moment—*un*intended to be a timeless work to which later writers will turn time and time again. Though this is in one sense a literary endeavor, I do not believe Wharton saw it in that light. She acted as editor and was hesitant to include her own contributions: the introduction and a single poem. Of all of her works it is the most explicit literary "product," a work Susan Goodman has referred to, accurately I think, as "propaganda."[92] *The Book of the Homeless* was assembled to achieve financial success for her political ends, demonstrating how deeply associated those two goals were to her mind and why they were inimical to her literary work more generally. The production of *The Book of the Homeless* is so unique in her career that it may indeed represent a shift in the way Wharton viewed the relationship between literature and politics. By this time, Wharton had become entrenched enough within the literary firmament to be able to marshal the brightest stars of the arts to produce such an anthology; the suspicion of political engagement on careerist terms was no longer a threat.

Nevertheless, Wharton is aware of the dangers of using sentimental literature to encourage political action. Just as Rebecca Harding Davis utilized subaltern characters who are themselves artists in order to lend them agency within their own representation, Wharton attempted to cast the beneficiaries of the anthology as subjects rather than charitable objects. Her description of the refugees housed in her hostels does not attempt to sentimentalize them nor romanticize her aid work:

> They are not all King Alberts and Queen Elizabeths, as some idealists apparently expected them to be. Some are hard to help, others unappreciative of what is done for them. But many, many more are grateful, appreciative, and eager to help us help them.

Her preface begins with an anecdote that resembles the plot of the artist's decline in miniature: "Last year, among the waifs swept to Paris by the great torrent of the flight from the North, there came to the American Hostels a little acrobat from a strolling circus." Her story of the acrobatic homeless waif goes on to describe how the material aid rendered to the child was insufficient:

> He was given good pay, and put into a good livery, and told to be a good boy . . . but the life was too lonely. Nobody knew anything about the only things *he* knew, or was particularly interested in the programme of the last performance the company had given. . . . The little acrobat could not understand. He told his friends at the Hostels how lonely and puzzled he was, and they tried to help him. But he couldn't sleep at night . . . and one night he went up to the attic of the hotel, broke open several trunks full of valuables stored there by rich lodgers, and made off with some of the contents. . . . They were the spangled dresses belonging to a Turkish family, and the embroidered coats of a lady's lap-dog.[93]

Wharton relates this incident to suggest that what the acrobat needs perhaps more than clothes and pay is spangles and embroidery—or the longing for the art and artistic community that these items represent. It is as though through this anecdote she is including him, a beneficiary of *The Book of the Homeless*, in the community of writers, painters, composers, and dramatic artists who contributed to it. Perhaps even more significantly, Wharton will later echo the language she uses to describe the acrobat in her own autobiography, *A Backward Glance*, in the passage cited in the epigraph to this chapter wherein she defines the "Land of Letters" that constituted her global citizenship. By referring to both herself and the acrobat as homeless "waifs" she demonstrates that the homelessness with which she identifies is both literal and metaphysical.

The rhetoric Wharton uses is curious: the daughter of the elite and well-heeled Rhinelander-Joneses casting herself as a homeless waif. Beyond curious, some might reasonably suggest, enlisting homelessness and political exile to describe the isolation of an artistic spirit in the suffocating privilege of New York high society borders on the insensitive or even offensive. In her work on illness as metaphor, Susan Sontag outlines the sociopolitical problems occasioned by the attractive and therefore frequent metaphorical use of real illness—tuberculosis and cancer in particular—in art and culture.[94] Perhaps a more apt example of the danger of sociopolitical metaphor in literature, however, is to be found in postcolonial studies. Writers and theorists of postcolonialism have long derided metaphors common to the English language as reifying a polar relationship between the normative and the exotic.[95] In Chinua Achebe's famous essayistic takedown of Conrad's *Heart of Darkness*, "An Image of Africa," he describes that novel's central metaphor—wherein the African continent represents the existential crisis of the narrator, Marlow—as "preposterous and perverse arrogance" and deems Conrad "A thoroughgoing racist."[96]

Surely a similarly structured critique might be lodged at Wharton, who not only compares herself to a homeless waif in her autobiography, but gives us picturesque descriptions of the suffering of war channeled through her own narrative perspective in *Fighting France*, which is, as Alice Kelly has observed, a very literary sort of propaganda that itself relies heavily on the uses of metaphor.[97] For Paul de Man and those engaged in the intellectual tradition his work inaugurated, his followers, the precise problem with such politicized metaphors is that they leverage what he calls a "protocol of identity," which he sees as a violent "totalization."[98] They rely on drawing similarities between two persons or groups of persons on the basis of one axis of identity and that axis subsequently supplants the other aspects and particulars of each respective identity. But, as more recent theorists of humanitarianism have come to see, some degree of such protocols of identity are necessary in order to create the political feeling that spurs real-world aid.

Martha Nussbaum describes how political action is impossible without what she calls a "circle of concern." We might imagine that all people have a ready "circle of concern" that includes their family, friends, and perhaps their neighbors and acquaintances. Broadening that circle of concern is the key to instigating political consciousness more broadly. And, as Nussbaum identifies, broadening that concern beyond nationalistic boundaries is the greatest challenge of all, as nationalism and patriotism—political feelings that, as Nussbaum notes, are capable of being evoked for the purposes of great violations of human rights such as war, crusades, and ethnic cleansing—may also be marshalled to achieve great good. It's easy to use patriotic sentiment to convince people to save "their own." But how can broader circles of concern that transcend the borders of nations and the confines of cultures be drawn? Nussbaum writes:

> If distant people and abstract principles are to get a grip on our emotions, therefore, these emotions must somehow position them within our circle of concern, creating a sense of "our" life in which these people and events matter as parts of our "us," our own flourishing. For this movement to take place, symbols and poetry are crucial.[99]

Symbols, poetry, and, perhaps most of all—metaphor. For Wharton, metaphor is not a tool of rhetoric but a humanitarian philosophy.

As far as humanitarian philosophies born out of literary and rhetorical devices go, historically metonymies have been preferred. Sigi Jöttkandt has described how deconstructivists tend to regard metonymy as a non-totalizing trope, because they see metaphor as "the paradigmatic trope of identity (with all of the negative connotations this term has since acquired—i.e., as involving the violent subjugation of otherness to the tyranny of the Same)," while metonymy is seen as "the trope of difference, capable of engaging with otherness in a more ethically attractive fashion."[100] Attractive because, as the linguists George Lakoff and Mark Johnson point out, the principal difference between the two devices is that while metaphors require two domains, metonymies have only one.[101] Or, as Roman Jakobson explains it, metonymy works on the axis of contiguity, metaphor on the axis of comparison.[102] Therefore, the problematic totalization or "tyranny of the Same" we find in some uses of metaphor is due to the necessary comparison metaphor must erect between the two different things it compares, whereas such a leap is not required of a metonymy because of the relatively low stakes of contiguity.

Most observations about the dangers of metaphor rely on assumptions that the relationship between the two parts of a metaphor will remain hierarchical. Lakoff and Johnson use the terms "source domain" and "target domain," to denote these parts rather than the more traditional "tenor" and "vehicle," to get at the way metaphors rely on the construction of whole areas of meaning.[103] In *Heart of Darkness*, the African is never given their own metaphysical crisis and therefore Africa remains only source domain. Laura Fisher has shown how Wharton critiques metaphors of suffering in *The House of Mirth*, where Lily Bart rather wrongly equates her own struggles to those of the women of the working club where she volunteers, arguing that "Wharton identifies both the success and the failure of comparison as a social practice."[104] Wharton's unique attention to the politics of metaphor results, I will argue here, in privileging the establishment of equivalencies rather than hierarchies.

To understand Wharton's idiosyncratic use of metaphors throughout her work, I'll examine the metaphor of the house—a favorite metaphor for Wharton and for two of her favorite writers. Walter Pater dwells on the details of good "literary architecture" in his 1889 essay on style.[105] Henry James later takes a page from Pater in the 1908 New York edition preface to *The Portrait of a Lady* with a complex metaphor that renders fiction a house of many windows, each window representing the "literary form" chosen by the author, the watcher out the window representing "the consciousness of the artist."[106] James neatly deconstructs his own metaphor for his reader, explicitly stating and therefore polarizing these representational relationships.

In contrast to James and Pater, for whom the house is an abstraction that enriches the discussion of their actual subject, Wharton uses metaphors of houses far more literally, even in the context of a source domain, perhaps because she identified as both a designer of houses and as an author. Writing to Ogden Codman Jr., with whom she coauthored the nonfiction work *The Decoration of Houses* (1897), "Decidedly, I'm a better landscape gardener than novelist, and this place [her home, The Mount, in Lenox], every line of which is my own work, far surpasses *The House of Mirth*."[107] Here, using the dual meaning of the word "line," Wharton employs the novel as the source domain, her house—the Mount—as the target. It is also significant that she calls her novel *The House of Mirth*, and that, within that novel, architecture offers the source domain for a great number of more abstract concepts.

In *The Decoration of Houses*, Wharton makes the argument that the best, and therefore most instructive, principles of architecture and decoration to be found in sixteenth-century Italian Palaces are not the grand rooms where the family lived their "spectacular" existence—the ballrooms and drawing rooms and libraries through which tourists are taken—but the private apartment, where the family actually lived, that was seldom seen by anyone else. Wharton notes in her introduction "the seeming lack of accord between the arguments used in this book and the illustrations chosen to interpret them," citing "that only such apartments as are accessible to the traveler might be given as examples."[108] So despite her central claim that the simplicity of the relatively unadorned private apartments is preferable, the book—like the public museums the palaces have become—does not exhibit them. One need not be extraordinarily imaginative to read the entire *Decoration of Houses* as a detailed and extended metaphor, but it is also really a book about the decoration of houses and has long been and continues to be read and utilized in that capacity. In her 1893 story "The Fulness of Life," the same principles about private rooms are brought to an explicitly metaphorical context:

> I have sometimes thought that a woman's nature is like a great house full of rooms: there is the hall, through which everyone passes in going in and out; the drawing room, where one receives formal visits; the sitting room, where the members of the family come and go as they list; but beyond that, far beyond, are other rooms, the handles of whose doors perhaps are never turned.[109]

The emotional tragedy of what Wharton calls a "spectacular existence" in *The Decoration of Houses* is laid out in the short story passage. Wharton returns to this concept repeatedly—the loneliness of crowds, the pain of being seen but never really known—but here in "the Fulness of Life" we see it explicitly connected to architecture through a metaphor. And then we have a new understanding of the deep significance of why Wharton prefers the architecture of the private apartment. It is a part of the house where only family members and intimate friends would be invited. Therefore, the exchanges that take place there would take on the character of intimacy more readily—not only because of who was involved, but because the space itself signals a particular kind of practice, just as placing a piano in a room with an open floor would encourage its inhabitants to play and dance, or as a conference room with a large table and office chairs would create a different kind of conversation than a private library with a few comfortable couches around a low coffee table. Reading the two passages together lends richer meaning to both and demonstrates how Wharton's architectural metaphors have a deep significance that transcends the hierarchies of metaphorical domains. Whartonian metaphors say something meaningful about both things rather than using one strictly in the service of the other.

Wharton's work also reminds us that metaphors do not always invent relationships between seemingly disparate things. They can also illuminate relationships that exist in practice. The conversation in the private library is not only intimate *like* the space in which it takes place, but also *because* of it. We see this at work in *The House of Mirth* when Lily and Selden abandon the public rooms of the Wellington Bry's for a tête-à-tête in the garden. Wharton uses her knowledge of sixteenth-century Italian palace architecture to create a spatial metaphor that demonstrates the contrast between the spectacular frivolity of the party and the private intimacy of Lily and Selden.

> [The Wellington Brys] recently built house, whatever it might lack as a frame for domesticity, was almost as well-designed for the display of a festal assemblage as one of those airy pleasure-halls which the Italian architects improvised to set off the hospitality of princes. . . . The seated throng, filling the immense room without undue crowding, presented a surface of rich tissues and jeweled shoulders in harmony with the festooned and gilded walls, and the flushed splendours of the Venetian ceiling . . . Selden, who had put one of these seats to the test, found himself, from an angle of the ball-room, surveying the scene with frank enjoyment . . . Selden had given [Lily] his arm without speaking. She took it in silence, and they moved away, not toward the supper-room, but against the tide which was setting thither . . . she hardly noticed where Selden was leading her, till they passed through a glass doorway at the end of the long suite of rooms and stood suddenly in the fragrant hush of a garden. Gravel grated beneath their feet . . . hanging lights made emerald caverns in the depths of foliage . . . the magic place was deserted . . . Selden and Lily stood still, accepting the unreality of the scene as a part of their own dream-like sensations.[110]

Here the environment in which Lily and Selden find themselves forces an honest conversation and the text explicitly acknowledges a slippage between the external architecture and their internal state of mind. It's not entirely clear if the garden itself is a product of their emotions or vice versa. This local instance of the Whartonian metaphor reflects broader such collapses in the way she understood the relation between literary realism and social change.

By supporting the hostels she built to house refugees through the creation of an anthology, Wharton deploys a cunning series of metaphors that extend beyond the boundaries of the literary text. In her preface to the *The*

Book of the Homeless, she uses a familiar metaphor to describe the genesis of the project:

> I appealed to my friends who write and paint and compose, and they to friends of theirs . . . and so the Book gradually built itself up, page by page and picture by picture. You will see from the names of the builders what a gallant piece of architecture it is, what delightful pictures hang on its walls, and what noble music echoes through them. . . . So I efface myself from the threshold and ask you to walk in.[111]

The Book of the Homeless is a metaphorical house designed to provide real-world shelter, and the psychological connection to place that shelter confers, to a community experiencing homelessness. The "homeless" of the title are both the refugees and the contributors in a metaphor that creates a productive equivalency. The book is a metaphorical house built by the artists who contribute to it that offers shelter to the readers who are asked to "walk in" and, in its philanthropic aim, literal shelter for the refugees. Therefore, its metaphorical structure places the donor/readers and the recipient/refugees in both domains.

Not only does Wharton include the acrobat in the "us" of the artistic community who create the book, she more broadly positions the entire nation of France within her own "circle of concern," and, thereby the "circle of concern" of her readers. The metaphor of losing a home or a connection to culture allows identification both with individuals and the personified nation state of France. As Susan Goodman has argued, "*The Book of the Homeless* provided both an argument for American intervention in the war and a reminder of the values uniting people across nations."[112] The means by which it accomplished this task—asking its readers to transcend the feelings of patriotism that more commonly motivated charitable works in this period—was a set of complex metaphorical relations centered on the book itself. By using the same figures of houses and homelessness; of artists and refugees; of literature, art, and music as both target and source domain in various contexts, she not only upsets the power dynamics that make such metaphorical relations politically problematic or even dangerous but also demonstrates the real relationships that can be forged between people, things, or ideas that we've come to think of as dissimilar.

Wharton was not only a citizen but an ardent patriot of the Land of Letters. Her experiment in reform realist fiction was less successful than the conflation of the real world with the literary that culminated in her production of *The Book of the Homeless*. Her ability to illuminate beauty ultimately created tangible social good, as did her literary work through its "imaginative reaches in life." While the conventional novel of purpose remains invested in the separation between the "real" world and the literary, Wharton understood good literature to be illustrative of the interdependent relationship between these two spheres. Her work encourages its readers to inhabit imaginary nations and build real and better houses within them.

THE LEGACY OF REFORM REALISM

In the nineteenth century, social causes were used to promote books and lecture tours. Early twentieth century suffrage china and accessories were fashionable in their own time and are valuable collectibles today. In our own moment, social scientists like Roberto Belloni, David Rieff, and Ilan Kapoor argue that the merchandizing of political engagement has become one of the most recognizable features of neoliberal humanitarianism.[113] The present-day trappings of progressive neoliberalism offer an astonishing variety and number of cause-related marketing efforts: shoes you can buy with a promise to shod the barefoot; fashionable glasses that help the vision-impaired; tote bags that promise to feed the hungry; iPhones that support research on AIDS; a broad array of t-shirts, hats, and leggings bearing catchy slogans that promote social causes; and "giving nights" at chain restaurant franchises. These nods towards ameliorating social problems offer the promise of progress within the gesture that has become the most familiar aspect of modern life: buying something. It is worth noting that among the earliest and most significant objects one could buy to support a social cause in the United States was a printed abolition text, the genre that—as Augusta Rohrbach has shown—gave rise to the realist protest novel in America.[114]

As the economist Zoltan Acs has argued, philanthropy and humanitarianism are the key factors behind the flourishing of global capitalism we see today, calling such areas of social and economic investment "the secret ingredient that fails to get mentioned in economic accounts of capitalism."[115] The popularity of these causes does not seem to have a direct relationship to their success in improving social conditions and, indeed, their use in cross-marketing campaigns can have a worsening effect. One example is a 2014 study on the impact of the highly profitable company TOMS shoes, often cited as a model for successful cause-related marketing. TOMS promises to donate a pair of shoes to children in need for every pair of shoes that it sells, but the study confirmed its hypothesis that "donated shoes exhibit negative impacts on local shoe markets," and additionally found that the shoes were not reaching those who would benefit most from receiving them.[116] Though this kind of aid is not effective in ameliorating poverty or improving the lives of those it purportedly benefits, it does have demonstrable financial and emotional benefits for both marketers and consumers. A 2016 study of the efficacy of these marketing strategies, which identifies cause-related marketing (CRM) programs as a $1.9 billion dollar business, found that such strategies garner more buy-in when they involve the "donation of a specific product rather than a donation of money that can be applied broadly to support a cause," because such models "evoke a more concrete mindset" among consumers.[117] The concern for consumer mindset is prioritized over the actual efficacy of the relief efforts.

This problem is precisely the kind of ill-conceived, profit-minded humanitarianism Edith Wharton wished to avoid when she established the garment factory in France during the First World War to fund the Hostels for Refugees. Her complaints about the sending of useless donations of blankets and clothing, donations which also hindered the profitability of the workhouses which were designed to offer both monetary aid to hostels that housed refugees and much-needed wage employment for their residents, mirrors the problems scholars and activists have identified with CRM efforts.[118] Recent scholarship has seen an even more dire need to address how humanitarian campaigns profit off of the suffering of their beneficiaries. An international research collective started in 2017 and funded by the Danish Council for Independent Research, Commodifying Compassion, states that it is "the first project to include the cause beneficiaries' regimes of value as an important component in understanding the ethical dilemmas of 'helping,'" performing research that, "will produce a better understanding by humanitarian organizations and businesses leading to more ethical fundraising, donors weighing consumption-based models as part of more effective aid, and consumers making more informed choices about 'helping' by buying brand aid products."[119] Just as buying CRM goods to alleviate inequity troubles these researchers, who have found demonstrable negative impacts of such practices, it was clear to Wharton that donations of goods rather than money represented a desire on the part of Americans to assuage their guilty consciences about the war rather than to actually aid the refugees or—what would help most—agitate for American intervention.

David Rieff describes how aid workers have learned that "while politics and political analyses matter desperately" to their causes, "moral fables matter more to the general public."[120] Similarly, James Baldwin's complaint about what he called "the protest novel" was that such moral fables in themselves become sufficient—they settle our discomfort with the injustices they depict rather than urging us to action:

> The "protest" novel, so far from being disturbing, is an accepted and comforting aspect of the American scene, ramifying that framework we believe to be so necessary. Whatever unsettling questions are raised are evanescent, titillating; remote, for this has nothing to do with us, it is safely ensconced in the social arena, where, indeed, it has nothing to do with anyone, so that finally we receive a very definite thrill of virtue from the fact that we are reading such a book at all. This report from the pit reassures us of its reality and its darkness and of our own salvation; and "as long as such books are being published," an American liberal once said to me, "everything will be alright."[121]

While aid efforts do provide some real benefits to the disenfranchised, they also—like Baldwin's protest novel—offer an out for the guilty consciences of those who benefit from the ever-increasing disparity in the distribution of resources across the globe.

It is no mere coincidence that the manifesto of modern philanthropy was written by a Gilded Age millionaire (an over 300 billionaire by today's standards) in 1889. Andrew Carnegie's "Gospel of Wealth" is a work that inspired an organization founded in 2010 called "The Giving Pledge," which encourages the world's richest citizens to promise to "give back" philanthropically. As of 2022 there are 236 pledgers. The original eighty-one Giving Pledge signers wrote letters explaining their decision to participate, which Giving Pledge founder Warren Buffet calls "The 81 Gospels of Wealth," after Carnegie's 1889 essay, a treatise in support of a capitalistic system that produces ever-increasing disparities in wealth with a philanthropic caveat.[122] Carnegie writes,

> Individualism, Private Property, the Law of Accumulation of Wealth, and the Law of Competition; for these are the highest results of human experience, the soil in which society so far has produced the best fruit. Unequally or unjustly, perhaps, as these laws sometimes operate, and imperfect as they appear to the Idealist, they are, nevertheless, like the highest type of man, the best and most valuable of all that humanity has yet accomplished. We start, then, with a condition of affairs under which the best interests of the race are promoted, but which inevitably gives

wealth to the few. Thus far, accepting conditions as they exist, the situation can be surveyed and pronounced good. The question then arises,—and, if the foregoing be correct, it is the only question with which we have to deal,—What is the proper mode of administering wealth after the laws upon which civilization is founded have thrown it into the hands of the few? And it is of this great question that I believe I offer the true solution.[123]

Here the modern idea of philanthropy itself is founded on the premise that wealth disparity is merely a side-effect of a system that serves the general good, not its fundamental product. Thus Buffet can write without irony in his own "Gospel of Wealth" that his "luck was accentuated by my living in a market system that sometimes produces distorted results, though overall it serves our country well."[124] The logical contradiction here remains the same as it was in 1889: how can a philanthropist recognize the urgent need to ameliorate such vast inequalities through drastic measures—Buffet promises to donate ninety-nine percent of his personal earnings to strangers—but continue to claim that the very system that produces this scenario "overall serves our country well"? Such an inherently contradictory philosophy of social justice fails to recognize its own participation in the inhumane conditions it seeks to correct.

Aesthetic realists were presciently attuned to how the popularity of social causes had become a valuable marketing tool above all else. But their concern was also how liberal politics oversimplified complex issues and furthered what they increasingly saw as an anti-intellectual agenda within American culture. Phillip Barrish suggests that high-art realist writers documented and cultivated the intellectual prestige that comes with literary knowledge; I've argued here that, on the other hand, such knowledge may indeed have served as a necessary bulwark against the prestige of shallow political engagement, which was and continues to be so easily transformed into cultural and financial capital.[125]

Today we see the continuation of their critique in what is perhaps an unlikely source: cultural critics who argue for revolution or abolition instead of reform. Dylan Rodriguez writes of how,

> the infrastructure of liberal philanthropy commodifies simplistic narratives of reform into tidy sound/text bites that are easily repeated, retweeted, and reposted by public-facing people and organizations. This dynamic not only insults the intelligence of those engaged in serious, collectively accountable forms of struggle against state violence; it also

glorifies clout-seeking laziness as a substitute for actual (abolitionist) activism.[126]

By recognizing the roots of such performative activism in the reform realism of the Progressive Era, we can begin to understand how our popular notion of social change has been shaped by the techniques of realist fiction and perhaps, even, how the study of aesthetic realism might help us to imagine a way out.

NOTES

INTRODUCTION: HIDEOUSLY POLITICAL

1 Fred Kaplan, *Henry James: The Imagination of Genius* (New York: Open Road Integrated Media, 2013), 422.

2 Rancière does not offer the full quotation, which can be found in "Louise Colet, 16 Jan. 1852," *Correspondance*, 5 vols. (Paris: Gallimard, 1973–2007), 231, translation mine. I refer here more generally to Ranciére's discussion in chapter one of *The Politics of Literature*, trans. Julie Rose (Cambridge, UK: Polity, 2011). "Flaubert, and in particular, *Madame Bovary* was a great influence to almost all of the writers in my study." James wrote that "Madame Bovary has a perfection that not only stamps it, but makes it stand almost alone: it holds itself with such a supreme unapproachable assurance as both excites and defies judgment." "Gustave Flaubert," *Literary Criticism, Volume Two: European Writers* (New York: Library of America, 1984), 325. Kate Chopin's *The Awakening* has long been called the "Creole Bovary" since its earliest reviews. Wharton admires Flaubert for his very contrariness, writing in *The Art of Fiction*, "Flaubert, for instance, so often cited as the example of the writer viewing his themes in a purely 'scientific' or amoral light, has disproved the claim by providing the other camp with the perfect formula: 'Plus la pensée est belle, plus la phrase est sonore'—not the metaphor, not the picture, but the thought." *The Art of Fiction* (New York: Touchstone, 1997), 24.

3 Fredric Jameson, *The Antinomies of Realism* (New York: Verso, 2016), 6.

4 Mark McGurl, *The Novel Art: Elevations of American Fiction after Henry James* (Princeton, NJ: Princeton University Press, 2001).

5 Nancy Bentley, *Frantic Panoramas: American Literature and Mass Culture, 1870–1920* (Philadelphia: University of Pennsylvania Press, 2009), 35.

6 Richard Hofstadter, *The Age of Reform* (New York: Vintage, 1955), 5.

7 Susan Ryan, "Reform," in *Keywords for American Cultural Studies*, 2nd ed., ed. Bruce Burgett and Glenn Hendler (New York: New York University Press, 2014), 9, http://hdl.handle.net/2333.1/280gb7cc.

8 Laura Hapke, "Social Purity Movement," in *Women's Studies Encyclopedia*, col. 3, ed. Helen Tierney (Westport, CT: Greenwood Press, 1991).

9 Richard White, *The Republic for Which It Stands: The United States During Reconstruction and the Gilded Age, 1865–1896* (New York: Oxford University Press, 2017), 3.

10 John Falsarella Dawson, *Combatting Injustice: The Naturalism of Frank Norris, Jack London, and John Steinbeck* (Baton Rouge: Louisiana State University Press, 2022); Mary Chapman, *Making Noise, Making News: Suffrage Print Culture and U.S. Modernism* (New York: Oxford University Press, 2014); Amanda Claybaugh, *The Novel of Purpose: Literature and Social Reform in the Anglo-American World* (Ithaca, NY: Cornell University Press, 2007); Laura Fisher, *Reading for Reform: The Social Work of American Literature in the Progressive Era* (Minneapolis: University of Minnesota Press, 2018); María Carla Sánchez, *Reforming the World: Social Activism and the Problem of Fiction in Nineteenth-Century America* (Iowa City: University of Iowa Press, 2008); Francesca Sawaya, *The Difficult Art of Giving: Patronage, Philanthropy, and the American Literary Market* (Philadelphia: University of Pennsylvania Press, 2014).

11 Sánchez, *Reforming the World*, 3.

12 Stowe's anger at the passage of the Fugitive Slave Act was the impetus for her composition of *Uncle Tom's Cabin*. Joan D. Hedrick describes Stowe's interest in literature (especially Byron, Dickens, and Charlotte Brönte) but maintains that Stowe's literary ambition was subordinate to her commitment to her religious and political convictions. *Harriet Beecher Stowe: A Life* (New York: Oxford University Press, 1994); Aleta Feinsod Cane and Susan Alves, eds., *"The Only Efficient Instrument": American Women Writers and the Periodical, 1837–1916* (Iowa City: University of Iowa Press, 2001). Cane and Alves's title comes from Margaret Fuller's assertion that literature is "the only efficient instrument for the general education of the people" in "American Literature: Its Position in the Present Time, and Prospects for the Future," *Papers on Literature and Art, Pt. II* (New York: Fowler and Wells, 1846), 137–38.

13 Justine Murison, *Faith in Exposure: Privacy and Secularism in the Nineteenth-Century United States* (Philadelphia: University of Pennsylvania Press, 2023).

14 Fisher, *Reading for Reform*.

15 Charlotte Perkins Gilman, "Why I Wrote 'The Yellow Wall-Paper,'" in *The Norton Anthology American Literature, Volume C: 1865–1914*, ed. N. Baym (New York: W. W. Norton, 2012), 804.

16 Russ Castronovo writes, more accurately, "rather than claim that *The Jungle* directly resulted in the passage of the Pure Food and Drug Act (a claim that many make but also one that historians have disputed), it might be better to say that *The Jungle* profited from timing its publication with the news that lawmakers were about to take on the meatpacking industry," in introduction to *The Jungle* by Upton Sinclair, ed. Russ Castronovo (New York: Oxford University Press, 2010), vii–xxv; xiii.

17 Fisher, *Reading for Reform*, 192.

18 See John S. Bak and Bill Reynolds, eds., *Literary Journalism across the Globe* (Amherst: University of Massachusetts Press, 2011).

19 Quoted in Owen Clayton, *Literature and Photography in Transition, 1850–1915* (London: Palgrave Macmillan, 2015), 24.

20 In her study of British Victorian fiction and photography, *Fiction in the Age of Photography: The Legacy of British Realism* (Cambridge, MA: Harvard University Press, 2002), Nancy Armstrong explores how photography introduced a language of the real that influenced how reality was represented in fiction. Daniel Akiva Novak, on the other hand, associates photography with the "unreal," demonstrating

how Victorian photographs were often manipulated and used as tools for the creative imagination in *Realism, Photography and Nineteenth-Century Fiction* (Cambridge: Cambridge University Press, 2008).

21 In Bonnie Yochelson and Daniel Czitrom, *Rediscovering Jacob Riis: Exposure Journalism and Photography in Turn-of-the-Century New York* (Chicago: University of Chicago Press, 2014), 131.

22 Amy Kaplan, *The Social Construction of American Literary Realism* (Chicago: University of Chicago Press, 1988), 10. See Kaplan's introduction for a longer history of the claim that realism orders the subjects it depicts. See also Mark Seltzer's *Henry James and the Art of Power* (Ithaca, NY: Cornell University Press, 1984).

23 Claybaugh, *Novel of Purpose*, 32–33.

24 Nancy Glazener, *Reading for Realism* (Durham, NC: Duke University Press, 1997), 44.

25 James William Sullivan, "Cohen's Figure," in *Tenement Tales of New York* (New York: Henry Holt and Company, 1895), 69–88, 69–71, 72.

26 W. D. Howells, *Novels: 1875–1886* (New York: Library of America, 1982), 327–28.

27 Henry Woodd Nevinson, *Slum Stories of London* (New York: Henry Holt and Company, 1895).

28 Keith Gandal suggests that while these works preceded that of the photographer Jacob Riis, "there is no evidence that [Riis] learned his outlook from them; in fact, it seems that he knew very little about their work," *The Virtues of the Vicious: Jacob Riis, Stephen Crane, and the Spectacle of the Slum* (New York: Oxford University Press, 1997), 145. It seems more likely that Crane had encountered these British predecessors, and practically certain that Crane's most important influence, Hamlin Garland, had. Keith Newlin shows Garland's extensive reading in British texts at the Boston Public Library in the 1880s in *Hamlin Garland: A Life* (Lincoln: University of Nebraska Press, 2008), 64.

29 Sharon Kim, "Puritan Realism: *The Wide, Wide World* and *Robinson Crusoe,*" *American Literature* 75, no. 4 (2003): 783–811; Ramón Saldívar, "Historical Fantasy, Speculative Realism, and Postrace Aesthetics in Contemporary American Fiction," *American Literary History* 23, no. 3 (2011): 574–99.

30 Brad Evans, "Realism as Modernism," in *The Oxford Handbook to American Literary Realism* (New York: Oxford University Press, 2019): 139–62, 141, 143.

31 Henry James, "Review of *Waiting for the Verdict* by Rebecca Harding Davis," *The Nation,* November 21, 1867, rpt. in *Literary Criticism: Essays on Literature; American Writers; English Writers,* ed. Leon Edel (New York: Library of America, 1984), 218–22.

32 Rebecca Harding Davis, "Life in the Iron-Mills," in *A Rebecca Harding Davis Reader,* ed. Jean Pfaelzer (Pittsburgh, PA: University of Pittsburgh Press, 1995), 3–34; 10.

33 Harriet Elizabeth Beecher Stowe, *Uncle Tom's Cabin: A Tale, or Life Among the Lowly* (London: George Routledge and Company, 1852), 30.

34 Wharton, *Art of Fiction*, 15.

35 Rebecca Harding Davis, *Bits of Gossip* (Edinburgh: Archibald Constable, 1904), 166.

36 Matthew Stratton, *The Politics of Irony in American Modernism* (New York: Fordham University Press, 2014), 15.

37 Howells is quoted in Glazener, *Reading for Realism*, 122; David E. Shi, *Facing Facts: Realism in American Thought and Culture, 1850–1920* (New York: Oxford University Press, 1995).

38 Vernon Louis Parrington, *The Beginnings of Critical Realism in America* (Piscataway: Transaction Publishers, 2013), 351.

39 Lionel Trilling, *The Liberal Imagination: Essays on Literature and Society* (New York: Viking, 1950).

40 Amy Kaplan, *Social Construction*, 7.

41 Dorothy Parker, "Reformers: A Hymn of Hate," in *Nonsensorship*, ed. Heywood Broun (New York: G. P. Putnam, 1922), 95–98.

42 Edith Wharton, *Hudson River Bracketed* (Oxford: Benediction Classics, 2011), 142.

43 Per Seyersted, ed., *The Complete Works of Kate Chopin* (Baton Rouge: Louisiana State University Press, 1997), 723.

44 Seyersted, *The Complete Works of Kate Chopin*, 699. Emily Toth adds to this that "Chopin despised most rules . . . [and] expressed anger though a bemused irony." *Unveiling Kate Chopin* (Jackson: University of Mississippi Press, 1999), 276.

45 Michele L. Mock, "'An Ardor That Was Human, and a Power That Was Art': Rebecca Harding Davis and the Art of the Periodical," in Cane and Alves, *"The Only Efficient Instrument,"* 126.

46 Kenneth Warren, *What Was African American Literature?* (Cambridge, MA: Harvard University Press, 2011).

47 Louis J. Budd, "The American Background," in *The Cambridge Companion to American Realism and Naturalism*, ed. Donald Pizer (Cambridge: Cambridge University Press, 2006), 32.

48 Rebecca Harding Davis, "The Disease of Money-Getting," *The Independent*, June 19, 1902, 1457.

49 Carol Singley, *Edith Wharton: Matters of Mind and Spirit* (Cambridge: Cambridge University Press, 1998), 68.

50 James Weldon Johnson, "Inside Measurement," in *The Selected Writings of James Weldon Johnson*, ed. Sondra K. Wilson (New York: Oxford University Press, 1995), 260–61.

51 T. J. Jackson Lears, *No Place of Grace* (Chicago: University of Chicago Press, 1982), xx.

52 Perhaps the most compelling recent accounts of this phenomenon occur in the field of Black Classicism, for example John Levi Barnard's *Empire of Ruin: Black Classicism and American Imperial Culture* (New York: Oxford University Press, 2018).

53 Lears, *No Place of Grace*, 256.

54 Amy Kaplan, *Social Construction*, 4.

55 Edith Wharton, *A Backward Glance* (New York: Simon & Schuster, 1998), 119. On Wharton and anti-Semitism, see Irene Goldman Price, "The Perfect Jew and *The House of Mirth*: A Study in Point of View," *Edith Wharton Review* 16, no. 1 (Spring 2000): 3–9.

56 Roman Jakobson recalls how different phases and schools of realists summarily identified against their predecessors in the European tradition, unpackaging a simplistic definition of verisimilitudinous realism, "the artistic intent to render life as it is," into subcategories; the subcategory he identifies as emerging most visibly in the late nineteenth century is "the tendency to deform given artistic

norms conceived as an approximation of reality." Roman Jakobson, *Language in Literature* (Cambridge, MA: Harvard University Press, 1987), 22–24. In his account, "new realist artists . . . were compelled to call themselves neo-realists," drawing a line "between quasi- or pseudo-realism and what they conceived to be genuine realism (i.e., their own)" (24). Aesthetic realists identified as realists of a privileged set—like Jakobson's Dostoevsky, who declares, "I am a realist, but only in the higher sense of the word" (25). What Jakobson's critique of these various forms of realist identification illuminates is the way in which realists responding to a previous tradition of literary realism must confront not only what they perceive as the relationship between their work and the previous tradition, but also what they perceive to be the relationship between their work and the world it represents. In negotiating both concerns, they find themselves rejecting not only the style of their forbears or followers, but also the worldview with which they understand that style to align.

57 Rancière, *Politics of Literature*, 22.

58 Rita Felski, *The Limits of Critique* (Chicago: University of Chicago Press, 2015), 182.

59 Bentley, *Frantic Panoramas*, 72.

60 See the discussion throughout the first chapter of Peter Brooks's *Realist Vision* (New Haven, CT: Yale University Press, 2005).

61 See Elizabeth Ammons, *Conflicting Stories: American Writers at the Turn into the Twentieth Century* (New York: Oxford University Press, 1991). See also Naomi Z. Sofer, *Making the "America of Art": Cultural Nationalism and Nineteenth-Century Women Writers* (Columbus: Ohio State University Press, 2005), and Anne E. Boyd, *Writing for Immortality: Women and the Emergence of High Literary Culture in America* (Baltimore: Johns Hopkins University Press, 2004).

62 Seyersted, *The Complete Works of Kate Chopin*, 881.

63 Candace Vogler, "Sex and Talk," *Critical Inquiry* 24, no. 2 (1998): 328–65, 328, 351.

64 Brent Edwards notes the ubiquity of dismals of Johnson's political significance, describing how "Johnson is usually portrayed as [a] stilted aesthetic aristocrat" in "The Seemingly Eclipsed Window of Form: James Weldon Johnson's Prefaces," in *The Jazz Cadence of American Culture*, ed. Robert G. O'Meally (New York: Columbia University Press, 1998), 580–601; 587.

65 Jennie Kasanoff, *Edith Wharton and the Politics of Race* (Cambridge: Cambridge University Press, 2004), 2.

CHAPTER ONE: REBECCA HARDING DAVIS AND CELEBRITY REFORM

Some sections of this chapter previously appeared in Arielle Zibrak, "Writing Behind a Curtain: Rebecca Harding Davis and Celebrity Reform," *ESQ: A Journal of the American Renaissance* 60, no. 4 (2014): 522–56; copyright 2024 by the Board of Regents of Washington State University.

1 Malcolm Cowley, "A Natural History of American Naturalism," in *Documents of Modern Literary Realism*, ed. George Joseph Becker (Princeton, NJ: Princeton

University Press, 1963), 429–51. Cowley particularly emphasizes the "tendency . . . to identify social laws with biological laws or physical laws" (433).

2 This argument is supported by Sharon Harris's reading of the final lines of the story as an ironic critique of simple Christian moralism in "Rebecca Harding Davis: From Romanticism to Realism," *American Literary Realism* 21, no. 2 (1989): 4–20.

3 Rebecca Harding Davis, "Life in the Iron-Mills," in *A Rebecca Harding Davis Reader*, ed. Jean Pfaelzer (Pittsburgh, PA: University of Pittsburgh Press, 1995), 3–34; 34. See Schurr who reads the story as a tale of conversion, and Rose, who reads Davis as a "devout Christian" (11). Hughes argues that the story is at once Christian and radical—classifying Davis's strategy as "liberationist."

4 See Caroline Miles, "Representing and Self-Mutilating the Laboring Male Body: Re-examining Rebecca Harding Davis's *Life in the Iron-Mills*," *American Transcendental Quarterly* 18 (2004): 89–104; and Mark Seltzer, *Bodies and Machines* (New York: Routledge, 1997).

5 Naomi Sofer sees Davis's portrayal of artists as a critique of "genius," arguing that Davis, along with other late-century women writers like Phelps, Alcott, and Woolson, saw the notion of the author as artistic genius limiting to women writers. Sofer turns to Davis's "Earthen Pitchers" and "Marcia" for her proof. I find these stories to lack the artistic optimism of "Life in the Iron-Mills" because, within them, the artist's work is not imputed particular merit, nor is it preserved.

6 Dana Seitler, "Strange Beauty: The Politics of Ungenre in Rebecca Harding Davis's *Life in the Iron-Mills*," *American Literature* 86, no. 3 (2014): 523–49; 523.

7 Jeff Nunokawa, *The Afterlife of Property* (Princeton, NJ: Princeton University Press, 2001), 6.

8 Sarah Ruffing Robbins, "Harriet Beecher Stowe, Starring as Benevolent Celebrity Traveler," in *Transatlantic Women: Nineteenth-Century American Women Writers and Great Britain*, ed. Beth Lynne Lueck, Brigitte Bailey, and Lucinda L. Damon-Bach (Durham: University of New Hampshire Press, 2012), 71–88.

9 See Sarah Meer, *Uncle Tom Mania: Slavery, Minstrelsy, and Transatlantic Culture in the 1850s* (Athens: University of Georgia Press, 2005); and Adena Spingarn, *Uncle Tom from Martyr to Traitor* (Redwood City: Stanford University Press, 2018).

10 Barbara Hochman, *"Uncle Tom's Cabin" and the Reading Revolution: Race, Literacy, Childhood, and Fiction, 1851–1911* (Amherst: University of Massachusetts Press, 2011), 201.

11 "Publishers Notes," *The Connecticut Magazine* 5 (1899): 251–52, 252.

12 Brenda R. Weber, *Women and Literary Celebrity in the Nineteenth Century: The Transatlantic Production of Fame and Gender* (New York: Routledge, 2012), 9.

13 Loren Glass, *Authors Inc.: Literary Celebrity in the Modern United States, 1880–1980* (New York: New York University Press, 2004), 11.

14 Sharon Harris observes Davis's reticence in this regard, pointing out that Davis responded to a reader's 1886 request for a photograph, "I should be very glad to send my photograph if it would give a moment's pleasure to [an] invalid who I am sure is trying to make the best of her suffering but there is no such thing to send. I have had no picture taken for nearly thirty years"; Harris goes on to conclude that Davis's "staunch belief in personal privacy had ingrained 'a great aversion to seeing a portrait of myself,' and she would not breach that aversion for readers or

NOTES TO PAGES 33–37   *199*

publishers." *Rebecca Harding Davis and American Realism* (Philadelphia: University of Pennsylvania Press, 1991), 222.

15 The photograph of Davis is undated but was likely taken before the publication of "Life in the Iron-Mills" and is extant in a private family collection. A second photograph, sometimes supposed to be of Davis, is dated after her death and therefore likely pictures a relative.

16 Michael Kearns, *Writing for the Street, Writing in the Garret: Melville, Dickinson, and Private Publication* (Columbus: Ohio State University Press, 2010), 27.

17 Mark Twain, *The Autobiography of Mark Twain*, vol. 1, ed. Harriet Elinor Smith (Berkeley: University of California Press, 2010), 230. It may be worth pointing out that the writer of the greatest "submerged renown" cited by Stevenson, according to Twain, is called Davis. There is, however, no way to prove any relation between the Davis considered by Twain and Stevenson in this anecdote and the Davis treated here.

18 Susan Ryan, *The Moral Economies of American Authorship: Reputation, Scandal, and the Nineteenth-Century Literary Marketplace* (New York: Oxford University Press, 2016), 11.

19 Stephen Knadler describes Davis's "own self-imagining as an outsider" because of her gender and, even more so, her regional identity. Stephen Knadler, "Miscegenated Whiteness: Rebecca Harding Davis, the 'Civil-izing' War, and Female Racism," *Nineteenth-Century Literature* 57, no. 1 (2002).

20 Rebecca Harding Davis, *A Rebecca Harding Davis Reader*, ed. Jean Pfaelzer (Pittsburgh, PA: University of Pittsburgh Press, 1995), 403. All subsequent page numbers for quotations from Davis works refer to this Davis Reader unless otherwise specified.

21 "Popular Birthdays," *Life* (June 23, 1910): 1152.

22 Rebecca Harding Davis, "A New National Trait," *The Independent,* October 31, 1889, 1.

23 For an expanded bibliography, see Jane Atteridge Rose, "A Complete Bibliography of Fiction and Non-Fiction by Rebecca Harding Davis," *American Literary Realism 1870–1910* 22, no. 3 (1990): 67–86.

24 Patricia Okker concludes that Davis's simultaneous publication in both magazines allowed her to divide her literary output between that intended to generate income (the *Peterson's* stories) and that intended to generate reputation (*The Atlantic* stories) in *Social Stories: The Magazine Novel in Nineteenth-Century America* (Charlottesville: University of Virginia Press, 2003).

25 For example, "Our Armchair" in the November 1885 issue states "[Peterson's] alone has such contributors as Mrs. Ann S. Stephens, Frank Leo Benedict, Rebecca Harding Davis, Mrs. John Sherwood, Edgar Fawcett . . . and the several authors of 'Josiah Allen's Wife,' . . . 'The Second Life,' etc., etc." Rebecca Harding Davis, "Our Armchair," *Peterson's Magazine* 88 (1885): 456.

26 David Dowling, "Davis, Inc.: The Business of Asylum Reform in the Periodical Press," *American Periodicals* 20, no. 1 (2010): 26.

27 We know, for example, that the Alcott family subscribed to both magazines. (Orchard House Museum; Concord, Massachusetts).

28 Michele L. Mock, "'An Ardor That Was Human, and a Power That Was Art': Rebecca Harding Davis and the Art of the Periodical," in *"The Only Efficient*

Instrument": American Women Writers and the Periodical 1837–1916, ed. Aleta Feinsod Cane and Susan Alves (Iowa City: University of Iowa Press, 2001), 126.

29 "Earthen Pitchers," in Pfaelzer, *A Rebecca Harding Davis Reader*, 215–86, 217.

30 We might examine the political implications of Davis's plagiarism—both of her own work and that of Dickens, discussed later—along the lines that scholars of Oscar Wilde use to consider his similar publication practices. Florina Tufescu reads Wilde's plagiarism as a refusal to accept romantic notions of authorship and creativity in *Oscar Wilde's Plagiarism: The Triumph of Art over Ego* (Dublin: Irish Academic Press, 2008). Paul Saint-Amour argues that Wilde's plagiarism is a form of protest against the commodification of the work of art in *Copywrights: Intellectual Property and the Literary Imagination* (Ithaca, NY: Cornell University Press, 2003).

31 Jane Atteridge Rose, *Rebecca Harding Davis* (New York: Twayne Publisher, 1993), 41; Harris, *Davis and American Realism*, 126.

32 Helen Woodward Sheaffer, "Rebecca Harding Davis: Pioneer Realist" (PhD diss., University of Pennsylvania, 1947), 117.

33 Dowling argues that Davis and her husband, the journalist and editor L. Clarke Davis, wielded their combined influence in the periodical press to widely disseminate the message of asylum reform.

34 Amanda Claybaugh, *The Novel of Purpose: Literature and Social Reform in the Anglo-American World* (Ithaca, NY: Cornell University Press, 2007), 52.

35 Juliet John, *Dickens and Mass Culture* (New York: Oxford University Press, 2010), 129.

36 Rose, *Rebecca Harding Davis*, 50.

37 Jean Pfaelzer, *Parlor Radical: Rebecca Harding Davis and the Origins of Social Realism* (Pittsburgh, PA: University of Pittsburgh Press, 1996), 7.

38 Davis, "Life," 6.

39 Pfaelzer characterizes the tone of the narration as "hostile" and Andrew Lawson identifies "the distance between speaker and addressee" as that between "embittered initiate and naive ingénue." Pfaelzer, *Parlor Radical*, 24; Andrew Lawson, *Downwardly Mobile: The Changing Fortunes of American Realism* (New York: Oxford University Press, 2012), 44. Jonathan Arac writes "the narrator remains at a meditative distance, not actively involved like 'personal' narrators, or, in her different way, like Stowe. The narrator's attitude to the working characters fluctuates between aesthetic and scientific and is never so fundamentally passional as in Stowe" in *The Emergence of American Literary Narrative, 1820–1860* (Cambridge, MA: Harvard University Press, 2005), 196–97.

40 Davis, "Life," 435.

41 Harriet Elizabeth Beecher Stowe, *Uncle Tom's Cabin: A Tale, or Life Among the Lowly* (London: George Routledge and Company, 1852), 30.

42 Rebecca Harding Davis, "John Lamar," in Pfaelzer, *A Rebecca Harding Davis Reader*, 35–53; 36.

43 Davis, "John Lamar," 45.

44 Keith Tester, *Humanitarianism and Modern Culture* (University Park: Penn State University Press, 2010), 1.

45 See also Ilan Kapoor, *Celebrity Humanitarianism: The Rise of Global Charity* (New York: Routledge, 2013).

46 See Tester and Kapoor, respectively, for descriptions and analyses of Live Aid and Save Darfur.

47 Tester, *Humanitarianism*, 58.

48 Frank Christianson, *Philanthropy in British and American Fiction: Dickens, Hawthorne, Eliot and Howells* (Edinburgh: Edinburgh University Press, 2007), 13.

49 Rebecca Harding Davis, "The Newly Discovered Woman," *The Independent*, November 30, 1893, 5.

50 Rebecca Harding Davis, "Bits of Gossip," in *Rebecca Harding Davis: Writing Cultural Autobiography*, ed. Janice Milner Lasseter and Sharon Harris (Nashville, TN: Vanderbilt University Press, 2001), 5.

51 Rebecca Harding Davis, *A Law Unto Herself* (Philadelphia, PA: J. B. Lippincott, 1878), 20.

52 Rebecca Harding Davis, *Kitty's Choice; or A Story of Berrytown* (Philadelphia: J. B. Lippincott, 1874), 5.

53 Charles Dickens, *Hard Times* (New York: Norton, 2001), 52.

54 Davis, "Life," 16.

55 Eric Schocket, "'Discovering Some New Race': Rebecca Harding Davis's 'Life in the Irons Mills' and the Literary Emergence of Working-Class Whiteness," *PMLA* 115, no. 1 (2001): 46–59.

56 Dickens, *Hard Times*, 20; Davis, "Life," 3.

57 Schocket, "'Discovering Some New Race,'" 49.

58 Michael Slater, *Charles Dickens* (New Haven, CT: Yale University Press, 2009), 185.

59 Charles Dickens, *American Notes for General Circulation*, ed. John S. Whitley and Arnold Goldman (New York: Penguin, 1972), 269.

60 See Slater, and the editorial comments in the Penguin *American Notes*. Weld did not sign his name as author to the pamphlet.

61 John, *Dickens and Mass Culture*, 5.

62 Quoted in Malcolm Andrews, *Charles Dickens and His Performing Selves: Dickens and the Public Readings* (New York: Oxford University Press, 2007), 31.

63 Letter of Sunday, March 1, 1868, to Annie Fields at the University of Virginia. I'm grateful to Sharon Harris for generously providing me with her transcript of this letter.

64 Charles Dickens, "Personal," *Household Words*, June 12, 1958, 601.

65 While rumors of the dissolution of the Dickens marriage were widespread among publishing circles in London, Slater points out "the result of the publication of Dickens's 'Personal' statement was, naturally, to publicise his domestic difficulties far beyond the world of the metropolitan literati," 455.

66 Elizabeth Gaskell, *The Letters of Mrs. Gaskell* (Cambridge, MA: Harvard University Press, 1967), 538.

67 Rebecca Harding Davis, "Blind Black Tom," *All the Year Round*, October 18, 1862, 126.

68 Critics have historically grouped "Blind Tom" with "David Gaunt," "John Lamar," and *Waiting for the Verdict* as her abolition stories.

69 For more on Bethune's life, see Deirdre O'Connell, *The Ballad of Blind Tom, Slave Pianist* (New York: Overlook, 2009) and Geneva Handy Southall, *Blind Tom, the Black Pianist-Composer (1849–1908): Continually Enslaved* (Lanham, MD: Scarecrow Press, 2002).

70 Rebecca Harding Davis, "Blind Tom," in Pfaelzer, *A Rebecca Harding Davis Reader*, 104–11; 105.

71 Davis, "Blind Tom," 107.

72 Davis, "Blind Tom," 109.

73 Davis, "Blind Tom," 106.

74 Davis, "Blind Tom," 110. Both Knadler and Schocket have described Davis's disturbing tendency to equate the position of suffering white, working-class characters to that of enslaved African Americans. Knadler describes how Davis uses such comparisons in her novel *Waiting for the Verdict* to undertake a larger project of redefining white subjecthood. Here, I argue that we see Davis imagining herself in the position of the African American artist. The shocking exaggeration of his racial characteristics performs Davis's perception of the white crowd viewing the outsider, as Knadler argues she imagined herself (a "backwoods" woman) to be viewed by the predominately male, New England *Atlantic* coterie.

75 Davis, "Life," 32.

76 Davis, "Blind Tom," 106.

77 Quoted in Jean Fagan Yellin's afterword to *Margret Howth* by Rebecca Harding Davis (New York: CUNY Feminist Press, 1990), 285.

78 Boyd describes how Fields "printed many of the women's stories, some of which he considered second-rate, with the intention of providing both 'leavening' and popularity for the magazine," emphasizing that especially in the 1880s and 1890s, "it rewarded those who conformed to its assumptions about women inhabiting a separate sphere in literature and in life. Thus, women writers gained the highest praise from editors for their local color literature, which was deemed of 'minor' importance in comparison to the great works that would be enshrined as America's high literature." Anne E. Boyd, "'What! Has She Got into the *Atlantic*?: Women Writers, the *Atlantic Monthly*, and the Formation of the American Canon," *American Studies* 39, no. 3 (1998): 5–36; 18, 10.

79 See Kirk Curnutt, "Direct Addresses, Narrative Authority, and Gender in Rebecca Harding Davis's 'Life in the Iron-Mills,'" *Style* 28, no. 2 (1994): 146–68. Curnutt reads the gender of the narrator as intentionally ambiguous, applying Robyn Warhol's term—"cross-gendered narrative"—to the story's voice. The *New York Times* 1910 obituary of Davis included the statement "When 'Life in the Iron-Mills' appeared in the *Atlantic Monthly*, many thought the author must be a man." Special to the *New York Times*, "Rebecca H. Davis, Novelist, Is Dead," *New York Times* (September 30, 1910), 13. Jane Atteridge Rose cites the story's "masculine narrative voice" in "Reading 'Life in the Iron-Mills' Contextually: A Key to Rebecca Harding Davis's Fiction," *Conversations: Contemporary Critical Theory and the Teaching of Literature*, ed. Charles Penfield and Elizabeth F. Moran (Urbana, IL: National Council of Teachers of English, 1990), 187–99; 191. Patricia Okker reads the narrator's political questioning as evidence of "realistic or naturalistic tendencies" in *Social Stories*, 133.

80 Cowley is quoted in Sarah Gooding Britton, "The Silent Partnership," in *Twisted from the Ordinary: Essays on American Literary Naturalism*, ed. Mary E. Papke (Knoxville: University of Tennessee Press, 2003), 1–22, 332.

81 Bill Brown reads the story as central to a history of nineteenth-century "disputes about the arts and the aesthetic in America" in "The Origin of the American Work of Art," *American Literary History* 25, no. 4 (2013): 772–802; 777.

82 Davis, "Life," 34.

83 Davis, "Life," 34.

84 Lawson reads them as "surface accomplishments of the bourgeoisie," Pfaelzer as the fruits of sublimation, arguing that they "suggest female incompletion and sterility" (*Downwardly Mobile*, 61; *Parlor Radical*, 53).

85 Seitler, "Strange Beauty," 545.

86 Brown suggests that we read the nakedness of the korl woman statue as a part of the mid-century tradition of divesting works of art of markers of historical particularity.

87 Davis, "Life," 5.

88 Seitler, "Strange Beauty," 546.

89 Caroline Miles sees the korl woman as Hugh's failed attempt to remake his own body and, coupled with Hugh's suicide, as the story's participation in the objectification and destruction of the worker. By contrast, I suggest that if we cease to consider the korl woman sculpture a failure—and its continuing power to inspire both the narrator and the readers surely testify to its success—we can, by extension, see that Davis is not failing to imagine Hugh as a subject but rather upsetting how we construct subjects, by offering art in the place of individuals.

90 Davis, "Life," 20.

91 Davis, "Life," 15–16.

92 Davis, "Life," 19.

93 Andrew Silver, "'Unnatural Unions': Picturesque Travel, Sexual Politics, and Working-Class Representation in 'A Night Under Ground' and 'Life in the Iron-Mills,'" *Legacy* 20, no. 2 (2003): 94–117.

94 Davis, "Life," 12.

95 Seitler, "Strange Beauty," 541.

96 Davis, "Life," 20.

97 Davis, "Life," 15.

98 Harris views the identification of Hugh with Mitchell as the worker's acceptance of capitalist ideas of beauty, while Pfaelzer acknowledges Mitchell's "complicated relationship with Hugh" and acknowledges that "ultimately it is Mitchell who politicizes the images of fire and light surrounding Hugh," *Davis and American Realism*, 37; *Parlor Radical*, 46.

99 Davis, "Life," 13.

100 Davis, "Life," 17.

101 Davis, "Life," 16.

102 Davis, "Life," 10.

103 Alan Bray, *Homosexuality in Renaissance England* (New York: Columbia University Press, 1982), 86.

104 Davis, "Life," 10–11.

105 Alan Sinfeld, *The Wilde Century: Effeminacy, Oscar Wilde, and the Queer Moment* (New York: Columbia University Press, 1994), 41.

106 Richard Dellamora, *Masculine Desire: The Sexual Politics of Victorian Aestheticism* (Durham: University of North Carolina Press, 1990), 198.

107 Charles Baudelaire, *The Painter of Modern Life and Other Essays*, trans. Jonathan Mayne (New York: Phaidon, 1995), 28–29.

108 Jules Barbey D'Aurevilly, *Dandyism*, trans. Doublas Ainslie (New York: PAJ, 1988), 33.

109 D'Aurevilly, *Dandyism*, 16.

110 Davis, "Life," 18.

111 Davis, "Life," 24.

112 Baudelaire, *Painter of Modern Life*, 28.

113 Davis, "Life," 25–26.

114 Davis, "Life," 11.

115 Davis, "Life," 7.

116 Regina Gagnier, *Idylls of the Marketplace: Oscar Wilde and the Victorian Public* (Redwood City: Stanford University Press, 1986), 79.

117 Miles, "Representing and Self-Mutilating the Laboring Male Body," 99, 100.

118 Sheila Hassell Hughes, "Between Bodies of Knowledge there is a Great Gulf Fixed: Liberationist Reading of Class and Gender in Life in the Iron-Mills," *American Quarterly* 49 (1997): 113–37; 127.

119 Davis, "Life," 10.

120 Davis, "Life," 5.

121 Davis, "Life," 14, 34, 34.

122 See "The Disease of Money-Getting" and "Is It All for Nothing?" for Davis's anti-consumerist articles. Her fictional works "Anne," "Marcia," and the novella *Earthen Pitchers* all grapple with female artists' struggle for expression and survival. All texts mentioned here are reprinted in Pfaelzer's *Rebecca Harding Davis Reader*.

123 Pfaezler, *Rebecca Harding Davis Reader*, 214.

124 Pfaezler, *Rebecca Harding Davis Reader*, 214.

CHAPTER TWO: KATE CHOPIN'S ART PANIC

1 Kate Chopin, "The Awakening," *Redbook* 140, no. 1 (November 1972): 199–221; 199.

2 Barbara Ewell, "Linked Fortunes: Kate Chopin, The Short Story (and Me)," in *Awakenings: The Story of the Kate Chopin Revival*, ed. Bernard Koloski (Baton Rouge: Louisiana State University Press, 2009): 32–46; 42.

3 Quoted in Emily Toth, *Unveiling Kate Chopin* (Jackson: University of Mississippi Press, 1999), 112.

4 Kate Chopin, *At Fault* (St. Louis: Nixon Jones, 1890), 214.

5 Ann Heilman, "*The Awakening* and New Woman Fiction" in *The Cambridge Companion to Kate Chopin*, ed. Janet Beer (Cambridge: Cambridge University Press, 2008): 87–104, 87.

6 Donna Campbell, *Bitter Tastes: Literary Naturalism and Early Cinema in American Women's Writing* (Athens: University of Georgia Press, 2016), 4.

7 See Burt Bender, *The Descent of Love: Darwin and the Theory of Sexual Selection in American Fiction, 1871–1926* (Philadelphia: University of Pennsylvania Press, 1996); Donald Pizer, "A Note on Kate Chopin's *The Awakening* as Naturalistic Fiction," *The Southern Literary Journal* 33, no. 2 (2001): 5–13; Eric Margraf, "Kate

Chopin's *The Awakening* as a Naturalistic Novel," *American Literary Realism* 37, no. 2 (2005): 93–116; Jean Witherow, "Flaubert's Vision and Chopin's Naturalistic Revision," *Southern Studies* 8, no. 1–2 (1997): 27–36; and Jennifer Fleissner, *Women, Compulsion, Modernity* (Chicago: University of Chicago Press, 2004).

8 Nancy Bentley, *Frantic Panoramas: American Literature and Mass Culture, 1870–1920* (Philadelphia: University of Pennsylvania Press, 2009), 140.

9 Toth, *Unveiling Kate Chopin*, 124.

10 Susan Wolstenholme. "Kate Chopin's Sources for 'Mrs. Mobry's Reason,'" *American Literature* 51, no. 4 (1980): 540–43.

11 Kate Chopin, "Emile Zola's 'Lourdes,'" in *The Complete Works of Kate Chopin*, ed. Per Seyersted (Baton Rouge: Louisiana State University Press, 1997), 697–99; 697.

12 Campbell, *Bitter Tastes*, 93.

13 Quoted in E. Maynial, *L'Epoque réaliste sous le Second Empire* (Paris: Hachette, 1913), 67. Translation by Marie Satya McDonough.

14 A. A. Cuvillier-Fleury, "Madame Bovary," *Journal des Débats,* May 26, 1857. Translation by Marie Satya McDonough.

15 Jill Kelly, "Photographic Reality and French Literary Realism: Nineteenth-Century Synchronism and Symbiosis," *The French Review* 65, no. 2 (1991): 195–205; 203.

16 Kate Chopin, "The Awakening," in Seyersted, *The Complete Works of Kate Chopin*, 881–1000; 881, 897.

17 Chopin, "The Awakening," 937.

18 Chopin, "The Awakening," 891.

19 Chopin, "The Awakening," 946.

20 See Patricia S. Yaeger, "'A Language Which Nobody Understood': Emancipatory Strategies in *The Awakening*," *NOVEL: A Forum on Fiction* 20, no. 3 (1987): 197–219. Yaeger argues that Edna lacks the language to articulate her dissent. Also, Cynthia Griffin Wolff, "Thanatos and Eros: Kate Chopin's *The Awakening*," *American Quarterly* 25 (1973): 449–71. Wolff argues that Edna's suicide is a regressive act. Lastly, Jennifer Gray sees Edna's feminist revolt as forestalled by an inescapable, Althusserian ideological paradigm in "The Escape of the 'Sea': Ideology and *The Awakening*," *Southern Literary Journal* 37, no. 1 (2004): 53–73.

21 Chopin, "The Awakening," 906.

22 Much has been written on commodity consumption in *The Awakening*. An excellent example of this criticism is Margit Stange, "Exchange Value and the Female Self in *The Awakening*," in *Personal Property: Wives, White Slaves, and the Market in Women* (Baltimore: Johns Hopkins University Press, 1998), 21–35.

23 Chopin, "The Awakening," 936, 904, 958.

24 Chopin, "The Awakening," 40, 43.

25 Chopin, "The Awakening," 43.

26 Chopin, "The Awakening," 46.

27 Nick Gaskill, "'The Light Which, Showing the Way, Forbids It': Reconstructing Aesthetics in *The Awakening*," *Studies in American Fiction* 34, no. 2 (2006): 161–88; 171.

28 Chopin, "The Awakening," 976.

29 Chopin, "The Awakening," 890.

30 Chopin, "The Awakening," 898.

31 Walter Benn Michaels, "The Contracted Heart," *New Literary History* 21, no. 3 (1990): 495–531; 503.

32 Chopin, "The Awakening," 967, 960, 971.

33 Emily Toth surmises that the painter and the writer may have met in *Unveiling Kate Chopin*, and Christopher Benfey explores their connection in a study of Degas's time in *New Orleans in Degas in New Orleans: Encounters in the Creole World of Kate Chopin and George Washington Cable* (Berkeley: University of California Press, 1999). The more relevant relation may actually be between Cézanne and Zola, who Chopin much admired. Meyer Schapiro suggests that the subject matter of a basket of apples held a personal resonance for Cézanne in addition to the more obvious associations with the fall: "In his later years [Cézanne] recalled in conversation that an offering of apples had sealed his friendship with Zola. At school in Aix Cezanne had shown his sympathy for the younger boy who had been ostracized by his fellow-students. Himself impulsive and refractory, Cezanne took a thrashing from the others for defying them and talking to Zola. 'The next day he brought me a big basket of apples. 'Ah, Cezanne's apples!' he said, with a playful wink, 'they go far back.'" Meyer Schapiro, *Modern Art* (New York: George Braziller, 1978), 4.

34 Peter Brooks devotes a chapter to Courbet in *Realist Vision* (New Haven, CT: Yale University Press, 2005), in which he argues that Courbet's primary aim in *A Burial at Ornans* and the other works that he hung in the 1850 Salon (*The Stone-Breakers* and *The Sowers*) was, like Flaubert's, to make the reader/viewer uncomfortable by portraying humble individuals on an epic scale (77).

35 Schapiro, *Modern Art*, 12.

36 Her 1867 composition on Christian Art, which survives in her commonplace book, also suggests a considerable degree of formal art education. Kate Chopin, *Private Papers*, ed. Emily Toth and Per Seyersted (Bloomington: Indiana University Press, 1998): 31–35.

37 Kate Chopin, "'Crumbling Idols' by Hamlin Garland," in Seyersted, *The Complete Works of Kate Chopin*, 693–94; Chopin, "Emile Zola's 'Lourdes'"; Kate Chopin, "Confidences," in Seyersted, *The Complete Works of Kate Chopin*, 700–702; 700–701.

38 While James O'Rourke claims that Lebrun's name is a reference to his racial ambiguity, I find it far more likely that Chopin had the painter in mind in "Secrets and Lies: Race and Sex in *The Awakening*," *Legacy* 16, no. 2 (1999): 168–76.

39 Chopin, *Private Papers*, 172; Henry Tyrrell, "The Paris Salon," *Frank Leslie's Popular Monthly* 36, no. 1 (July 1893): 2–18. Other examples include "The Royal Academy of Painting and Sculpture in France" by Lady Dilke, an article from the London *Fortnightly Review* reprinted in the United States in *The Eclectic Magazine of Foreign Literature* in January of 1887; "A History of French Art," and an anonymously authored review of the Brownell's comprehensive history *French Art* in the October 1893 *The Art Amateur*.

40 Paul Duro notes that these debates themselves were an imitation of the lectures on art theory in the Roman and Florentian academies and the debate over the reproduction of older works by younger artists was surely nothing new in "'The Surest Measure of Perfection': Approaches to Imitation in Seventeenth-Century French Art and Theory," *Word & Image* 25, no. 4 (2009): 363–83, 366.

NOTES TO PAGES 74–78   *207*

41 Duro, "Surest Measure of Perfection," 374.

42 Nathaniel Hawthorne, *The Marble Faun*, vol. 1 (Boston: Ticknor and Fields, 1860), 158.

43 The National Vigilance Association, "Pernicious Literature," in *Documents of Modern Literary Realism*, ed. George J. Becker (Princeton, NJ: Princeton University Press, 1963): 350–82; 352.

44 Molly McGarry, "Spectral Sexualities: Nineteenth-Century Spiritualism, Moral Panics, and the Making of U.S. Obscenity Law," *Journal of Women's History* 12, no. 2 (2000): 8–29; 17.

45 Nicola K. Beisel, *Anthony Comstock & Family Reproduction in Victorian America* (Princeton, NJ: Princeton University Press, 1996), 163.

46 Aaron Powell, ed., *The National Purity Congress: Its Papers, Addresses, and Portraits* (New York: The American Purity Alliance, 1896), 9.

47 New Woman novelists like Sarah Grand, Ouida, Charlotte Perkins Gilman, Victoria Woodhull, and Grant Allen held widely varying social and political opinions.

48 See Lucy Bland, *Banishing the Beast: Sexuality and the Early Feminists* (New York: New Press, 1995) for more about Social Purity feminism in the American context.

49 See, for example: David J. Pivar, *Purity and Hygiene: Women, Prostitution, and the "American Plan," 1900–1930* (Westport, CT; Greenwood Press, 2002); Katherine Mullin, *James Joyce, Sexuality and Social Purity* (Cambridge: Cambridge University Press, 2003); Christopher Pittard, *Purity and Contamination in Late Victorian Detective Fiction* (Surrey: Ashgate, 2011); Christine DeVine, "Marginalized Maisie: Social Purity and What Maisie Knew," *Victorian Newsletter* 99 (2001): 7–15.

50 Chopin, "Mrs. Mobry's Reason," in Seyersted, *The Complete Works of Kate Chopin*, 79.

51 Elaine Showalter, "Syphilis, Sexuality, and the Fiction of the Fin de Siècle," in *Sex, Politics and Science in the Nineteenth-Century Novel*, ed. Ruth Bernard Yeazel (Baltimore: Johns Hopkins University Press, 1986): 88–115; 95.

52 B. O. Flower, "Prostitution Within the Marriage Bond," *The Arena* 13 (1895): 59–73; 60.

53 Roger N. Lancaster, *Sex Panic and the Punitive State* (Berkeley: University of California Press, 2011), 232.

54 Margaret Oliphant, "The Anti-Marriage League," *Blackwood's Edinburgh Magazine*, January 1896, 135–49; 144, 142.

55 The most influential library, with the largest circulation, was Mudie's—an organization that demanded its selections be family-friendly and published in three volumes. Paul Delany writes that "The name 'Mudie's Select Library' meant that Mudie himself guaranteed that all his fiction would be decent and moral.... In 1840–70 all the major novels were put out by seven publishers, and Mudie's might order more than half of a novel's press run." *Literature, Money, and the Market: From Trollope to Amis* (New York: Palgrave, 2002), 104–5. Several authors protested the power and censorship practices of Mudie's, including George Moore, whose scathing pamphlet "Literature at Nurse, or Circulating Morals" was published by Vizetelly in 1885. In 1894, Mudie's, and its only rival even roughly equivalent in size, Smith's, issued a decree that they would pay no more than 4s. per volume, a decision which ostensibly ended their reign of control as from then on publishers would produce volumes at a price point that would allow private individuals to purchase them

208 NOTES TO PAGES 78–85

directly. For a more detailed account of this history, see Guinevere L. Greist, *Mudie's Circulating Library and the Victorian Novel* (Bloomington: Indiana University Press, 1970).

56 Delany, *Literature, Money, and the Market*, 106.

57 Rita [Eliza Margaret Humpreys], "The Modern Young Person," *Belgravia* 86 (1895): 61–64; 61.

58 Powell, *National Purity Congress*, 357, 375.

59 Kate Chopin, "As You Like It," in Seyersted, *The Complete Works of Kate Chopin*, 706–20; 714, 713–14, 715.

60 Ewell, "Linked Fortunes," 40.

61 Kate Chopin, "In the Confidence of a Story-Writer," in Seyersted, *The Complete Works of Kate Chopin*, 703–5; 703.

62 Aaron Matz, *Satire in an Age of Realism* (Cambridge: Cambridge University Press, 2010), xiv.

63 Chopin, "As You Like It," 709.

64 Chopin, "As You Like It."

65 Kate Chopin, "Miss Witherwell's Mistake," in Seyersted, *The Complete Works of Kate Chopin*, 59–66; 59.

66 Chopin, "Miss Witherwell's Mistake," 62. If the reader somehow misses the implied quality of the *Boredomville Battery* and the kind of periodical it's meant to lambaste, Chopin's naming of the guard "Cerberus" at the top of the stairs also signals her opinion of the editorial offices that publish work like Miss Witherwell's.

67 Chopin, "Miss Witherwell's Mistake," 65. Nancy Walker, one of the story's few critics, also sees Miss Witherwell as Chopin's satire of a female journalist bent on "conventional melodramatic fiction" in "'A Group of People at My Disposal': Humor in the Works of Kate Chopin," *Legacy* 17, no. 1 (2000): 48–58; 50.

68 Chopin, "The Awakening," 898.

69 Chopin, "The Awakening," 882.

70 Chopin, "The Awakening," 887.

71 Chopin, "The Awakening," 931.

72 Ivy Schweitzer, "Maternal Discourse and the Romance of Self-Possession in Kate Chopin's *The Awakening*," *boundary 2* 17, no. 1 (1990): 158–86; 175, 177.

73 Both Philip Fisher, *Still the New World* (Cambridge, MA: Harvard University Press, 1999) and Gillian Brown, *Domestic Individualism* (Berkeley: University of California Press, 1990) argue that though "sentimentalism has operated as a representational tactic for extending human rights to the disenfranchised, it nevertheless retains the slave or woman or child within the inventory of human proprietorship" (Brown 41). Edna begins to acknowledge and reject proprietorship as the mechanism of her subjugation.

74 Chopin, "The Awakening," 984.

75 John W. Crowley, "Kate Chopin, Frédéric Chopin, and the Music of the Future," *American Literary Realism* 47, no. 2 (2015): 95–116; 111.

76 Silas Weir Mitchell (1829–1914) was a successful nerve doctor who prescribed the "rest cure" for women and the "West cure" for men who were suffering from neurasthenia. Charlotte Perkins Gilman sought treatment from Mitchell in 1887,

which she later felt only worsened her symptoms, prompting her to write "The Yellow Wall-Paper" (1892). Mitchell also treated Rebecca Harding Davis and Edith Wharton.

77 Chopin, "The Awakening," 916.

78 Chopin, "The Awakening," 890.

79 Chopin, "The Awakening," 900.

80 Chopin, "The Awakening."

81 Chopin, "The Awakening," 927.

82 Pierre Bourdieu, *Distinction: A Social Critique of the Judgment of Taste*, trans. Richard Nice (Cambridge, MA: Harvard University Press, 1984), 26.

83 Chopin, "The Awakening," 957; Linda Dowling, "The Decadent and the New Woman in the 1890's," *Nineteenth-Century Fiction* 33, no. 4 (1979): 434–53; 435.

84 Ellen Moers, *The Dandy* (New York: The Viking Press, 1960), 311.

85 Dowling, "The Decadent and the New Woman," 438.

86 Chopin, "The Awakening," 881–1000, 969.

87 Chopin, "The Awakening," 957, 970; 972.

88 See, for example, Lawrence Thornton, *"The Awakening*: A Political Romance," *American Literature* 52, no. 2 (1980): 50–66. Thornton argues that "Whereas Flaubert is interested in exposing the dry-rot of romanticism, Chopin is concerned with a woman whose susceptibility to romantic codes ultimately gives way to at least a partial understanding of the lie that animated her visions" (51).

89 Mary E. Papke, "So Long as We Read Chopin," in Koloski, *Awakenings*, 77–93; 77.

90 Henry James, "The Art of Fiction," in *A Victorian Art of Fiction: Essays on the Novel in British Periodicals 1870-1900*, ed. John Charles Olmsted (New York: Routledge, 2016): 285–306; 304.

CHAPTER THREE: POLITICAL INTIMACY IN HENRY JAMES

1 Henry James, *The Bostonians*, vol. 1 (London: Macmillan and Co., 1921), 193.

2 Joyce L. Jenkins, "Art Against Equality," in "Jane Austen's Darwinian Gambit," special issue, *Philosophy and Literature*, suppl. 22, no. 1 (1998): 108–18; 108.

3 Kent Puckett, "Make No Mistake: Getting it Right in *The Princess Casamassima*," *NOVEL: A Forum on Fiction* 43, no. 1 (2010): 60–66; 64.

4 Henry James, *The Princess Casamassima* (New York: Penguin, 1977), 352.

5 Lionel Trilling, *The Liberal Imagination: Essays on Literature and Society* (New York: Viking, 1950), 82.

6 James, *The Princess Casamassima*, 530

7 James, *The Princess Casamassima*, 368, 353.

8 Thomas J. Otten, "Slashing Henry James (On Painting and Political Economy, Circa 1900)," *Yale Journal of Criticism* 13, no. 2 (2000): 293–320; 296.

9 Peter Brooks, *Realist Vision* (New Haven, CT: Yale University Press, 2005), 16.

10 Henry James, *Portrait of a Lady* (Boston: Houghton, Mifflin and Company, 1882), 175.

11 James, *The Bostonians*, 18.

12 James, *The Bostonians*, 34, 31.

13 James, *The Bostonians*, 184.
14 Jonathan L. Freedman, *Professions of Taste: Henry James, British Aestheticism, and Commodity Culture* (Stanford, CA: Stanford University Press, 1990), xix.
15 Autumn M. Womack, "Object Lesson(s)," *Women & Performance: a journal of feminist theory* 27, no. 1 (2017): 59–66; 62.
16 Lulu Chang, "Remember Joe the Plumber, Guys?," *Bustle*, May 22, 2014, https://www.bustle.com/articles/25343-whatever-happened-to-joe-the-plumber-the-average-joe-who-wasnt-actually-a-plumber.
17 Scott Detrow, "A Few Minutes with Joe the Plumber," *State House Sound Bites* (blog), February 13, 2010, https://scottdetrow.wordpress.com/2010/02/13/a-few-minutes-with-joe-the-plumber/.
18 Terry Castle and Hugh Stevens both see the ending of *The Bostonians* as James's depiction of a tragic scenario sympathetic to Olive and therefore same-sex love, and Sarah Daugherty sees Miss Chancellor as a character open to multiple interpretations, dependent upon the reader's orientation. Terry Castle, *The Apparitional Lesbian: Female Homosexuality and Modern Culture* (New York: Columbia University Press, 1993); Hugh Stevens, *Henry James and Sexuality* (Cambridge: Cambridge University Press, 1999); Sarah Daugherty, "*The Bostonians* and the Crisis of Vocation," in *A Companion to Henry James*, ed. Greg W. Zacharias (Malden, MA: Wiley Blackwell, 2008), 88–99.
19 James, *The Bostonians*, 41.
20 James, *The Bostonians*, 133.
21 Philip Fisher, *Still the New World* (Cambridge, MA: Harvard University Press, 1999), 29–30.
22 James, *The Bostonians*, 134, 119, 193.
23 James, *The Bostonians*, 3, 199, 191, 135, 116, 130.
24 Donna J. Haraway, *Manifestly Haraway* (Minneapolis: University of Minnesota Press, 2016), 5.
25 James, *Portrait of a Lady*, 506.
26 Peter Coviello, for example, notes *The Bostonians'* "strange and often torturous generosity to Olive Chancellor." *Tomorrow's Parties* (New York: New York University Press, 2013), 170.
27 Beryl Rowland writes, "The popular significance of the mill derives from earliest times when the grinding of corn into life-giving flour was seen as analogous to the creative act" (70), further citing the Talmud's commentary on the Samson story, "Grind means nothing else than [sexual] transgression and thus it is stated: Then let my wife grind unto another" (71). "The Mill in Popular Metaphor," *Southern Folklore Quarterly* 33, no. 2 (1969): 69–91. James is, of course, no stranger to sexual punning and this double meaning underscores that it is almost always characters in relationships marked by sexual tension who "grind" one another in his novels.
28 Henry James, *The Tragic Muse, Vol. 2* (Boston: Houghton, Mifflin and Company, 1890), 829.
29 Henry James, *Roderick Hudson* (Boston: James R. Osgood and Company, 1876), 237
30 James, *The Princess Casamassima*, 352.
31 Henry James, *Autobiography*, ed. Frederick W. Dupee (Princeton, NJ: Princeton University Press, 1983), 69.

32 Charles Dickens, *David Copperfield* (New York: Penguin, 2004), 303.

33 Dickens, *David Copperfield*, 303,

34 Dickens, *David Copperfield*, 806.

35 Lauren N. Hoffer, "'She Brings Everything to a Grindstone': Sympathy and the Paid Female Companion's Critical Work in *David Copperfield*," *Dickens Studies Annual* 41, no. 1 (2010): 191–213; 202–3.

36 Henry James, "Review of *Waiting for the Verdict* by Rebecca Harding Davis," *The Nation*, November 21, 1867, rpt. in *Literary Criticism: Essays on Literature; American Writers; English Writers*, ed. Leon Edel (New York: Library of America, 1984), 218–22; 222.

37 Lauren Berlant, *The Female Complaint* (Durham, NC: Duke University Press, 2008), 35.

38 James, *The Bostonians*, 200.

39 James, *The Bostonians*, 43.

40 James, *The Bostonians*, 133.

41 Alfred Habegger, *Henry James and the Woman Business* (Cambridge: Cambridge University Press, 1989), 211–12.

42 James, *The Bostonians*, 32.

43 James, *The Bostonians*, 31.

44 Eva-Lynn Jagoe, "Depersonalized Intimacy: The Cases of Sherry Turkle and Spike Jonze," *English Studies in Canada* 42 (2016): 155–73; 155, 155.

45 Laura Fisher, "Forms of Mediation: Undercover Literature," in *Reading for Reform: The Social Work of American Literature* (Minneapolis: University of Minnesota Press, 2018), 240–304.

46 Augusta Rohrbach, *Truth Stranger Than Fiction: Race, Realism, and the U.S. Literary Market Place* (New York: Springer, 2002), 58.

47 Marjorie Garber, *Bisexuality and the Eroticism of Everyday Life* (New York: Routledge, 2013), 465.

48 Michael Kearns, "Narrative Discourse and the Imperative of Sympathy in *The Bostonians*," *The Henry James Review* 17, no. 2 (1996): 162–76; 162.

49 Kearns, "Narrative Discourse," 300.

50 Joseph Conrad, "Henry James: An Appreciation," *North American Review* 203, no. 725 (1916): 585–91; 591.

51 Joseph Conrad, *The Secret Agent* (New York: Doubleday/Anchor Books, 1953), 143.

52 Henry James, *The Art of the Novel* (Chicago: University of Chicago Press, 2011), 62.

53 James, *The Bostonians*, 74.

54 James, *The Art of the Novel*, 78.

55 Quoted in Candace Vogler, "Sex and Talk," *Critical Inquiry* 24, no. 2 (1998): 328–65; 351.

56 Jean Laplanche, *Life & Death in Psychoanalysis*, trans. Jeffrey Mehlman (Baltimore: Johns Hopkins University Press, 1985).

57 Sigmund Freud, *The Ego and the Id and Other Works,* vol. 19 of *The Standard Edition of the Complete Psychological Works of Sigmund Freud*, ed. James Strachey, Anna Freud, Alix Strachey, Alan Tyson, and Angela Richards (London: Hogarth Press and the Institute of Psycho-analysis, 1995), 170.

58 Bersani and Edelman (particularly in *No Future* [Durham, NC: Duke University Press, 2004]) are the primary theorists associated with the queer theoretical embrace of the death drive. José Esteban Muñoz suggests we turn away from the association between queer jouissance and "sexual abandon or self-styled risky behavior" and instead imagine "going beyond the singular shattering that a version of jouissance suggests" by positioning queer time as the "not yet here but nonetheless always potentially dawning." *Cruising Utopia* (New York: New York University Press, 2009), 14, 187.

59 Vogler, "Sex and Talk," 342, 331, 329, 330.

60 James, *The Bostonians*, 94, 96, 163.

61 James, *The Bostonians*, 143.

62 Leo Bersani, *A Future for Astyanax: Character and Desire in Literature* (New York: Columbia University Press, 1984), 129.

63 James, *The Bostonians*, 199.

64 Jagoe, "Depersonalized Intimacy,"155.

65 Amanda Claybaugh, *The Novel of Purpose: Literature and Social Reform in the Anglo-American World* (Ithaca, NY: Cornell University Press, 2007), 139, 148.

66 James, *The Bostonians*, 228.

67 Habegger, *Woman Business*, 227.

68 Henry James, *The Notebooks of Henry James* (Chicago: University of Chicago Press, 1981), 47.

69 Adelais Mills, "'Absolutely Irresponsible': Representations of Life in *The Bostonians*," *Henry James Review* 40, no. 2 (2019): 91–109.

70 Habegger, *Woman Business*, 197.

71 Andrew Taylor, *Henry James and the Father Question* (Cambridge: Cambridge University Press, 2002), 81.

72 Henry James, "Henry James on Carlyle," *The Albion*, January 20, 1866, 3–44; 3.

73 Bersani, *A Future for Astyanax*, 293.

74 Henry James Jr., "The Correspondence of Carlyle and Emerson," *Century Illustrated Magazine*, June 1883, 265–72; 266.

75 James Jr., "The Correspondence of Carlyle and Emerson," 270.

76 James Jr., "The Correspondence of Carlyle and Emerson."

77 Julia C. Obert, "What We Talk About When We Talk About Intimacy," *Emotion, Space and Society* 21 (2016): 25–32; 30.

CHAPTER FOUR: JAMES WELDON JOHNSON'S POLITICAL FORMALISM

1 Walter White, *A Man Called White: The Autobiography of Walter White* (Bloomington: Indiana University Press, 1948), 43.

2 November 5, 1937, box 10, folder 223, JWJMSS49, James Weldon Johnson and Grace Nail Johnson Papers, Beinecke Rare Book and Manuscript Library, Yale University Library (hereafter cited as Johnson Papers).

3 Caroline Levine, *Forms: Whole, Rhythm, Hierarchy, Network* (Princeton, NJ: Princeton University Press, 2015).

4 James Baldwin, "Preface to the 1984 Edition," *Notes of a Native Son* (New York: Beacon Press, 2012), xxii. The full sentence reads: "The people who think of themselves as White have a choice of becoming human or irrelevant."

5 W. E. B. Du Bois, *Writings* (New York: Penguin, 1986), 372; Johnson Address, box 76, folder 485, Johnson Papers.

6 See, for example, Cary D. Wintz, *Black Culture and the Harlem Renaissance* (Houston, TX: Rice University Press, 1998), 112. The other two men are Alain Locke and Charles S. Johnson.

7 W. E. B. Du Bois, "Criteria of Negro Art," *The Crisis*, October 1926, 290–97; Gene Andrew Jarrett, *Representing the Race: A New Political History of African American Literature* (New York: New York University Press, 2011), 78.

8 Upton Sinclair, *Mammonart: An Essay in Economic Interpretation* (Pasadena, CA: Published by the author, 1925), 8–9.

9 See, for example, W. E. B. Du Bois's comment that, after reading Claude McKay's *Home to Harlem*, he felt he needed to take a bath. "The Browsing Reader," *The Crisis* (May 1928): 165.

10 James Weldon Johnson, *James Weldon Johnson Writings*, ed. William J. Andrews (New York: Library of America, 2004), 741.

11 Quoted in Chidi Ikonné, *From Du Bois to Van Vechten: The Early New Negro Literature, 1903–1926* (Westport, CT: Greenwood Press, 1981), 26.

12 See Kenneth W. Warren, *What Was African American Literature?* (Cambridge, MA: Harvard University Press, 2011).

13 Warren, *What Was African American Literature?*, 11.

14 Kenneth W. Warren, "Does African American Literature Exist?," *Chronicle of Higher Education*, February 24, 2011.

15 Gene Andrew Jarrett, "African American Literature Lives On, Even as Black Politics Expire," *Chronicle of Higher Education*, March 27, 2011, https://www.chronicle.com/article/african-american-literature-lives-on-even-as-black-politics-expire/.

16 Fisk Contemporary American Literature Notes 1933, box 76, folder 57, Johnson Papers.

17 James Weldon Johnson, *The Selected Writings of James Weldon Johnson*, ed. Sondra K. Wilson (New York: Oxford University Press, 1995), 289.

18 "Misc Noted and General Ideas before 1933," box 45, folder 87, Johnson Papers.

19 "Misc Noted and General Ideas before 1933."

20 Brian Russell Roberts, *Artistic Ambassadors: Literary and International Representation of the New Negro Era* (Charlottesville: University of Virginia Press, 2013), 42.

21 Richard Wright, "Blueprint for Negro Writing," in *Within the Circle: An Anthology of African American Literary Criticism from the Harlem Renaissance to the Present*, ed. Angelyn Mitchell (Durham, NC: Duke University Press, 1994), 97–106; 97; Brent Hayes Edwards, "The Seemingly Eclipsed Window of Form: James Weldon Johnson's Prefaces," in *The Jazz Cadence of American Culture*, ed. Robert G. O'Meally (New York: Columbia University Press, 1998), 580–601; 587.

22 September 26, 1937, box 13, folder 309, Johnson Papers.

23 Nathan Irvin Huggins, *Harlem Renaissance* (New York: Oxford University Press, 2007); David Levering Lewis, *When Harlem Was in Vogue* (New York: Penguin Books, 1997); Lawrence P. Jackson, *The Indignant Generation: A Narrative History of African American Writers and Critics, 1934–1960* (Princeton, NJ: Princeton University Press, 2010); Warren, *What Was African American Literature?*

24 Jean Andrew Jarrett, "The Harlem Renaissance and Its Indignant Aftermath: Rethinking Literary History and Political Action after Black Studies," *American Literary History* 24, no. 4 (2012): 775–95; 793.

25 Johnson, *Selected Writings*, 314.

26 Johnson, *Selected Writings*, 210.

27 Addison Gayle, *The Addison Gayle Jr. Reader*, ed. Nathaniel Norment Jr. (Urbana: University of Illinois Press, 2009), 15.

28 Maggie Sale, "Critiques from Within: Antebellum Projects of Resistance," *American Literature* 64, no. 4 (1992): 695–718; 711–12.

29 Shelley Fisher Fishkin and Carla L. Peterson, "'We Hold These Truths to Be Self-Evident': The Rhetoric of Frederick Douglass's Journalism," in *Frederick Douglass: New Literary and Historical Essays*, ed. Eric J. Sundquist (Cambridge: Cambridge University Press, 1990), 189–204; Ivy Wilson, *Specters of Democracy: Blackness and the Aesthetics of Politics in the Antebellum U.S.* (New York: Oxford University Press, 2011).

30 Du Bois, *Writings*, 545, 370.

31 Johnson, *Writings*, 738, 620.

32 James Weldon Johnson, *Along This Way* (New York: De Capo Press, 2000), 328.

33 Johnson, *Writings*, 709.

34 Johnson, *Writings*, 642, 619.

35 Johnson, *Writings*, 42.

36 Johnson, *Writings*, 738.

37 Brent Hayes Edwards, *The Practice of Diaspora* (Cambridge, MA: Harvard University Press, 2003), 47.

38 Noelle Morrissette, *James Weldon Johnson's Modern Soundscapes* (Iowa City: University of Iowa Press, 2013), 71.

39 "Misc Noted and General ideas before 1933—planning *Along This Way*," box 45, folder 87, Johnson Papers.

40 Chris Mustazza, "James Weldon Johnson and the Speech Lab Recordings," *Oral Tradition* 30, no. 1 (2016): 95–110.

41 Warren, *What Was African American Literature?*, 7.

42 "The Negro in American Literature: ENG 123," box 81, folder 589, Johnson Papers.

43 Johnson Papers.

44 Johnson, *Along This Way*, 188.

45 Johnson, *Along This Way*, 188.

46 Brenda Ellis, "John Rosamond Johnson," in *Encyclopedia of the Harlem Renaissance*, ed. Cary D. Wintz and Paul Finkelman (New York: Taylor and Francis, 2004). ProQuest Ebook Central.

47 See Constance Valis Hill, *Tap Dancing America: A Cultural History* (New York: Oxford University Press, 2010).

48 See Albert "Prodigy" Johnson and Laura Checkoway, *My Infamous Life: The Autobiography of Mobb Deep's Prodigy* (New York: Simon & Schuster, 2012), 1–4. Albert "Prodigy" Johnson was Bernice Johnson's grandson. See also Cholly Atkins and Jacqui Malone, *Class Act: The Jazz Life of Choreographer* (New York: Columbia University Press, 2012); 104–5.

49 Justin Timberlake, "Suit and Tie," dir. David Fincher (Filmed: January 2013), Vevo video; Janelle Monae, "Tight Rope," dir. Wendy Morgan (Filmed: March 2010), Vevo video., P Square, "Personally" (Filmed: 2014), YouTube video.

50 Box 81, folder 593, NYU class on "Racial Contributions to American Culture" claims "Bill Robinson, the greatest tap dancer of all time, has been the teacher of the Roxy dancing girls."

51 Box 81, folder 593, Johnson Papers.

52 Levine, *Forms*, 13.

53 Morrissette, *James Weldon Johnson's Modern Soundscapes*, 11.

54 John Sekora, "Black Message/White Envelope: Genre, Authenticity, and Authority in the Antebellum Slave Narrative," *Callaloo* no. 32 (1987): 482–515; 511.

55 Quoted in Sekora, "Black Message," 507.

56 Masami Sugimori includes a strong critical summary of the reading of the ex-colored man as "Black passing for white" in his "Narrative Order, Racial Hierarchy, and 'White' Discourse in James Weldon Johnson's *The Autobiography of an Ex-colored Man* and *Along This Way*," *MELUS* 36, no. 3 (2011): 37–62.

57 Mark Twain, *Pudd'nhead Wilson and Those Extraordinary Twins* (New York: Harper and Brothers, 1922), 12.

58 Werner Sollors, *Neither Black Not White Yet Both* (Cambridge, MA: Harvard University Press, 1997).

59 James Weldon Johnson, *The Autobiography of an Ex-Colored Man* (New York: Dover, 1995), 66.

60 Bruce Barnhart, *Jazz in the Time of the Novel: The Temporal Politics of American Race and Culture* (Tuscaloosa: University of Alabama Press, 2013), 14.

61 Johnson, *Autobiography of an Ex-Colored Man*, 47.

62 Johnson, *Autobiography of an Ex-Colored Man*, 100.

63 Lisa Hinrichsen, "'A Curious Study': *The Autobiography of an Ex-Colored Man*, Pedagogy, and the Post-Plantation Imagination," *African American Review* 48, no. 1–2 (2015): 175–89; 185.

64 Autumn Womack, *The Matter of Black Living: The Aesthetic Experiment of Racial Data, 1880–1930* (Chicago: University of Chicago Press, 2022), 107.

65 Daphne Lamothe observes the connection between the protagonist's mission and the ethnographic work that was being conducted by sociologists such as Franz Boas and W. E. B. Du Bois at the beginning of the century, reminding us that while the novel itself engages in its own ethnographic project, it also "questions the usefulness of the ethnographic imagination to the collective good, suggesting that its efficacy lies in the attitudes the Black intellectual brings with him when he goes into the field to collect, preserve, and disseminate his culture." *Inventing the New Negro: Narrative, Culture, and Ethnography* (Philadelphia: University of Pennsylvania Press, 2008), 90. Lamothe highlights Johnson's view that the "how" and the "who" of historical narrative-making is far more significant than the "what."

66 Augusta Rohrbach, *Truth Stranger Than Fiction: Race, Realism, and the U.S. Literary Market Place* (New York: Springer, 2002), 25.

67 Johnson, *Autobiography of an Ex-Colored Man*, vii.

68 Edwards, *Practice of Diaspora*, 41.

69 "Interview on Negro Literature for a Radio Broadcast," box 81, folder 609, Johnson Papers.

70 Jacqueline Goldsby, "Introduction," *The Autobiography of an Ex-Colored Man* (New York: Norton Critical Editions, 2015), ix–lvi.

71 Carl Van Vechten, "Introduction to Mr. Knopf's New Edition," *The Autobiography of an Ex-Colored Man*, ed. Jacqueline Goldsby (New York: Norton Critical Editions, 2015), 121–23; 122.

72 Endorsement from Clarence Darrow sent from JWJ to Blanche Knopf December 23, 1927, Johnson Papers.

216 NOTES TO PAGES 145–151

73 Van Vechten, "Introduction," 123.

74 Van Vechten, "Introduction," 123.

75 Harper Barnes, *Never Been a Time: The 1917 Race Riot that Sparked the Civil Rights Movement* (New York: Walker & Company), 2008.

76 Johnson describes how the executive committee of the Harlem branch of the NAACP met to discuss a reaction to the St. Louis riots and "the plan most favored was a mass meeting at Carnegie Hall . . . I suggested a silent protest parade" in Johnson, *Along This Way*, 320.

77 Barnes, *Never Been a Time*, 188.

78 "Memorandum for NAACP Branches: Mottoes Used in the Negro Silent Protest Parade New York," NAACP Silent Protest Parade Flyer & Memo, July 1917, National Humanities Center, https://nationalhumanitiescenter.org/pds/maai2/forward/text4/silentprotest.pdf.

79 Soyica Diggs Colbert, *Black Movements: Performance and Cultural Politics* (New Brunswick: Rutgers University Press, 2017), 148.

80 Johnson, *Along This Way*, 321.

81 Chad Williams, "From the Silent Protest Parade to Black Lives Matter: 100 Years On, the First Mass African American Demo Remains Shamefully Relevant," *Newsweek*, July 28, 2017, https://www.newsweek.com/black-lives-matter-silent-protest-parade-first-mass-african-american-642322.

82 Benjamin Fagan, *Acting Chosen* (Atlanta: University of Georgia Press, 2016), 30.

83 Stephen G. N. Tuck, *We Ain't What We Ought to Be: The Black Freedom Struggle from Emancipation to Obama* (Cambridge, MA: Harvard University Press, 2010), 137.

84 Toni Morrison, *Jazz* (New York: Alfred Knopf, 1992), 53.

85 Paul Finkelman, ed., *Thirty Years of Lynching in the United States (1889–1918)* (Clark, NJ: The Lawbook Exchange, Ltd., 2012), 11.

86 In his excellent chapter on the aesthetic struggles of the NAACP and, more specifically, the politico-aesthetic dialectic according to W. E. B. Du Bois, Russ Castronovo articulates a central question of the struggle Black turn-of-the-century writer/activists faced on the question of aesthetics: "Did not the aesthetic aspects of lynching itself—its cruel drama, ritual orchestration, and spectacular atmosphere—invalidate political aesthetics even before it got underway?" Russ Castronovo, "Beauty along the Color Line: Lynching, Form, and Aesthetics," in *Beautiful Democracy: Aesthetics and Anarchy in a Global Era* (Chicago: University of Chicago Press, 2007): 106–35; 118.

87 Finkelman, *Thirty Years*, 25.

88 Finkelman, *Thirty Years*, 25.

89 "Campaigning in Support of the United States Constitution," box 76, folder 478, Johnson Papers.

90 Leigh Raiford, *Imprisoned in a Luminous Glare* (Chapel Hill: University of North Carolina Press, 2011), 32.

91 Womack, *The Matter of Black Living*, 106.

92 White writes of their efforts, "It was Jim's skillful hand which guided the efforts for passage of legislation against lynching during the twenties. I frequently joined him in appearing before the Senate and the House committees and in the laborious work of buttonholing congressmen and senators to get them to work more

NOTES TO PAGES 151–157   *217*

vigorously. Year after year and session after session of congress went by, and still no anti-lynching bill was enacted," *Man Called White*, 43.

93 Johnson, *Along This Way*, 363.

94 Box 24, folder 539, Johnson Papers.

95 Johnson, *Along This Way*, 369

96 Johnson, *Along This Way*, 371.

97 "Emmett Till Bill Making Lynching a Federal Crime Passes House," ABC News, February 26, 2020, https://abcnews.go.com/Politics/emmett-till-bill-making-lynching-federal-crime-passes/story?id=69229940.

98 Box 8, folder 189, Johnson Papers.

99 Jacqueline Goldsby, *A Spectacular Secret: Lynching in American Life and Literature* (Chicago: University of Chicago Press, 2006), 212–13.

100 Johnson, *Along This Way*, 560.

101 Box 14, folder 343, Johnson Papers.

102 Box 14, folder 343, Johnson Papers.

103 Johnson, *Along This Way*, 374.

104 Johnson, *Along This Way*, 374.

105 Elijah Anderson, "The White Space," *Sociology of Race and Ethnicity* 1, no. 1 (2015): 10.

106 Johnson, *Along This Way*, 219.

CHAPTER FIVE: EDITH WHARTON AT WAR IN THE LAND OF LETTERS

1 Letter to Upton Sinclair from Edith Wharton, *The Letters of Edith Wharton*, ed. Richard Warrington Baldwin Lewis and Nancy Lewis (New York: Charles Scribner's Sons, 1988), 500.

2 Wharton, *The Letters of Edith Wharton*, 500.

3 In *The Great Tradition*, F. R. Leavis claims *Daniel Deronda*'s two plots "stand apart, in fairly neatly separable masses . . . as for the bad part . . . there is nothing to do but cut it away." Leavis went so far as to produce an edition of *Daniel Deronda* alternatively titled *Gwendolen Harleth* with the Deronda plot removed as he suggests. See Richard Storer, "Leavis and 'Gwendolen Harleth,'" in *F. R. Leavis: Essays and Documents*, ed. Ian MacKillop, Richard Storer, and Frank Raymond Leavis (London: Bloomsbury, 1995), 40–52; 40.

4 Robert Grant to Edith Wharton, November 17, 1907, Beinecke Library.

5 Elizabeth Ammons, *Edith Wharton's Argument with America* (Athens: University of Georgia Press, 1980), 44.

6 Lyall H. Powers, ed., *Henry James and Edith Wharton: Letters, 1900–1915* (New York: Scribner's, 1990), 79.

7 Dale Bauer, *Edith Wharton's Brave New Politics* (Madison: University of Wisconsin Press, 1994), xiii.

8 Deborah Hecht, "Literary Biography: The Poisoned Well: Percy Lubbock and Edith Wharton," *The American Scholar* 62, no. 2 (1993): 255–59; 256.

9 Percy Lubbock, *Portrait of Edith Wharton* (New York: D. Appleton-Century Co., 1947), 15.

10 Jennie Kasanoff, *Edith Wharton and the Politics of Race* (Cambridge: Cambridge University Press, 2004), 2.

NOTES TO PAGES 157–167

11 Gaillard Lapsley Reminiscence, Beinecke Library.

12 Bauer, *Wharton's Brave New Politics*, 18, 189.

13 Robin Peel, *Apart from Modernism: Edith Wharton, Politics, and Fiction Before World War One* (Teaneck, NJ: Farleigh Dickinson University Press, 2005), 231, 229.

14 Penelope Vita-Finzi argues that Wharton's career was defined by her competing allegiances to the conservativism of classical sources and traditional forms and to the innovation of imagination and creativity. *Edith Wharton and the Art of Fiction* (New York: Pinter Publishing, 1994).

15 Edith Wharton, *The Fruit of the Tree* (New York: Charles Scribner's Sons, 1914), 21–22.

16 Wharton, *The Fruit of the Tree*, 22.

17 Wharton, *The Fruit of the Tree*, 208, 580.

18 Wharton, *The Fruit of the Tree*, 218, 356.

19 Cynthia J. Davis, *Pain and the Aesthetics of US Literary Realism* (New York: Oxford University Press, 2022), 111, 627–28.

20 Edith Wharton, *The Reef* (London: Macmillan, 1913), 38.

21 Edith Wharton, *Twilight Sleep* (New York: Scribner, 1997), 11.

22 Edith Wharton, *Hudson River Bracketed* (Oxford: Benediction Classics, 2011), 142, 143.

23 Wharton, *Hudson River*, 4, 364.

24 Wharton, *Hudson River*, 355.

25 Letter of December 14, 1935, from Edith Wharton to her niece, Beatrix Farrand, Beinecke Library.

26 Bauer convincingly reads *Twilight Sleep*, Wharton's satire of modern childbirth techniques, as a work of feminist criticism: "Wharton's target is the contradictory nature of these choices offered to women," *Wharton's Brave New Politics*, 95. See also Jennifer Fleissner, *Women, Compulsion, Modernity* (Chicago: University of Chicago Press, 2004).

27 Reminiscence from Mrs. Gordon K. Bell, Beinecke Library.

28 February 17, 1906, letter from Edith Wharton to George B. Dorr, Beinecke Library.

29 April 28, 1915, letter from Edith Wharton to Margaret Chanler, Beinecke Library; April 30, 1933, letter from Edith Wharton to Mrs. Thomas Seton, Beinecke Library.

30 Edith Wharton, *The Marne* (New York: D. Appleton and Company, 1918), 33–34, 35 (emphasis mine), 43.

31 Sheila Liming includes a breakdown of Wharton's personal library holdings by genre. Highly represented categories include literature, history, science, religion, art history, travel, philosophy, horticulture, psychology, design, and music. *What a Library Means to a Woman: Edith Wharton and the Will to Collect Books* (Minneapolis: University of Minnesota Press, 2020), 126.

32 Liming, *What a Library Means to a Woman*, 73.

33 Liming, *What a Library Means to a Woman*.

34 Cynthia Griffin Wolff, *A Feast of Words: The Triumph of Edith Wharton* (Reading, MA: Merloyd Lawrence, 1995), 27.

35 Edith Wharton, *The Uncollected Critical Writings*, ed. Frederick Wegener (Princeton, NJ: Princeton University Press, 1996), 132.

36 Edith Wharton, *A Backward Glance* (New York: Simon & Schuster, 1998), 35.

37 Quoted in Grace Ann Hovet and Theodore R. Hovet, *Tableaux Vivants: Female Identity Development Through Everyday Performance* (New York: X-Libris Corporation, 2009), 88.

38 Liming writes, "For Wharton (and for Wharton's characters), book collecting amounts to a perceived investment in the precapitalist world of cultural specificity and authenticity . . . Wharton never lived in such a world, but she dreamed of accessing it through her library," *What a Library Means*, 103.

39 Irene Goldman Price, "The Perfect Jew and *The House of Mirth*: A Study in Point of View," *Edith Wharton Review* 16, no. 1 (Spring 2000): 172.

40 Edith Wharton, "A Reconsideration of Proust," *The Saturday Review of Literature*, October 27, 1934, 15.

41 Karl Marx, "On the Jewish Question," in *Works of Karl Marx, March 1843–August 1844*, vol. 3 of *Karl Marx & Frederick Engels: Collected Works* (London: Lawrence & Wishart, 1975), 146–74; 147.

42 Draft of Collected Lubbock Reminiscences, Beinecke Library.

43 Edith Wharton letter to Mary Cadwallader Jones, February 21, 1914, Beinecke Library.

44 Robin Peel argues that Wharton's objection is to the politics, rather than the form, of modernism in *Apart from Modernism*.

45 Wharton, *The Letters of Edith Wharton*, 481.

46 Noted in Wharton, *The Letters of Edith Wharton*, 482.

47 R. W. B. Lewis, *Edith Wharton: A Biography* (New York: Fromm International Publishing Corporation, 1975), 461.

48 Bentley discusses Wharton's love affair with the trappings of modernism, if not its effects on culture, documenting her well-known affinity for the automobile and fast travel in general (trains, yachts). Haytock demonstrates how Wharton engaged with contemporary discourses about birth control, the effect of technology on society, and sexual politics in her late fictions, which Dale Bauer argues have not enjoyed the popularity of her earlier works because of their connection to issues too specific to their moment. Nancy Bentley, *Frantic Panoramas: American Literature and Mass Culture, 1870–1920* (Philadelphia: University of Pennsylvania Press, 2009); Jennifer Haytock, *Edith Wharton and the Conversations of Literary Modernism* (New York: Palgrave, 2008).

49 Edith Wharton, *The Writing of Fiction* (New York: Simon & Schuster, 1925), 17

50 More specifically, Janet Beer and Avril Horner suggest that the "corruption, economic volatility, and political instability of eighteenth-century Italy in Wharton's novel obliquely mirror the Panic of 1893 in the United States and echo the conditions leading to the formation of the progressive movement in the 1890s . . . what emerges in Wharton's first novel is a sense that change is desirable and inevitable; that evolution is preferable to revolution; that the aesthetic identity of a nation and continuity with its past must be respected but also developed if that nation is to remain vital and distinctive; that individual liberty needs to be balanced with social responsibility and democratic freedom with good government" (75). Janet Beer, "'The Great Panorama': Edith Wharton as Historical Novelist," *The Modern Language Review* 110, no. 1 (January 2015): 69–84.

51 Betsy Klimasmith, "Salvaging History: Modern Philosophies of Memory and Time in *The Age of Innocence*," *American Literature* 80, no. 3 (2008): 555–81.

52 Quoted in Lewis, *Edith Wharton*, 423–24.

53 In his 2012 introduction to an omnibus edition of three Wharton novels, also published as an essay in the *New Yorker*, Jonathan Franzen asserts that "Wharton's work is still commonly assumed to be as dated as the hats she wore." Franzen, "Introduction," *Three Novels of New York: "The House of Mirth," "The Custom of the Country," "The Age of Innocence"* (New York: Penguin, 2012).

54 Edith Wharton, *The Age of Innocence* (New York: Oxford University Press, 2008), 180.

55 Amy Kaplan, "Crowded Spaces in *The House of Mirth*," in *Edith Wharton's "The House of Mirth": A Casebook*, ed. Carol J. Singley (New York: Oxford University Press, 2003): 85–106; 90.

56 Edith Wharton, *The Custom of the Country* (New York: Oxford University Press, 2009), 50–51.

57 Stephanie Foote, *The Parvenu's Plot: Gender, Culture, and Class in the Age of Realism* (Durham: University of New Hampshire Press, 2014), 127.

58 Wharton, *Hudson River Bracketed*, 46.

59 Edith Wharton, "The Vice of Reading," *North American Review* 177, no. 563 (1903): 513–21; 517.

60 Wharton, "The Vice of Reading," 515.

61 Wharton, *The Letters of Edith Wharton*, 424.

62 James W. Tuttleton suggests "the parallels between Mrs. Wharton and Vance are many," in "Edith Wharton: Form and the Epistemology of Artistic Creation," *Criticism* 10, no. 4 (1968): 334–51; 335.

63 Lewis, *Edith Wharton*, 236.

64 Wharton, *Custom of the Country*, 50.

65 Susan Goodman, "Edith Wharton's 'Sketch of an Essay on Walt Whitman,'" *Walt Whitman Quarterly Review* 10, no. 1 (1992): 3–9; 4.

66 Wharton, *Custom of the Country*, 88.

67 Wharton, *Custom of the Country*, 97.

68 Wharton, *Custom of the Country*, 178.

69 Ana Quiring, "What's Dark About Dark Academia," *Avidly*, March 31, 2020, https://avidly.lareviewofbooks.org/2021/03/31/whats-dark-about-dark-academia/.

70 Edith Wharton, *The Unpublished Writings of Edith Wharton*, vol. 2, ed. Laura Rattray (New York: Taylor & Francis, 2009), 212.

71 Debra MacComb understands *The Custom of the Country* to be in dialogue with other divorce problem novels by Wharton's friends and contemporaries, such as *The Orchid* (1905) by Robert Grant in "New Wives for Old: Divorce and the Leisure-Class Marriage Market in Edith Wharton's *The Custom of the Country*," *American Literature* 68, no. 4 (1996): 765–97.

72 Shafquat Towheed takes issue with Elaine Showalter's assessment that Wharton mocks "Undine's ignorance in reading 'When the Kissing Had to Stop,'" by pointing out that Undine "remembers Browning's words precisely" (Ed. Rattray, 31). My argument falls in between these. Like Showalter, I think *When the Kissing Had to Stop* is a popular novel named after the Browning poem, not a fragment of the poem Undine mistakes for its title. (It is referred to in the text as a "new book.") I think the point here is, though, not simply that Undine is ignorant, but that she has lost sight of the channels through which her "culture" reaches her, that her cultural identity is as fragmented and dislocated as the bag of newspaper clippings that Mrs. Heeny carries.

73 Wharton, *Age of Innocence*, 92.

74 Edith Wharton, *The House of Mirth* (New York: Charles Scribner's Sons, 1905), 15.

75 Wharton, *Custom of the Country*, 363.

76 Wharton, *Custom of the Country*, 108.

77 Barbara Hochman draws a connection between Selden's Republic of the Spirit and the "paysage choisi of the spirit" that Wharton describes in "The Vice of Reading" in "The Rewards of Representation: Edith Wharton, Lily Bart and the Writer/Reader Interchange," *NOVEL: A Forum on Fiction* 24, no. 2 (1991): 147–61.

78 Wharton, *House of Mirth*, 113.

79 Wharton, *House of Mirth*, 7.

80 Wharton, *House of Mirth*, 10.

81 In a letter from Wharton to John Hugh Smith of July 21, 1909, she writes "Well, I say to you, as Howard [Sturgis] says to me in his last: 'keep it up—run your race—fly your flight—live your romances—drain the cup of pleasure to the dregs.'" Wharton, *The Letters of Edith Wharton*, 188. Likewise, James references Wharton's "power to go and to consume and to enjoy" in a letter to Mary Cadwallader Jones quoted in Millicent Bell, *Edith Wharton and Henry James* (New York: George Braziller, 1965), 116.

82 Wharton, *House of Mirth*, 39.

83 Edith Wharton, *Fighting France: From Dunkerque to Belfort*, ed. Alice Kelly (Edinburgh: Edinburgh University Press, 2015), 193.

84 Wharton, *Fighting France*, 196.

85 Sharon Kehl Califano, "'The Necessities of the Hour': Edith Wharton's Reluctant Volunteerism," *Forum on Public Policy: A Journal of the Oxford Round Table* (Summer 2012), Gale Academic OneFile.

86 Letter of August 22, 1914, to Bernard Berenson, Beinecke Library.

87 January 15 letter to Mary Berenson quoted in Wharton, *Fighting France*, 23; letter to Mary Cadwallader Jones, January 3, 1915, Beinecke Library.

88 Myrto Drizou, "Citizenship in the 'Land of Letters': Edith Wharton's Literary Home in Exile," in *Critical Insights: American Writers in Exile*, ed. Jeff Birkenstein and Robert C. Hauhart (Ipswich, MA: Grey House Publishing, 2015), 73–87.

89 Drizou, "Citizenship in the 'Land of Letters.'"

90 Bauer, *Wharton's Brave New Politics*, 145.

91 List of Donors, Beinecke Library.

92 Susan Goodman, "Bearing Witness: Edith Wharton's *The Book of the Homeless*," *Mosaic: A Journal for the Interdisciplinary Study of Literature* 46, no. 2 (2013): 87–103.

93 Edith Wharton, ed., *The Book of the Homeless* (New York: Charles Scribner's Sons, 1916), xxi, xix.

94 Susan Sontag, *Illness as Metaphor* (New York: Farrar, Strauss and Giroux, 1978).

95 See David Punter, "Metaphor and the Postcolonial Turn," in *Metaphor* (New York: Routledge, 2007): 113–24.

96 Chinua Achebe, "An Image of Africa: Racism in Conrad's *Heart of Darkness*," *The Massachusetts Review* 57, no. 2 (2016): 14–27; 21.

97 Alice Kelly, "Introduction: Wharton in Wartime," in *Fighting France*, 1–75.

98 Paul de Man, "The Epistemology of Metaphor," in *Aesthetic Ideology*, ed. Andrzej Warminski (Minneapolis: University of Minnesota Press, 1996): 34–50.

99 Martha Nussbaum, *Political Emotions: Why Love Matters for Justice* (Cambridge, MA: Belknap Press, 2013), 11.

100 Sigi Jöttkandt, "Effectively Equivalent," *Nineteenth Century Literature* 60, no. 2 (2005): 163–98; 165.

101 George Lakoff and Mark Johnson, *Metaphors We Live By* (Chicago: University of Chicago Press, 2003).

102 Roman Jakobson, "Two Aspects of Language and Two Types of Aphasic Disturbances," in *On Language* (Cambridge, MA: Harvard University Press, 1995): 115–33.

103 Lakoff and Johnson, *Metaphors We Live By*.

104 Laura Fisher, *Reading for Reform: The Social Work of American Literature in the Progressive Era* (Minneapolis: University of Minnesota Press, 2018), 122.

105 Walter Pater, "Style," in *Appreciations with an Essay on Style* (New York: MacMillan and Co., 1895): 1–36; 20.

106 Henry James, *The Art of the Novel* (Chicago: University of Chicago Press, 2011), 46.

107 Wharton, *The Letters of Edith Wharton*, 242.

108 Edith Wharton and Ogden Codman, *The Decoration of Houses* (New York: Charles Scribner's Sons, 1897), xxii.

109 Edith Wharton, "The Fulness of Life," *Edith Wharton: Collected Stories*, vol. 1 (New York: Library of America, 2001), 12–22.

110 Wharton, *House of Mirth*, 212–22.

111 Wharton, *Book of the Homeless*, xxiv.

112 Goodman, "Bearing Witness," 87.

113 Roberto Belloni, "The Trouble with Humanitarianism" *Review of International Studies* 33, no. 3 (2007): 451–74; Ilan Kapoor, *Celebrity Humanitarianism: The Rise of Global Charity* (New York: Routledge, 2013); David Rieff, *A Bed for the Night: Humanitarianism in Crisis* (New York: Simon & Schuster, 2003).

114 Augusta Rohrbach, *Truth Stranger Than Fiction: Race, Realism, and the U.S. Literary Market Place* (New York: Springer, 2002).

115 Zoltan J. Acs, *Why Philanthropy Matters: How the Wealthy Give, and What it Means for Our Economic Well-Being* (Princeton, NJ: Princeton University Press, 2013), 7.

116 In 2014, TOMS sold half of its shares to the investment firm BAIN capital LLC, founded by Mitt Romney. T. Coleman Andrews III, and Eric Kriss. At that time, the company was valued at $625 million. See Greg Roumeliotis and Oliva Oran, "Exclusive: Bain Capital to invest in shoemaker TOMS—sources," Reuters, August 20, 2014, online; Bruce Wydick, Elizabeth Katz, and Brendan Janet, "Do In-Kind Transfers Damage Local Markets? The Case of TOMS Shoe Donations in El Salvador," *Journal of Development Effectiveness* 6, no. 3 (2014): 249–67; 265. Wydick, Katz, and Janet noted that the shoes were only distributed in schools, which required shoes as a part of their dress code; therefore, the company's claims to provide shoes to those who did not have them were unfounded.

117 Anne Hamby, "One for Me, One for You: Cause-Related Marketing with Buy-One-Give-One Promotions," *Psychology and Marketing* 33, no. 9 (2016): 692–703; 692.

118 "When I think of the money those blankets represent I can only 'curse and swear'–and Mrs. Augie Belmont has just sent me 50 more!" Edith Wharton to Mary Cadawallder Jones, January 3, 1915, Beinecke Library.

119 Commodifying Compassion, "Implications of Turning People and Humanitarian Causes into Marketable Things," https://www.commodifyingcompassion.com/, accessed December 20, 2021.

120 Rieff, *A Bed for the Night*, 24.

121 James Baldwin, "Everybody's Protest Novel," *Partisan Review* 16 (1949): 578–85.

122 See "Spreading Gospels of Wealth," *The Economist*, May 19, 2012, online.

123 Andrew Carnegie, *The Gospel of Wealth Essays and Other Writings* (New York: Penguin, 2006), 5.

124 Quoted in Acs, *Why Philanthropy Matters*, 208.

125 Phillip Barrish, *American Literary Realism, Critical Theory, and Intellectual Prestige, 1880–1995* (Cambridge: Cambridge University Press, 2001).

126 Dylan Rodriguez, "The Magical Thinking of Reformism," *Level*, October 19, 2020, https://level.medium.com/reformism-isnt-liberation-it-s-counterinsurgency-7ea oa1ce11eb.

WORKS CITED

Achebe, Chinua. "An Image of Africa: Racism in Conrad's *Heart of Darkness*." *Massachusetts Review* 57, no. 2 (2016): 14–27.

Acs, Zoltan J. *Why Philanthropy Matters: How the Wealthy Give, and What It Means for Our Economic Well-Being*. Princeton, NJ: Princeton University Press, 2013.

Ammons, Elizabeth. *Conflicting Stories: American Writers at the Turn into the Twentieth Century*. New York: Oxford University Press, 1991.

———. *Edith Wharton's Argument with America*. Athens: University of Georgia Press, 1980.

Anderson, Elijah. "The White Space." *Sociology of Race and Ethnicity* 1, no. 1 (2015): 10.

Andrews, Malcolm. *Charles Dickens and His Performing Selves: Dickens and the Public Readings*. New York: Oxford University Press, 2007.

Arac, Jonathan. *The Emergence of American Literary Narrative, 1820–1860*. Cambridge, MA: Harvard University Press, 2005.

Armstrong, Nancy. *Fiction in the Age of Photography: The Legacy of British Realism*. Cambridge, MA: Harvard University Press, 2002.

Atkins, Cholly, and Jacqui Malone. *Class Act: The Jazz Life of Choreographer*. New York: Columbia University Press, 2012.

Bak, John S., and Bill Reynolds, eds. *Literary Journalism across the Globe*. Amherst: University of Massachusetts Press, 2011.

Baldwin, James. "Everybody's Protest Novel." *Partisan Review* 16 (1949): 578–85.

———. "Preface to the 1984 Edition." In *Notes of a Native Son*. New York: Beacon Press, 2012.

Barnard, John Levi. *Empire of Ruin: Black Classicism and American Imperial Culture*. New York: Oxford University Press, 2018.

Barnes, Harper. *Never Been a Time: The 1917 Race Riot That Sparked the Civil Rights Movement*. New York: Walker & Company, 2008.

Barnhart, Bruce. *Jazz in the Time of the Novel: The Temporal Politics of American Race and Culture*. Tuscaloosa: University of Alabama Press, 2013.

Barrish, Phillip. *American Literary Realism, Critical Theory, and Intellectual Prestige, 1880–1995*. Cambridge: Cambridge University Press, 2001.

Baudelaire, Charles. *The Painter of Modern Life and Other Essays*. Translated by Jonathan Mayne. New York: Phaidon, 1995.

Bauer, Dale. *Edith Wharton's Brave New Politics*. Madison: University of Wisconsin Press, 1994.

Bell, Millicent. *Edith Wharton and Henry James*. New York: George Braziller, 1965.

Beer, Janet. "'The Great Panorama': Edith Wharton as Historical Novelist." *Modern Language Review* 110, no. 1 (January 2015): 69–84.

Beisel, Nicola K. *Anthony Comstock & Family Reproduction in Victorian America*. Princeton, NJ: Princeton University Press, 1996.

Belloni, Roberto. "The Trouble with Humanitarianism." *Review of International Studies* 33, no. 3 (2007): 451–74.

Bender, Burt. *The Descent of Love: Darwin and the Theory of Sexual Selection in American Fiction, 1871–1926*. Philadelphia: University of Pennsylvania Press, 1996.

Benfey, Christopher. *New Orleans in Degas in New Orleans: Encounters in the Creole World of Kate Chopin and George Washington Cable*. Berkeley: University of California Press, 1999.

Bentley, Nancy. *Frantic Panoramas: American Literature and Mass Culture, 1870–1920*. Philadelphia: University of Pennsylvania Press, 2009.

Berlant, Lauren. *The Female Complaint*. Durham, NC: Duke University Press, 2008.

Bersani, Leo. *A Future for Astyanax: Character and Desire in Literature*. New York: Columbia University Press, 1984.

Bland, Lucy. *Banishing the Beast: Sexuality and the Early Feminists*. New York: New Press, 1995.

Bourdieu, Pierre. *Distinction: A Social Critique of the Judgment of Taste*. Translated by Richard Nice. Cambridge, MA: Harvard University Press, 1984.

Boyd, Anne E. "'What! Has she got into the *Atlantic?*': Women Writers, the *Atlantic Monthly*, and the Formation of the American Canon." *American Studies* 39, no. 3 (1998): 5–36.

———. *Writing for Immortality: Women and the Emergence of High Literary Culture in America*. Baltimore: Johns Hopkins University Press, 2004.

Bray, Alan. *Homosexuality in Renaissance England*. New York: Columbia University Press, 1982.

Britton, Sarah Gooding. "The Silent Partnership." In *Twisted from the Ordinary: Essays on American Literary Naturalism*, edited by Mary E. Papke, 1–22. Knoxville: University of Tennessee Press, 2003: 1–22.

Brooks, Peter. *Realist Vision*. New Haven, CT: Yale University Press, 2005.

Brown, Bill. "The Origin of the American Work of Art." *American Literary History* 25, no. 4 (2013): 772–802.

Brown, Gillian. *Domestic Individualism*. Berkeley: University of California Press, 1990.

Budd, Louis J. "The American Background." In *The Cambridge Companion to American Realism and Naturalism*, edited by Donald Pizer, 32. Cambridge: Cambridge University Press, 2006.

Califano, Sharon Kehl. "'The Necessities of the Hour': Edith Wharton's Reluctant Volunteerism." *Forum on Public Policy: A Journal of the Oxford Round Table*, (Summer 2012): Gale Academic OneFile.

Campbell, Donna. *Bitter Tastes: Literary Naturalism and Early Cinema in American Women's Writing*. Athens: University of Georgia Press, 2016.

Cane, Aleta Feinsod, and Susan Alves, eds. *"The Only Efficient Instrument": American Women Writers and the Periodical 1837–1916*. Iowa City: University of Iowa Press, 2001.

Carnegie, Andrew. *The Gospel of Wealth Essays and Other Writings*. New York: Penguin, 2006.

Castle, Terry. *The Apparitional Lesbian: Female Homosexuality and Modern Culture*. New York: Columbia University Press, 1993.

Castronovo, Russ. *Beautiful Democracy: Aesthetics and Anarchy in a Global Era*. Chicago: University of Chicago Press, 2007.

———. Introduction to *The Jungle*, by Upton Sinclair, vii–xxv. Edited by Russ Castronovo. New York: Oxford University Press, 2010.

Chang, Lulu. "Remember Joe the Plumber, Guys?" *Bustle*, May 22, 2014. https://www.bustle.com/articles/25343-whatever-happened-to-joe -the-plumber-the-average-joe-who-wasnt-actually-a-plumber.

Chapman, Mary. *Making Noise, Making News: Suffrage Print Culture and U.S. Modernism*. New York: Oxford University Press, 2014.

Chopin, Kate. "As You Like It." In Seyersted, *The Complete Works of Kate Chopin*, 706–20.

———. *At Fault*. St. Louis: Nixon Jones, 1890.

———. "The Awakening." In Seyersted, *The Complete Works of Kate Chopin*, 881–1000.

———. "The Awakening," *Redbook* 140, no. 1 (November 1972): 199–221.

———. "Confidences." In Seyersted, *The Complete Works of Kate Chopin*, 700–702.

———. "'Crumbling Idols' by Hamlin Garland." In Seyersted, *The Complete Works of Kate Chopin*, 693–94.

———. "Emile Zola's 'Lourdes.'" In Seyersted, *The Complete Works of Kate Chopin*, 697–99.

———. "In the Confidence of a Story-Writer." In Seyersted, *The Complete Works of Kate Chopin*, 703–5.

———. "Miss Witherwell's Mistake." In Seyersted, *The Complete Works of Kate Chopin*, 59–66.

———. "Mrs. Mobry's Reason." In Seyersted, *The Complete Works of Kate Chopin*, 71–79.

———. *Private Papers*. Edited by Emily Toth and Per Seyersted. Blooming-ton: Indiana University Press, 1998.

Christianson, Frank. Edinburgh: Edinburgh University Press, 2007.

Claybaugh, Amanda. *The Novel of Purpose: Literature and Social Reform in the Anglo-American World*. Ithaca, NY: Cornell University Press, 2007.

Clayton, Owen. *Literature and Photography in Transition, 1850–1915*. London: Palgrave Macmillan, 2015.

Colbert, Soyica Diggs. *Black Movements: Performance and Cultural Politics*. New Brunswick: Rutgers University Press, 2017.

Conrad, Joseph. "Henry James: An Appreciation." *North American Review* 203, no. 725 (1916): 585–91.

———. *The Secret Agent*. New York: Doubleday/Anchor Books, 1953.

Coviello, Peter. *Tomorrow's Parties*. New York: New York University Press, 2013.

Cowley, Malcolm. "A Natural History of American Naturalism." In *Documents of Modern Literary Realism*, edited by George Joseph Becker, 429–51. Princeton: Princeton University Press, 1963.

Crowley, John W. "Kate Chopin, Frédéric Chopin, and the Music of the Future." *American Literary Realism* 47, no. 2 (2015): 95–116.

Cuvillier-Fleury, A. A. "Madame Bovary." *Journal des Débats*, May 26, 1857.

Curnutt, Kirk. "Direct Addresses, Narrative Authority, and Gender in Rebecca Harding Davis's 'Life in the Iron Mills.'" *Style* 28, no. 2 (1994): 146–68.

Daugherty, Sarah. "*The Bostonians* and the Crisis of Vocation." In *A Companion to Henry James*, edited by Greg W. Zacharias, 88–99. Malden, MA: Wiley Blackwell, 2008.

D'Aurevilly, Jules Barbey. *Dandyism*. Translated by Doublas Ainslie. New York: PAJ, 1988.

Davis, Cynthia J. *Pain and the Aesthetics of US Literary Realism*. New York: Oxford University Press, 2022.

Davis, Rebecca Harding. *Bits of Gossip*. Edinburgh: Archibald Constable, 1904.

———. "Bits of Gossip." In *Rebecca Harding Davis: Writing Cultural Autobiography*, edited by Janice Milner Lasseter and Sharon Harris. Nashville, TN: Vanderbilt University Press, 2001.

———. "Blind Black Tom." *All the Year Round*, October 18, 1862, 126.

———. "Blind Tom." In Pfaelzer, *A Rebecca Harding Davis Reader*, 104–111.

———. "The Disease of Money-Getting." *The Independent*, June 19, 1902, 1457.

———. "Earthen Pitchers." In Pfaelzer, *A Rebecca Harding Davis Reader*, 215–86.

———. "John Lamar." In Pfaelzer, *A Rebecca Harding Davis Reader*, 35–53

———. *Kitty's Choice; or A Story of Berrytown*. Philadelphia: J. B. Lippincott, 1874.

———. *A Law Unto Herself*. Philadelphia: J. B. Lippincott, 1878.

———. "Life in the Iron-Mills." In Pfaelzer, *A Rebecca Harding Davis Reader*, 3–34.

———. "The Newly Discovered Woman." *The Independent*, November 30, 1893, 5.

———. "A New National Trait." *The Independent*, October 31, 1889, 1.

———. "Our Armchair." *Peterson's Magazine* 88 (1885): 456.

Dawson, John Falsarella. *Combatting Injustice: The Naturalism of Frank Norris, Jack London, and John Steinbeck*. Baton Rouge: Louisiana State University Press, 2022.

Delany, Paul. *Literature, Money, and the Market: From Trollope to Amis*. New York: Palgrave, 2002.

Dellamora, Richard. *Masculine Desire: The Sexual Politics of Victorian Aestheticism*. Durham: University of North Carolina Press, 1990.

de Man, Paul. "The Epistemology of Metaphor." In *Aesthetic Ideology*, edited by Andrzej Warminski, 34–50. Minneapolis: University of Minnesota Press, 1996.

Detrow, Scott. "A Few Minutes with Joe the Plumber." *State House Sound Bites* (blog), February 13, 2010. https://scottdetrow.wordpress.com/2010/02/13/a-few-minutes-with-joe-the-plumber/.

DeVine, Christine. "Marginalized Maisie: Social Purity and What Maisie Knew." *Victorian Newsletter* 99 (2001): 7–15.

Dickens, Charles. *American Notes for General Circulation*. Edited by John S. Whitley and Arnold Goldman. New York: Penguin, 1972.

———. *David Copperfield*. New York: Penguin, 2004.

———. *Hard Times*. New York: Norton, 2001.

———. "Personal." *Household Words*, June 12, 1958, 601.

Dowling, David. "Davis, Inc.: The Business of Asylum Reform in the Periodical Press." *American Periodicals* 20, no. 1 (2010): 26.

Dowling, Linda. "The Decadent and the New Woman in the 1890's." *Nineteenth-Century Fiction* 33, no. 4 (1979): 434–53.

Drizou, Myrto. "Citizenship in the 'Land of Letters': Edith Wharton's Literary Home in Exile." In *Critical Insights: American Writers in Exile*, edited by Jeff Birkenstein and Robert C. Hauhart, 73–87. Ipswich, MA: Grey House Publishing, 2015.

Du Bois, W. E. B. "The Browsing Reader." *The Crisis*, May 1928, 165.

———. "Criteria of Negro Art." *The Crisis*, October 1926, 290–97.

———. *Writings*. New York: Penguin, 1986.

Duro, Paul. "'The Surest Measure of Perfection': Approaches to Imitation in Seventeenth-Century French Art and Theory." *Word & Image* 25, no. 4 (2009): 363–83.

Edelman, Lee. *No Future*. Durham: Duke University Press, 2004.

Edwards, Brent Hayes. *The Practice of Diaspora*. Cambridge, MA: Harvard University Press, 2003.

———. "The Seemingly Eclipsed Window of Form: James Weldon Johnson's Prefaces." In *The Jazz Cadence of American Culture*, edited by Robert G. O'Meally, 580–601. New York: Columbia University Press, 1998.

Ellis, Brenda. "John Rosamond Johnson." In *Encyclopedia of the Harlem Renaissance*, edited by Cary D. Wintz and Paul Finkelman, 635–37. New York: Taylor and Francis, 2004. ProQuest Ebook Central.

Evans, Brad. "Realism as Modernism." In *The Oxford Handbook to American Literary Realism, edited by Keith Newlin*, 139–62. New York: Oxford University Press, 2019.

Ewell, Barbara. "Linked Fortunes: Kate Chopin, The Short Story (and Me)." In Koloski, *Awakenings*, 32–46.

Fagan, Benjamin. *Acting Chosen*. Atlanta: University of Georgia Press, 2016.

Felski, Rita. *The Limits of Critique*. Chicago: University of Chicago Press, 2015.

Finkelman, Paul, ed., *Thirty Years of Lynching in the United States (1889-1918)*. Clark, NJ: The Lawbook Exchange, Ltd., 2012.

Fisher, Laura. *Reading for Reform: The Social Work of American Literature in the Progressive Era*. Minneapolis: University of Minnesota Press, 2018.

Fisher, Philip. *Still the New World*. Cambridge, MA: Harvard University Press, 1999.

Fishkin, Shelley Fisher, and Carla L. Peterson. "'We Hold These Truths to Be Self-Evident': The Rhetoric of Frederick Douglass's Journalism." In *Frederick Douglass: New Literary and Historical Essays*, edited by Eric J. Sundquist, 189–204. Cambridge: Cambridge University Press, 1990.

Fleissner, Jennifer. *Women, Compulsion, Modernity*. Chicago: University of Chicago Press, 2004.

Flower, B. O. "Prostitution Within the Marriage Bond." *The Arena* 13 (1895): 59–73.

Foote, Stephanie. *The Parvenu's Plot: Gender, Culture, and Class in the Age of Realism*. Durham: University of New Hampshire Press, 2014.

Franzen, Jonathan. Introduction to *Three Novels of New York: "The House of Mirth," "The Custom of the Country," "The Age of Innocence,"* 85–106. New York: Penguin, 2012.

Freedman, Jonathan L. *Professions of Taste: Henry James, British Aestheticism, and Commodity Culture*. Stanford, CA: Stanford University Press, 1990.

Freud, Sigmund. *The Ego and the Id and Other Works*. Vol. 19 of *The Standard Edition of the Complete Psychological Works of Sigmund Freud*, edited by James Strachey, Anna Freud, Alix Strachey, Alan Tyson, and Angela Richards. London: Hogarth Press and the Institute of Psycho-analysis, 1995.

Fuller, Margaret. "American Literature: Its Position in the Present Time, and Prospects for the Future." In *Papers on Literature and Art, Pt. II*. New York: Fowler and Wells, 1846.

Gagnier, Regina. *Idylls of the Marketplace: Oscar Wilde and the Victorian Public*. Redwood City: Stanford University Press, 1986.

Gandal, Keith. *The Virtues of the Vicious: Jacob Riis, Stephen Crane, and the Spectacle of the Slum*. New York: Oxford University Press, 1997.

Garber, Marjorie. *Bisexuality and the Eroticism of Everyday Life*. New York: Routledge, 2013.

Gaskell, Elizabeth. *The Letters of Mrs. Gaskell*. Cambridge, MA: Harvard University Press, 1967.

Gaskill, Nick. "'The Light Which, Showing the Way, Forbids It': Reconstructing Aesthetics in *The Awakening*." *Studies in American Fiction* 34, no. 2 (2006): 161–88.

Gayle, Addison. *The Addison Gayle Jr. Reader*. Edited by Nathaniel Norment Jr. Urbana: University of Illinois Press, 2009.

Gilman, Charlotte Perkins. "Why I Wrote 'The Yellow Wall-Paper.'" In *The Norton Anthology American Literature, Volume C: 1865–1914*, edited N. Baym, 804. New York: W. W. Norton, 2012.

Glass, Loren. *Authors Inc.: Literary Celebrity in the Modern United States, 1880–1980*. New York: New York University Press, 2004.

Glazener, Nancy. *Reading for Realism*. Durham, NC: Duke University Press, 1997.

Goldsby, Jacqueline. Introduction to *The Autobiography of an Ex-Colored Man* by James Weldon Johnson, ix–lvi. New York: Norton Critical Editions, 2015.

———. *A Spectacular Secret: Lynching in American Life and Literature*. Chicago: University of Chicago Press, 2006.

Goodman, Susan. "Bearing Witness: Edith Wharton's *The Book of the Homeless. Mosaic: A Journal for the Interdisciplinary Study of Literature* 46, no. 2 (2013): 87–103.

———. "Edith Wharton's 'Sketch of an Essay on Walt Whitman,'" *Walt Whitman Quarterly Review* 10, no. 1 (1992): 3–9.

Gray, Jennifer. "The Escape of the 'Sea': Ideology and *The Awakening*." *Southern Literary Journal* 37, no. 1 (2004): 53–73.

Greist, Guinevere L. *Mudie's Circulating Library and the Victorian Novel.* Bloomington: Indiana University Press, 1970.

Habegger, Alfred. *Henry James and the Woman Business.* Cambridge: Cambridge University Press, 1989.

Hamby, Anne. "One for Me, One for You: Cause-Related Marketing with Buy-One-Give-One Promotions." *Psychology and Marketing* 33, no. 9 (2016): 692–703.

Hapke, Laura Hapke. "Social Purity Movement." In *Women's Studies Encyclopedia*, col. 3, edited by Helen Tierney. Westport, CT: Greenwood Press, 1991.

Haraway, Donna J. *Manifestly Haraway.* Minneapolis: University of Minnesota Press, 2016.

Harris, Sharon. *Rebecca Harding Davis and American Realism.* Philadelphia: University of Pennsylvania Press, 1991.

———. "Rebecca Harding Davis: From Romanticism to Realism." *American Literary Realism* 21, no. 2 (1989): 4–20.

Hawthorne, Nathaniel. *The Marble Faun.* Vol. 1. Boston: Ticknor and Fields, 1860.

Haytock, Jennifer. *Edith Wharton and the Conversations of Literary Modernism.* New York: Palgrave, 2008.

Hecht, Deborah. "Literary Biography: The Poisoned Well: Percy Lubbock and Edith Wharton." *The American Scholar* 62, no. 2 (1993): 255–59.

Hedrick, Joan D. *Harriet Beecher Stowe: A Life.* New York: Oxford University Press, 1994.

Heilman, Ann. "*The Awakening* and New Woman Fiction." In *The Cambridge Companion to Kate Chopin*, edited by Janet Beer, 87–104. Cambridge: Cambridge University Press, 2008.

Hill, Constance Valis. *Tap Dancing America: A Cultural History.* New York: Oxford University Press, 2010.

Hinrichsen, Lisa. "'A Curious Study': *The Autobiography of an Ex-Coloured Man*, Pedagogy, and the Post-Plantation Imagination." *African American Review* 48, no. 1–2 (2015): 175–89.

Hochman, Barbara. "The Rewards of Representation: Edith Wharton, Lily Bart and the Writer/Reader Interchange," *NOVEL: A Forum on Fiction* 24, no. 2 (1991): 147–61.

———. *"Uncle Tom's Cabin" and the Reading Revolution: Race, Literacy, Childhood, and Fiction, 1851–1911*. Amherst: University of Massachusetts Press, 2011.

Hoffer, Lauren N. "'She Brings Everything to a Grindstone': Sympathy and the Paid Female Companion's Critical Work in *David Copperfield*." *Dickens Studies Annual* 41, no. 1 (2010): 191–213.

Hofstadter, Richard. *The Age of Reform*. New York: Vintage, 1955.

Hovet, Grace Ann, and Theodore R. Hovet. *Tableaux Vivants: Female Identity Development Through Everyday Performance*. New York: X-Libris Corporation, 2009.

Howells, W. D. *Novels: 1875–1886*. New York: Library of America, 1982.

Huggins, Nathan Irvin. *Harlem Renaissance*. New York: Oxford University Press, 2007.

Hughes, Sheila Hassell. "Between Bodies of Knowledge There is a Great Gulf Fixed: Liberationist Reading of Class and Gender in *Life in the Iron Mills*." *American Quarterly* 49 (1997): 113–37.

Ikonné, Chidi. *From Du Bois to Van Vechten: The Early New Negro Literature, 1903–1926*. Westport, CT: Greenwood Press, 1981.

Jackson, Lawrence P. *The Indignant Generation: A Narrative History of African American Writers and Critics, 1934–1960*. Princeton, NJ: Princeton University Press, 2010.

Jagoe, Eva-Lynn. "Depersonalized Intimacy: The Cases of Sherry Turkle and Spike Jonze." *English Studies in Canada* 42 (2016): 155–73.

Jakobson, Roman. *Language in Literature*. Cambridge, MA: Harvard University Press, 1987.

———. "Two Aspects of Language and Two Types of Aphasic Disturbances." In *On Language*, 115–133. Cambridge: Harvard University Press, 1995.

James, Henry. "The Art of Fiction." In *A Victorian Art of Fiction: Essays on the Novel in British Periodicals 1870–1900*, edited by John Charles Olmsted, 285–306. New York: Routledge, 2016.

———. *The Art of the Novel*. Chicago: University of Chicago Press, 2011.
———. *Autobiography*. Edited by Frederick W. Dupee. Princeton, NJ: Princeton University Press, 1983.
———. *The Bostonians*. Vol. 1. London: Macmillan and Co., 1921.
———. *The Bostonians*. Vol. 2. London: Macmillan and Co., 1921.
———. "The Correspondence of Carlyle and Emerson." *Century Illustrated Magazine*, June 1883, 265–72.
———. "Henry James on Carlyle." *The Albion*, January 20, 1866, 3–44.
———. "Gustave Flaubert." In *Literary Criticism, Volume Two: European Writers*. New York: Library of America, 1984.
———. *The Notebooks of Henry James*. Chicago: University of Chicago Press, 1981.
———. *Portrait of a Lady*. Boston: Houghton, Mifflin and Company, 1882.
———. *The Princess Casamassima*. New York: Penguin, 1977.
———. "Review of *Waiting for the Verdict* by Rebecca Harding Davis." *The Nation*, November 21, 1867. Rpt. in *Literary Criticism: Essays on Literature; American Writers; English Writers*, edited by Leon Edel, 218–22. New York: Library of America, 1984.
———. *Roderick Hudson*. Boston: James R. Osgood and Company, 1876.
———. *The Tragic Muse*, Vol. 2. Boston: Houghton, Mifflin and Company, 1890.
Jameson, Fredric. *The Antinomies of Realism*. New York: Verso, 2016.
Jarrett, Gene Andrew. "African American Literature Lives On, Even as Black Politics Expire." *Chronicle of Higher Education*, March 27, 2011. https://www.chronicle.com/article/african-american-literature-lives-on-even-as-black-politics-expire/.
———. "The Harlem Renaissance and Its Indignant Aftermath: Rethinking Literary History and Political Action after Black Studies." *American Literary History* 24, no. 4 (2012): 775–95.
———. *Representing the Race: A New Political History of African American Literature*. New York: New York University Press, 2011.
Jenkins, Joyce L. "Art Against Equality." *Philosophy and Literature, suppl. Special Issue: Jane Austen's Darwinian Gambit* 22, no. 1(1998): 108–18.
John, Juliet. *Dickens and Mass Culture*. New York: Oxford University Press, 2010.

Johnson, Albert "Prodigy," and Laura Checkoway. *My Infamous Life: The Autobiography of Mobb Deep's Prodigy.* New York: Simon & Schuster, 2012.

Johnson, James Weldon. *Along This Way.* New York: De Capo Press, 2000.

———. *The Autobiography of an Ex-Colored Man.* New York: Dover, 1995.

———. "Inside Measurement." In *The Selected Writings of James Weldon Johnson,* edited by Sondra K. Wilson, 260–61. New York: Oxford University Press, 1995.

———. *James Weldon Johnson Writings.* Edited by William J. Andrews. New York: Library of America, 2004.

———. *The Selected Writings of James Weldon Johnson,* edited by Sondra K. Wilson. New York: Oxford University Press, 1995

Jöttkandt, Sigi. "Effectively Equivalent." *Nineteenth Century Literature* 60, no. 2 (2005): 163–98.

Kaplan, Amy. "Crowded Spaces in *The House of Mirth.*" In *Edith Wharton's "The House of Mirth": A Casebook,* edited by Carol J. Singley, 85–106. Oxford: Oxford University Press, 2003.

———. *The Social Construction of American Literary Realism.* Chicago: University of Chicago Press, 1988.

Kaplan, Fred. *Henry James: The Imagination of Genius.* New York: Open Road Integrated Media, 2013.

Kapoor, Ilan. *Celebrity Humanitarianism: The Rise of Global Charity.* New York: Routledge, 2013.

Kasanoff, Jennie. *Edith Wharton and the Politics of Race.* Cambridge: Cambridge University Press, 2004.

Kearns, Michael. "Narrative Discourse and the Imperative of Sympathy in *The Bostonians.*" *Henry James Review* 17, no. 2 (1996): 162–76.

———. *Writing for the Street, Writing in the Garret: Melville, Dickinson, and Private Publication.* Columbus: Ohio State University Press, 2010.

Kelly, Jill. "Photographic Reality and French Literary Realism: Nineteenth-Century Synchronism and Symbiosis." *The French Review* 65, no. 2 (1991): 195–205.

Kim, Sharon. "Puritan Realism: *The Wide, Wide World* and *Robinson Crusoe.*" *American Literature* 75, no. 4 (2003): 783–81.

Klimasmith, Betsy. "Salvaging History: Modern Philosophies of Memory and Time in *The Age of Innocence.*" *American Literature* 80, no. 3 (2008): 555–81.

Knadler, Stephen. "Miscengenated Whiteness: Rebecca Harding Davis, the 'Civil-izing' War, and Female Racism." *Nineteenth-Century Literature* 57, no. 1 (2002): 64–99.

Koloski, Bernard, ed. *Awakenings: The Story of the Kate Chopin Revival.* Baton Rouge: Louisiana State University Press, 2009.

Lakoff, George, and Mark Johnson. *Metaphors We Live By.* Chicago: University of Chicago Press, 2003.

Lamothe, Daphne. *Inventing the New Negro: Narrative, Culture, and Ethnography.* Philadelphia: University of Pennsylvania Press, 2008.

Lancaster, Roger N. *Sex Panic and the Punitive State.* Berkeley: University of California Press, 2011.

Laplanche, Jean. *Life & Death in Psychoanalysis.* Translated by Jeffrey Mehlman. Baltimore: Johns Hopkins University Press, 1985.

Lawson, Andrew *Downwardly Mobile: The Changing Fortunes of American Realism.* New York: Oxford University Press, 2012.

Lears, T. J. Jackson. *No Place of Grace.* Chicago: University of Chicago Press, 1982.

Levine, Caroline. *Forms: Whole, Rhythm, Hierarchy, Network.* Princeton, NJ: Princeton University Press, 2015.

Lewis, David Levering. *When Harlem Was in Vogue.* New York: Penguin Books, 1997.

Lewis, R. W. B. *Edith Wharton: A Biography.* New York: Fromm International Publishing Corporation, 1975.

Liming, Sheila. *What a Library Means to a Woman: Edith Wharton and the Will to Collect Books.* Minneapolis: University of Minnesota Press, 2020.

Lubbock, Percy. *Portrait of Edith Wharton.* New York: D. Appleton-Century Co., 1947.

MacComb, Debra. "New Wives for Old: Divorce and the Leisure-Class Marriage Market in Edith Wharton's *The Custom of the Country.*" *American Literature* 68, no. 4 (1996): 765–97.

Margraf, Eric. "Kate Chopin's *The Awakening* as a Naturalistic Novel." *American Literary Realism* 37, no. 2 (2005): 93–116.

Marx, Karl. "On the Jewish Question." In *Works of Karl Marx, March 1843–August 1844,* 146–74. Vol. 3 of *Karl Marx & Frederick Engels: Collected Works.* London: Lawrence & Wishart, 1975.

WORKS CITED

Matz, Aaron. *Satire in an Age of Realism*. Cambridge: Cambridge University Press, 2010.

Maynial, E. *L'Epoque réaliste sous le Second Empire*. Paris: Hachette, 1913.

McGarry, Molly. "Spectral Sexualities: Nineteenth-Century Spiritualism, Moral Panics, and the Making of U.S. Obscenity Law." *Journal of Women's History* 12, no. 2 (2000): 8–29.

McGurl, Mark. *The Novel Art: Elevations of American Fiction after Henry James*. Princeton, NJ: Princeton University Press, 2001.

Meer, Sarah. *Uncle Tom Mania: Slavery, Minstrelsy, and Transatlantic Culture in the 1850s*. Athens: University of Georgia Press, 2005.

Michaels, Walter Benn. "The Contracted Heart." *New Literary History* 21, no. 3 (1990): 495–531.

Miles, Caroline. "Representing and Self-Mutilating the Laboring Male Body: Re-examining Rebecca Harding Davis's *Life in the Iron-Mills*." *American Transcendental Quarterly* 18 (2004): 89–104.

Mills, Adelais. "'Absolutely Irresponsible': Representations of Life in *The Bostonians*." *Henry James Review* 40, no. 2 (2019): 91–109.

Mock, Michele L. "'An Ardor That Was Human, and a Power That Was Art': Rebecca Harding Davis and the Art of the Periodical." In Cane and Alves, *"The Only Efficient Instrument."*

Moers, Ellen. *The Dandy*. New York: The Viking Press, 1960.

Morrison, Toni. *Jazz*. New York: Alfred Knopf, 1992,

Morrissette, Noelle. *James Weldon Johnson's Modern Soundscapes*. Iowa City: University of Iowa Press, 2013.

Mullin, Katherine. *James Joyce, Sexuality and Social Purity*. Cambridge: Cambridge University Press, 2003.

Muñoz, José Esteban. *Cruising Utopia*. New York: New York University Press, 2009.

Murison, Justine. *Faith in Exposure: Privacy and Secularism in the Nineteenth-Century United States*. Philadelphia: University of Pennsylvania Press, 2023.

Mustazza, Chris. "James Weldon Johnson and the Speech Lab Recordings." *Oral Tradition* 30, no. 1 (2016): 95–110.

The National Vigilance Association. "Pernicious Literature." In *Documents of Modern Literary Realism*, edited by George J. Becker, 350–82. Princeton, NJ: Princeton University Press, 1963.

Nevinson, Henry Woodd. *Slum Stories of London.* (New York: Henry Holt and Company, 1895.

Newlin, Keith. *Hamlin Garland: A Life.* Lincoln: University of Nebraska Press, 2008.

Novak, Daniel Akiva. *Realism, Photography and Nineteenth-Century Fiction.* Cambridge: Cambridge University Press, 2008.

Nunokawa, Jeff. *The Afterlife of Property.* Princeton, NJ: Princeton University Press, 2001.

——. *Political Emotions: Why Love Matters for Justice.* Cambridge, MA: Belknap Press, 2013.

Obert, Julia C. "What We Talk About When We Talk about Intimacy." *Emotion, Space and Society* 21 (2016): 25–32.

Oliphant, Margaret. "The Anti-Marriage League." *Blackwood's Edinburgh Magazine,* January 1896, 135–49.

Parker, Dorothy. "Reformers: A Hymn of Hate." In *Nonsensorship,* edited by Heywood Broun, 95–98. New York: G. P. Putnam, 1922.

Pater, Walter. "Style." In *Appreciations with an Essay on Style,* 1–36. New York: MacMillan and Co., 1895.

Peel, Robin. *Apart from Modernism: Edith Wharton, Politics, and Fiction before World War One.* Teaneck, NJ: Farleigh Dickinson University Press, 2005.

Pittard, Christopher. *Purity and Contamination in Late Victorian Detective Fiction.* Surrey: Ashgate, 2011.

Pivar, David J. *Purity and Hygiene: Women, Prostitution, and the "American Plan," 1900–1930.* Westport, CT: Greenwood Press, 2002.

Pizer, Donald. "A Note on Kate Chopin's *The Awakening* as Naturalistic Fiction." *Southern Literary Journal* 33, no. 2 (2001): 5–13.

Powers, Lyall H., ed. *Henry James and Edith Wharton: Letters, 1900–1915.* New York: Scribner's, 1990.

Puckett, Kent. "Make No Mistake: Getting It Right in *The Princess Casamassima." NOVEL: A Forum on Fiction* 43, no. 1 (2010): 60–66.

O'Connell, Deirdre. *The Ballad of Blind Tom, Slave Pianist.* New York: Overlook, 2009.

Okker, Patricia. *Social Stories: The Magazine Novel in Nineteenth-Century America.* Charlottesville: University of Virginia Press, 2003.

O'Rourke, James. "Secrets and Lies: Race and Sex in *The Awakening." Legacy* 16, no. 2 (1999): 168–76.

Otten, Thomas J. "Slashing Henry James (On Painting and Political Economy, Circa 1900)." *Yale Journal of Criticism* 13, no. 2 (2000): 293–320.

Papke, Mary E. "So Long as We Read Chopin." In Koloski, *Awakenings*, 77–93.

Parrington, Vernon Louis. *The Beginnings of Critical Realism in America*. Piscataway: Transaction Publishers, 2013.

Pfaelzer, Jean. *Parlor Radical: Rebecca Harding Davis and the Origins of Social Realism*. Pittsburgh, PA: University of Pittsburgh Press, 1996.

———, ed. *A Rebecca Harding Davis Reader*. Pittsburgh, PA: University of Pittsburgh Press, 1995.

Powell, Aaron, ed. *The National Purity Congress: Its Papers, Addresses, and Portraits*. New York: The American Purity Alliance, 1896.

Price, Irene Goldman, "The Perfect Jew and *The House of Mirth*: A Study in Point of View." *Edith Wharton Review* 16, no. 1 (Spring 2000): 3–9.

Punter, David. "Metaphor and the Postcolonial Turn." In *Metaphor*, 113–24. New York: Routledge, 2007.

Quiring, Ana. "What's Dark about Dark Academia." *Avidly*, March 31, 2020. https://avidly.lareviewofbooks.org/2021/03/31/whats-dark -about-dark-academia/.

Raiford, Leigh. *Imprisoned in a Luminous Glare*. Chapel Hill: University of North Carolina Press, 2011.

Rancière, Jacques. *The Politics of Literature*. Translated by Julie Rose. Cambridge, UK: Polity, 2011.

Rieff, David. *A Bed for the Night: Humanitarianism in Crisis*. New York: Simon & Schuster, 2003.

Rita [Eliza Margaret Humpreys]. "The Modern Young Person." *Belgravia* 86 (1895): 61–64.

Robbins, Sarah Ruffing. "Harriet Beecher Stowe, Starring as Benevolent Celebrity Traveler." In *Transatlantic Women: Nineteenth-Century American Women Writers and Great Britain*, edited by Beth Lynne Lueck, Brigitte Bailey, and Lucinda L. Damon-Bach, 71–88. Durham: University of New Hampshire Press, 2012.

Roberts, Brian Russell. *Artistic Ambassadors: Literary and International Representation of the New Negro Era*. Charlottesville: University of Virginia Press, 2013.

Rohrbach, Augusta. *Truth Stranger Than Fiction: Race, Realism, and the U.S. Literary Market Place*. New York: Springer, 2002.

Rodriguez, Dylan. "The Magical Thinking of Reformism." *Level*, October 19, 2020. https://level.medium.com/reformism-isnt-liberation-it-s-counterinsurgency-7ea0a1ce11eb.

Rose, Jane Atteridge. "A Complete Bibliography of Fiction and Non-Fiction by Rebecca Harding Davis." *American Literary Realism 1870–1910* 22, no. 3 (1990): 67–86.

———. "Reading 'Life in the Iron-Mills' Contextually: A Key to Rebecca Harding Davis's Fiction." In *Conversations: Contemporary Critical Theory and the Teaching of Literature*, edited by Charles Penfield and Elizabeth F. Moran, 187–99. Urbana, IL: National Council of Teachers of English, 1990.

———. *Rebecca Harding Davis*. New York: Twayne Publisher, 1993.

Rowland, Beryl. "The Mill in Popular Metaphor." *Southern Folklore Quarterly* 33, no. 2 (1969): 69–91.

Ryan, Susan. "Reform." In *Keywords for American Cultural Studies*, edited by Bruce Burgett and Glenn Hendler. 2nd ed. New York: New York University Press, 2014. http://hdl.handle.net/2333.1/280gb7cc.

———. *The Moral Economies of American Authorship: Reputation, Scandal, and the Nineteenth-Century Literary Marketplace*. New York: Oxford University Press, 2016.

Saint-Amour, Paul. *Copywrights: Intellectual Property and the Literary Imagination*. Ithaca, NY: Cornell University Press, 2003.

Saldívar, Ramón. "Historical Fantasy, Speculative Realism, and Postrace Aesthetics in Contemporary American Fiction." *American Literary History* 23, no. 3 (2011): 574–99.

Sale, Maggie. "Critiques from Within: Antebellum Projects of Resistance," *American Literature* 64, no. 4 (1992): 695–718.

Sánchez, María Carla. *Reforming the World: Social Activism and the Problem of Fiction in Nineteenth-Century America*. Iowa City: University of Iowa Press, 2008.

Sawaya, Francesca. *The Difficult Art of Giving: Patronage, Philanthropy, and the American Literary Market*. Philadelphia: University of Pennsylvania Press, 2014.

Sekora, John. "Black Message/White Envelope: Genre, Authenticity, and Authority in the Antebellum Slave Narrative." *Callaloo*, no. 32 (1987): 482–515.

Schapiro, Meyer. *Modern Art*. New York: George Braziller, 1978.

Schocket, Eric. "'Discovering Some New Race': Rebecca Harding Davis's 'Life in the Iron Mills' and the Literary Emergence of Working-Class Whiteness." *PMLA* 115, no. 1 (2001): 46–59.

Schweitzer, Ivy. "Maternal Discourse and the Romance of Self-Possession in Kate Chopin's *The Awakening*." *boundary* 2 (1990): 158–86.

Seitler, Dana. "Strange Beauty: The Politics of Ungenre in Rebecca Harding Davis's *Life in the Iron-Mills*." *American Literature* 86, no. 3 (2014): 523–49.

Seltzer, Mark. *Bodies and Machines*. New York: Routledge, 1997.

———. *Henry James and the Art of Power*. Ithaca, NY: Cornell University Press, 1984.

Seyersted, Per, ed. *The Complete Works of Kate Chopin*. Baton Rouge: Louisiana State University Press, 1998.

Sheaffer, Helen Woodward. "Rebecca Harding Davis: Pioneer Realist." PhD diss., University of Pennsylvania, 1947.

Shi, David E. *Facing Facts: Realism in American Thought and Culture, 1850–1920*. New York: Oxford University Press, 1995.

Showalter, Elaine. "Syphilis, Sexuality, and the Fiction of the Fin de Siècle." In *Sex, Politics, and Science in the Nineteenth-Century Novel*, edited by Ruth Bernard Yeazall, 88–115. Baltimore: Johns Hopkins University Press, 1986.

Silver, Andrew. "'Unnatural Unions: Picturesque Travel, Sexual Politics, and Working-Class Representation in 'A Night Under Ground' and 'Life in the Iron-Mills.'" *Legacy* 20, no. 2 (2003): 94–117.

Sinclair, Upton. *Mammonart: An Essay in Economic Interpretation*. Pasadena, CA: Published by the author, 1925.

Sinfeld, Alan. *The Wilde Century: Effeminacy, Oscar Wilde, and the Queer Moment*. New York: Columbia University Press, 1994.

Singley, Carol, *Edith Wharton: Matters of Mind and Spirit*. Cambridge: Cambridge University Press, 1998).

Slater, Michael. *Charles Dickens*. New Haven: Yale University Press, 2009.

Sofer, Naomi Z. *Making the "America of Art": Cultural Nationalism and Nineteenth-Century Women Writers*. Columbus: Ohio State University Press, 2005.

Sollors, Werner. *Neither Black Not White Yet Both*. Cambridge, MA: Harvard University Press, 1997.

Sontag, Susan. *Illness as Metaphor*. New York: Farrar, Strauss, and Giroux, 1978.

Southall, Geneva Handy. *Blind Tom, the Black Pianist-Composer (1849–1908): Continually Enslaved*. Lanham, MD: Scarecrow Press, 2002.

Sugimori, Masami. "Narrative Order, Racial Hierarchy, and 'White' Discourse in James Weldon Johnson's *The Autobiography of an Ex-Colored Man* and *Along This Way*." *MELUS* 36, no. 3 (2011): 37–62.

Spingarn, Adena. *Uncle Tom: From Martyr to Traitor*. Redwood City: Stanford University Press, 2018.

Stange, Margit. "Exchange Value and the Female Self in *The Awakening*." In *Personal Property: Wives, White Slaves, and the Market in Women*, 21–35. Baltimore: The Johns Hopkins University Press, 1998.

Stevens, Hugh. *Henry James and Sexuality*. Cambridge: Cambridge University Press, 1999.

Storer, Richard. "Leavis and 'Gwendolen Harleth.'" In *F. R. Leavis: Essays and Documents*, edited by Ian MacKillop, Richard Storer, and Frank Raymond Leavis, 40–52. London: Bloomsbury, 1995.

Stowe, Harriet Elizabeth Beecher. *Uncle Tom's Cabin: A Tale, or Life Among the Lowly*. London: George Routledge and Company, 1852.

Stratton, Matthew. *The Politics of Irony in American Modernism*. New York: Fordham University Press, 2014.

Sullivan, James William. "Cohen's Figure." In *Tenement Tales of New York*, 69–88. New York: Henry Holt and Company, 1895.

Taylor, Andrew. *Henry James and the Father Question*. Cambridge: Cambridge University Press, 2002.

Tester, Keith. *Humanitarianism and Modern Culture*. University Park: Penn State University Press, 2010.

Thornton, Lawrence. "*The Awakening*: A Political Romance." *American Literature* 52, no. 2 (1980): 50–66.

Toth, Emily. *Unveiling Kate Chopin*. Jackson: University of Mississippi Press, 1999.

Trilling, Lionel. *The Liberal Imagination: Essays on Literature and Society*. New York: Viking, 1950.

Tuck, Stephen G. N. *We Ain't What We Ought to Be: The Black Freedom Struggle from Emancipation to Obama*. Cambridge, MA: Harvard University Press, 2010.

Tufescu, Florina. *Oscar Wilde's Plagiarism: The Triumph of Art over Ego.* Dublin: Irish Academic Press, 2008.

Tuttleton, James W. "Edith Wharton: Form and the Epistemology of Artistic Creation," *Criticism* 10, no. 4 (1968): 334–51.

Twain, Mark. *The Autobiography of Mark Twain, Vol. 1.* Edited by Harriet Elinor Smith. Berkeley: University of California Press, 2010.

———. *Pudd'nhead Wilson and Those Extraordinary Twins.* New York: Harper and Brothers, 1922.

Tyrrell, Henry. "The Paris Salon." *Frank Leslie's Popular Monthly* 36, no. 1 (July 1893): 2–18.

Van Vechten, Carl. "Introduction to Mr. Knopf's New Edition." In *The Autobiography of an Ex-Colored Man*, edited by Jacqueline Goldsby, 121–23. New York: Norton Critical Editions, 2015.

Vita-Finzi, Penelope. *Edith Wharton and the Art of Fiction.* New York: Pinter Publishing, 1994.

Vogler, Candace. "Sex and Talk." *Critical Inquiry* 24, no. 2 (1998): 328–65.

Walker, Nancy. "'A Group of People at My Disposal': Humor in the Works of Kate Chopin." *Legacy* 17, no. 1 (2000): 48–58.

Warren, Kenneth. "Does African American Literature Exist?" *Chronicle of Higher Education*, February 24, 2011.

———. *What Was African American Literature?* Cambridge, MA: Harvard University Press, 2011.

Weber, Brenda R. *Women and Literary Celebrity in the Nineteenth Century: The Transatlantic Production of Fame and Gender.* New York: Routledge, 2012.

Wharton, Edith. *The Age of Innocence.* New York: Oxford University Press, 2008.

———. *The Art of Fiction.* New York: Touchstone, 1997.

———. *A Backward Glance.* New York: Simon & Schuster, 1998.

———, ed. *The Book of the Homeless.* New York: Charles Scribner's Sons, 1916.

———. *The Custom of the Country.* New York: Oxford University Press, 2009.

———, and Ogden Codman. *The Decoration of Houses.* New York: Charles Scribner's Sons, 1897.

———. *Fighting France: From Dunkerque to Belfort.* Edited by Alice Kelly. Edinburg: Edinburgh University Press, 2015.

———. *The Fruit of the Tree*. New York: Charles Scribner's Sons, 1914.

———. "The Fulness of Life." *Edith Wharton: Collected Stories, 1891–1910*. Edited by Maureen Howard, New York: Library of America, 2001.

———. *The House of Mirth*. New York: Charles Scribner's Sons, 1905.

———. *Hudson River Bracketed*. Oxford: Benediction Classics, 2011.

———. *The Letters of Edith Wharton*. Edited by Richard Warrington Baldwin Lewis and Nancy Lewis. New York: Charles Scribner's Sons, 1988.

———. *The Marne*. New York: D. Appleton and Company, 1918.

———. "A Reconsideration of Proust." *The Saturday Review of Literature*, October 27, 1934, 15.

———. *The Reef*. London: Macmillan, 1913.

———. *Twilight Sleep*. New York: Scribner, 1997.

———. *The Uncollected Critical Writings*. Edited by Frederick Wegener. Princeton, NJ: Princeton University Press, 1996.

———. *The Unpublished Writings of Edith Wharton: Novels and Life Writing*. Edited by Laura Rattray. New York: Taylor & Francis, 2009.

———. "The Vice of Reading." *North American Review* 177, no. 563 (1903): 513–21.

———. *The Writing of Fiction*. New York: Simon & Schuster, 1925.

White, Richard. *The Republic for Which It Stands: The United States During Reconstruction and the Gilded Age, 1865–1896*. New York: Oxford University Press, 2017.

White, Walter. *A Man Called White: The Autobiography of Walter White*. Bloomington: Indiana University Press, 1948.

Williams, Chad. "From the Silent Protest Parade to Black Lives Matter: 100 Years On, the First Mass African American Demo Remains Shamefully Relevant." *Newsweek*, July 28, 2017. https://www.newsweek. com/black-lives-matter-silent-protest-parade-first-mass-african -american-642322.

Wilson, Ivy. *Specters of Democracy: Blackness and the Aesthetics of Politics in the Antebellum U.S.* New York: Oxford University Press, 2011.

Wintz, Cary D. *Black Culture and the Harlem Renaissance*. Houston, TX: Rice University Press, 1998.

Witherow, Jean. "Flaubert's Vision and Chopin's Naturalistic Revision." *Southern Studies* 8, no. 1–2 (1997): 27–36.

Wolff, Cynthia Griffin. *A Feast of Words: The Triumph of Edith Wharton*. Reading, MA: Merloyd Lawrence, 1995.

———. "Thanatos and Eros: Kate Chopin's *The Awakening*." *American Quarterly* 25 (1973): 449–71.

Wolstenholme, Susan. "Kate Chopin's Sources for 'Mrs. Mobry's Reason,'" *American Literature* 51, no. 4 (1980): 540–43.

Womack, Autumn M. The Matter of Black Living: The Aesthetic Experiment of Racial Data, 1880–1930. Chicago: University of Chicago Press, 2022.

———. "Object Lesson(s)." *Women & Performance: a journal of feminist theory* 27, no. 1 (2017): 59–66.

Wright, Richard. "Blueprint for Negro Writing." In *Within the Circle: An Anthology of African American Literary Criticism from the Harlem Renaissance to the Present*, edited by Angelyn Mitchell, 97–106. Durham, NC: Duke University Press, 1994.

Wydick, Bruce, Elizabeth Katz, and Brendan Janet, "Do In-Kind Transfers Damage Local Markets? The Case of TOMS Shoe Donations in El Salvador." *Journal of Development Effectiveness* 6, no. 3 (2014): 249–67.

Yaeger, Patricia S. "'A Language Which Nobody Understood': Emancipatory Strategies in *The Awakening*." *NOVEL: A Forum on Fiction* 20, no. 3 (1987): 197–219.

Yellin, Jean Fagan. Afterword to *Margret Howth* by Rebecca Harding Davis. New York: CUNY Feminist Press, 1990.

Yochelson, Bonnie, and Daniel Czitrom. *Rediscovering Jacob Riis: Exposure Journalism and Photography in Turn-of-the-Century New York.* Chicago: University of Chicago Press, 2014.

INDEX

Page numbers in *italics* refer to illustrations.

Achebe, Chinua, 182
Acs, Zoltan, 188
Addison, Joseph, 46
aesthetes: in Chopin's *The Awakening*, 69–71, 96; in Davis's "Life in the Iron-Mills," 11, 30, 55; in James's *Bostonians*, 96, 99; in James's *Portrait of a Lady*, 99; in James's *Princess Casamassima*, 11; New Woman movement and, 86
aestheticism: the dandy and, 57; Davis and, 30; James's critique of, 94; James's *Princess Casamassima* and *The Bostonians*, 94–99, 116; realism and, 11; Van Wyck Brooks on James and, 18
aesthetic realism, 9, 12–19, 197n56
African American culture, 132–39
African American life narrative genre, 139–45
African American literature, 15–17. *See also* Johnson, James Weldon
African American protest novel genre, 124–25
The Age of Innocence (Wharton), 170–72, 176
Aïdé, Charles Hamilton, 78–79
Allen, Grant, 77–78
All the Year Round (Dickens), 46–48
Along This Way (Johnson), 133, 135–38, 146–47, 151–52
American Hostels for Refugees, 179–80, 189

American Notes for General Circulation (Dickens), 45–46
American Purity Alliance (APA), 75–76
"American Slavery As It Is" (Weld), 45–46
Anderson, Elijah, 154
antimodern tradition, 17–18
"Apples" (Cézanne), *73*
Arac, Jonathan, 200n39
The Architecture of Humanism (Scott), 166–67
"The Art of Fiction" (James), 88–89, 116
The Art of Fiction (Wharton), 12, 193n2
Astaire, Fred, 137
At Fault (Chopin), 63
authorship: celebrity and, 31–32, 45; Davis and, 32–39; Dickens and, 45; Johnson and, 143–44; slave narratives and, 139
The Autobiography of an Ex-Colored Man (Johnson), 4, 125, 139–45
The Awakening (Chopin), 3–4, 62–63, 65–74, 83–89, 193n2

A Backward Glance (Wharton), 168
Baldwin, James, 125, 190
Balzac, Honoré de, 57, 65
Barbey d'Aurevilly, Jules, 57, 65
Barnes, Harper, 145
Barnhart, Bruce, 141
Barrish, Phillip, 191
Baudelaire, Charles, 56, 58
Bauer, Dale, 156–57, 180, 218n26, 219n48
Beer, Janet, 219n50

Belloni, Roberto, 188
Bentley, Nancy, 4, 20, 64, 219n48
Bergson, Henri, 171
Berlant, Lauren, 107
Bersani, Leo, 112–15, 118
Bethune, Thomas ("Blind Tom Wiggins"), 48–49
Bits of Gossip (Davis), 42
"Black Message/White Envelope" (Sekora), 139–40
Bleak House (Dickens), 6
"Blind Tom" ("Blind Black Tom") (Davis), 47–50, 140
"Blueprint for Negro Writing" (Wright), 129
The Book of American Negro Poetry (Johnson), 133
The Book of Negro Spirituals (Johnson), 137, 144
The Book of the Homeless (Wharton), 180–82, 186–88
The Bostonians (James): aesthetic realism and, 9; demographic realism and, 99–104, 108, 120; intimacy, depersonalizing vs. self-conscious, 112–15; intimacy, political, 115–20; narrative asides, 93; reform and aestheticism in, 96–99; suffering under domination, value of, 104–10
Bourdieu, Pierre, 86
Boyd, Anne E., 202n78
Bradford, Roark, 136
Bray, Allan, 56
Britton, Sara Gooding, 51
Brooks, Peter, 21, 97–98, 206n34
Brown, Bill, 203n81, 203n86
Brown, Gillian, 208n73
Brown, William Wells, 124, 131
Browning, Robert, 176
Budd, Louis J., 16
Buffet, Warren, 190–91
A Burial at Ornans (Courbet), 71, 206n34
Butler, Josephine, 76

Caird, Mona, 88
Califano, Sharon Kehl, 178–79
Campbell, Donna, 64

capitalism, global, 188–92
Carlyle, Thomas, 118–19
Carnegie, Andrew, 190–91
Carroll, Ellen, 37–38
Castle, Terry, 210n18
Castronovo, Russ, 194n16, 216n86
cause-related marketing (CRM), 188–89
celebrity culture: celebrity reform paradigm, 33–34, 51; common-sense humanitarianism and, 41–42; Davis and, 31–39; emergence of the celebrity author, 32; Stowe and, 31–32
Cézanne, Paul, 71, 73, 206n33
Child, Lydia Maria, 34
Children of Flanders Rescue Committee, 180
Chopin, Kate: feminism, New Woman movement, and, 62–63, 76, 86; influences on, 64–65; literary canon and, 62–63; naturalism and, 64–65; photographic realism and, 64–74; as reviewer, 19; review of Zola's *Lourdes*, 15; satirical realism and, 81–82; on smoking, 15; Social Purity movement, sex panic, and "art panic" of, 64, 75–83; as transitional figure, 21; visual art, interest in, 71–72
—works: *At Fault*, 63; *The Awakening*, 3–4, 62–63, 65–74, 83–89, 193n2; "Miss Witherwell's Mistake," 12, 63, 82–83; "Mrs. Mobry's Reason," 62, 65, 76–77; review of Hardy's *Jude the Obscure*, 80–81; review of Zola's *Lourdes*, 65; "A Shameful Affair," 72, 73; "Wiser Than a God," 63, 68
circle of concern, 182–83, 187
Clarke, James, 139–40
"class act" form, 136–38
Claybaugh, Amanda, 8–9, 38, 76, 116
Codman, Ogden, Jr., 184
"Cohen's Figure" (Sullivan), 9–10
Colbert, Soyica Diggs, 146
Cole, Bob, 136–37
Comstock, Anthony, 75
Conrad, Joseph: *The Heart of Darkness*, 182–84; *The Secret Agent*, 110–11; in Wharton's *The Book of the Homeless*, 180

"Contributions of the Negro to American Culture" (Johnson), 123
Cooke, Rose Terry, 109
Coolidge, Calvin, 153
Cooper, James Fenimore, 34
Courbet, Gustave, 71, 72, 206n34
Cowley, Malcolm, 51
Crane, Stephen, 10, 29, 195n28
"Criteria of Negro Art" (Du Bois), 126
Crowley, John W., 84
Curnutt, Kirk, 202n79
The Custom of the Country (Wharton), 172–76
Cuvillier-Fleury, A. A., 65

"daguerreotyping," 12, 65
dandyism, 56–59, 86–87
Daniel Deronda (G. Eliot), 156, 217n3
"dark academia" aesthetic, 175
Darrow, Clarence, 145
Daugherty, Sarah, 210n18
David Copperfield (Dickens), 105–6
"David Gaunt" (Davis), 36
Davis, Cynthia, 160
Davis, Rebecca Harding: authorial identity and personal privacy, 32–39; clubs and societies, rejection of, 15; as critic, 19; Dickens and, 38–39, 44–48; genre and, 29–30; identity- and property-based culture, rejection of, 30–31; Mitchell's "rest cure" and, 209n76; objects of reform depicted as artists, 48–51, 61; as pioneer, 21; plagiarism and, 37–38, 200n30; on progress, 16; readerships as distinct demographics, 36–37; reform individualism, celebrity reform, and, 39–44; representation strategies and, 30; Wharton compared to, 181; on Women's Exhibition, Chicago World's Fair, 42
—works: *Bits of Gossip*, 42; "Blind Tom" ("Blind Black Tom"), 47–50, 140; "David Gaunt," 36; *The Deaf and the Dumb*, 50; "Earthen Pitchers," 37, 198n5; "Ellen," 37–38; "A Faded Leaf of History," 36; "George Bedillion,

Knight," 35–36; "Ingenuity in Earning a Living," 60; "In the Market," 60–61; "John Lamar," 36; *Kitty's Choice; or, a Story of Berrytown*, 29, 43; *A Law Unto Herself*, 43; "Marcia," 198n5; *Margret Howth*, 36, 50; "The Murder in the Glen Ross," 36; *The Second Life*, 36; *Waiting for the Verdict*, 11, 106, 202n74; "Women in Literature," 34. *See also* "Life in the Iron-Mills"
Dawson, Jon Falsarella, 5
The Deaf and the Dumb (Davis), 50
The Decoration of Houses (Wharton and Codman), 184–86
Defoe, Daniel, 10–11
Degas, Edgar, 71, 206n33
Delany, Paul, 78, 207n55
Dellamora, Richard, 56
de Man, Paul, 182
demographic realism, 93, 99–104, 108, 120
depersonalizing intimacy, 112–15
"Dialogue" (Rich), 112–13
Dickens, Charles: as celebrity reformer, 38–40; Davis and, 38–39, 44–47; marriage, dissolution of, 47; reform writers, influence on, 6
—works: *All the Year Round*, 46–48; *American Notes for General Circulation*, 45–46; *Bleak House*, 6; *David Copperfield*, 105–6; *Hard Times*, 6, 38, 44–47; *Household Words*, 46–47
Dickinson, Emily, 33
"The Dilemma of the Negro Author" (Johnson), 152–53
direct address, 109–10
"Don Giovanni" (Mozart), 67
Douglass, Frederick, 131, 135
Dowling, David, 36, 38, 200n33
Dowling, Linda, 86–87
Dreiser, Theodore, 13, 29
Du Bois, W. E. B., 125–27, 132, 143–44, 215n65
Dumas, Alexandre, 18
Dunbar, Paul Laurence, 124, 133
Duro, Paul, 74, 206n40
Dyer Anti-Lynching Bill, 151–53

"Earthen Pitchers" (Davis), 37, 198n5
Edelman, Lee, 77
Edwards, Brent, 129, 135, 197n64
Einstein, Albert, 171
Eliot, George: *Daniel Deronda*, 156, 217n3
Eliot, T. S.: *Sweeney Agonistes*, 139; Wharton on, 170
"Ellen" (Davis), 37–38
Ellis, Brenda, 136–37
Ellison, Ralph, 147
Elmar, Karl, 67
Emerson, Ralph Waldo, 119, 174
Ethan Frome (Wharton), 128
Evans, Brad, 11
Ewell, Barbara, 62–63, 81

"A Faded Leaf of History" (Davis), 36
Fagan, Benjamin, 147
Faulkner, William, 170
Fauset, Jessie Redmond, 124
Felski, Rita, 19–20
feminism: Chopin and, 62–63, 67, 88; in James's *The Bostonians*, 96; Social Purity movement and, 5, 76–77; Wharton and, 218n26
Fields, James T., 50, 202n78
Fighting France (Wharton), 178, 182
Fisher, Laura, 6–7, 109, 184
Fisher, Philip, 101–2, 208n73
Fishkin, Shelley Fisher, 131
Fitzgerald, F. Scott, 170
Flaubert, Gustave: Brooks on, 206n34; *Madame Bovary*, 65, 87–88, 193n2; realism and, 2, 65
Flower, Benjamin Orange, 77
Foote, Stephanie, 173
formalism, 124, 132–33, 136–37
Forster, John, 46
Foucault, Michel, 13
Franzen, Jonathan, 220n53
Freedman, Jonathan L., 99
Freud, Sigmund, 112
The Fruit of the Tree (Wharton), 155–56, 158–62
Fuller, Margaret, 194n12
"The Fulness of Life" (Wharton), 185

Gagnier, Regina, 59
Gandal, Keith, 195n28
Garber, Marjorie, 109
Garland, Hamlin, 72, 195n28
Garnet, Henry Highland, 131
Gaskell, Elizabeth, 44, 47
Gaskill, Nicholas, 69
Gayle, Addison, Jr., 131
"George Bedillion, Knight" (Davis), 35–36
Gestefeld, Ursula Newel, 88
Ghosts (Ibsen), 65
Gilman, Charlotte Perkins, 7, 208n76
Giving Pledge, 190
Glass, Loren, 32
Glazener, Nancy, 9
The Gods Arrive (Wharton), 172
Goldsby, Jacqueline, 144, 152
Goodman, Susan, 174, 180, 187
"Gospel of Wealth" (Carnegie), 190–91
Grand, Sarah, 78–79
Grant, Robert, 156, 169, 220n71
Gray, Jennifer, 205n20
The Great Gatsby (Fitzgerald), 170
Green, Paul, 136
Greet, W. Cabell, 135
Griggs, Sutton, 127
"grinding" trope, 104–7, 210n18

Habegger, Alfred, 101, 117
Hagar (Johnston), 88
Haines, John Peter, 164
Haraway, Donna, 104
Hard Times (Dickens), 6, 38, 44–47
Hardy, Thomas, 22, 77–78, 80–81, 89
Harlem Renaissance, 123–24, 129–30
Harper, Frances, 124
Harris, Sharon, 37, 198n2, 198n14, 203n98
Hawthorne, Nathaniel, 74
Haytock, Jennifer, 219n48
The Heart of Darkness (Conrad), 182–84
The Heavenly Twins (Grand), 78
Heilmann, Ann, 63–64
Hérold, Ferdinand, 67
Heyward, DuBose, 136
Hibbitt, George W., 135
Hinrichsen, Lisa, 142
historical novels, 171

Hochman, Barbara, 31, 176–77
Hoffer, Lauren, 106
Hofstadter, Richard, 4
Hopkins, Pauline Elizabeth, 124
Horner, Avril, 219n50
Household Words (Dickens), 46–47
The House of Mirth (Wharton), 167, 172, 176–78, 186
Howells, William Dean, 10, 13, 18
Hudson River Bracketed (Wharton), 14, 162–64, 170, 172–73
Huggins, Nathan Irvin, 129–30
Hughes, Langston, 129, 135
Hughes, Sheila Hassell, 59
humanitarianism: common-sense, 41–42; demographic realism and, 108; neoliberal and profit-minded, 188–92
Hume, Beverly, 174
Hurston, Zora Neale, 123–24

Ibsen, Henrik, 65
impersonal intimacy, 112–15
Impressionism, 71–72, 88
individualism, 39–40. *See also* celebrity culture
"Ingenuity in Earning a Living" (Davis), 60
interiority, 97–98
"In the Market" (Davis), 60–61
intimacy: depersonalizing/impersonal vs. self-conscious, 112–15; political, 115–20
irony: aesthetic realism, ironic stance in, 12–13; Chopin and, 196n44; in Davis's "Life in the Iron-Mills," 51, 57; in James's *The Bostonians*, 103–4; in Wharton's *The Fruit of the Tree*, 156, 161

Jackson, Lawrence P., 129–30
Jagoe, Eva-Lynn, 109, 115
Jakobson, Roman, 183, 196n56
James, Henry, Jr.: Conrad on, 110; as critic, 19; demographic realism, critique of, 93; discomfort of feeling and, 110; "grinding" trope and, 104–7, 210n18; Johnson on, 128; Lears on, 18; on

London as "hideously political," 1, 12; misogyny, purported, 104; in Paris, 1; reform realism vs. affective responses and, 93–94, 109; Sargent's portrait of, 96; as transitional figure, 21; on Wharton's *The Fruit of the Tree*, 156, 221n81
—works: "The Art of Fiction," 88–89, 116; *The Portrait of a Lady*, 97, 104, 184; review of Davis's *Waiting for the Verdict*, 106; *Roderick Hudson*, 94, 104–5; *The Tragic Muse*, 104. See also *The Bostonians*; *The Princess Casamassima*
James, Henry, Sr., 118
Jameson, Fredric, 2–3
Jarrett, Gene Andrew, 126–27, 130–31
Jazz (Morrison), 147
Jenkins, Joyce L., 94
Jewett, Lillian, 100
Jewishness, Wharton and, 168–69
John, Juliet, 38
"John Lamar" (Davis), 36
Johnson, Bernice, 137
Johnson, James Weldon: African American life writing and, 139–45; on Coolidge, 153; as critic, 19; as diplomat, 125; Dyer Bill campaign, 151–53; ethnographic recordings, 135; form, genre, and primacy of Black culture, 132–39; Hampton Institute address, 125; Harlem Renaissance and, 123–25, 129–30; James, Wharton, and, 18; on James and Wharton, 128; lynching investigations, 147–51; NAACP work, 124–25, 145–53; "Negro in American Literature" course, 136; politics and literature, separation of, 152–53; on progress, 16–17; "race problem," African American arts, and project of, 124–32; Silent Protest Parade and, 145–47
—works: *Along This Way*, 133, 135–38, 146–47, 151–52; *The Autobiography of an Ex-Colored Man*, 4, 125, 139–45; *The Book of American Negro Poetry*, 133; *The Book of Negro Spirituals*, 137, 144;

—works (*continued*)
"Contributions of the Negro to American Culture" (address), 123; "The Dilemma of the Negro Author," 152–53; "Race Prejudice and the Negro Artist," 130–31; *The Second Book of Negro Spirituals*, 132, 137
Johnson, Mark, 183
Johnson, Rosamund, 136–37, 154
Johnston, Mary, 88
Jones, Lucretia Rhinelander, 166
Jöttkandt, Sigi, 183
Joyce, James, 170
Jude the Obscure (Hardy), 22, 77–78, 80–81, 89
The Jungle (Sinclair), 7, 194n16

Kaplan, Amy, 8, 13–14, 18, 172
Kapoor, Ilan, 188
Kasanoff, Jennie, 157
Kearns, Michael, 33, 109–10
Kelly, Alice, 182
Kelly, Jill, 65
Kim, Sharon, 10–11
Kitty's Choice; or, a Story of Berrytown (Davis), 29, 43
Klimasmith, Betsy, 171–72
Knadler, Stephen, 199n19, 202n74

Lakoff, George, 183
Lamothe, Daphne, 215n65
Lancaster, Roger, 77
Laplanche, Jean, 112
Lapsley, Gaillard, 156–57
Lawrence, D. H., 78
Lawson, Andrew, 52, 203n84
A Law Unto Herself (Davis), 43
Lears, T. J. Jackson, 17–18
Leavis, F. R., 217n3
Le Brun, Charles, 73–74
Levering, Joshua, 76
Levine, Caroline, 124, 138
Lewis, David Levering, 129–30
"Life in the Iron-Mills" (Davis): anonymous publication of, 35; dandyism in, 56–59; Dickens's *Hard Times* and, 38–39; ending of, 52, 60; Evans

on aestheticism and, 11–12; Hugh's crime and suicide, 57–59; korl woman sculpture, 51–60; narrator in, 40, 50–53; naturalism vs. sentimental realism and, 29–30; racism and eugenicism, assault on, 50; tourism and, 39–40, 54
life narrative genre, 139–45
Liming, Sheila, 218n31, 219n38
Locke, Alain, 127
London, Jack, 5
London Labour and the London Poor (Mayhew), 8
Lourdes (Zola), 15, 65
Lubbock, Percy, 156–57
Lukács, György, 171

MacComb, Debra, 220n71
Madame Bovary (Flaubert), 65, 87–88, 193n2
Mammonart (Sinclair), 126
The Marble Faun (Hawthorne), 74
"Marcia" (Davis), 198n5
Margret Howth (Davis), 36, 50
The Marne (Wharton), 165
Marx, Karl, 169
Mary Barton (Gaskell), 44
Masson, David, 8
Matz, Aaron, 81–82
Maupassant, Guy de, 64–65, 72
Mayhew, Henry, 8, 109
McCain, John, 100
McGarry, Molly, 75
McGurl, Mark, 3
McKay, Claude, 127, 129, 135, 152
Melville, Herman, 33
Mérimée, Prosper, 67
metaphor, politics of, 183–87
metonymy, 183
Michaels, Walter Benn, 70
Miles, Caroline, 59, 203n89
Miller, Michael Vincent, 113
minstrelsy, 130
"Miss Witherwell's Mistake" (Chopin), 12, 63, 82–83
Mitchell, Silas Weir, 85, 208n76
Mock, Michele, 36–37

A Modern Instance (Howells), 10
modernism: aesthetic realism and, 18;
    antimodern tradition, 17–18; James
    and, 21, 116–17; realism and, 3, 11;
    Wharton and, 157, 170–72, 219n48
"The Modern Young Person" (Aïdé),
    78–79
Moers, Ellen, 86
Moore, George, 207n55
Morrisette, Noelle, 135, 139
Morrison, Toni, 147
Mozart, Wolfgang Amadeus, 67
"Mrs. Mobry's Reason" (Chopin), 62,
    65, 76–77
Mudie's Select Library, 78, 81, 207n55
Muñoz, José Esteban, 212n58
"The Murder in the Glen Ross" (Davis), 36
Murison, Justine, 6
Mustazza, Chris, 135

NAACP, 145–52
National Vigilance Association (NVA),
    75–76, 79–80
naturalism: Chopin and, 64–65; dandy
    figures and, 57; Davis and, 29–30,
    44; poverty, descriptions of, 40–41;
    realism vs., 13; reform fiction and, 5;
    Zola and, 65, 71
neoliberalism, 188–92
Nevinson, Henry Woodd, 10
new journalists, 7–8
New Woman movement, 63–64, 76,
    86, 168
New York Society for the Suppression of
    Vice (NYSSV), 75
N——Heaven (Van Vechten), 126–27
Nordau, Max, 76
Norris, Frank, 5, 17, 29
North & South (Gaskell), 47
Novak, Daniel Akiva, 194n20
Nunokawa, Jeff, 30
Nussbaum, Martha, 155, 182–83

Obert, Julia, 120
Odum, Howard W., 136
L'Oeuvre (Zola), 71
Oil (Sinclair), 155

Okker, Patricia, 199n24
Oliphant, Margaret, 77–78
The Orchid (Grant), 220n71
O'Rourke, James, 206n38
Otten, Thomas, 96

Palin, Sarah, 100
Papke, Mary E., 88
Parker, Dorothy, 14
Parrington, Vernon L., 13, 157
Pater, Walter, 184
Peel, Robin, 157
The People of Paper (Plascencia), 10–11
Person, Ell, 148–49
Peterkin, Julia, 136
Peters, Michael, 137
Peterson, Carla L., 131
Pfaelzer, Jean, 39, 52, 203n84, 203n98
Phelps, Elizabeth Stuart, 29, 67, 88
philanthropy, 162, 188–92
photography: in Chopin's *The Awakening*,
    86; Davis's rejection of, 33, 198n14;
    realism, photographic, 65–74; Social
    Purity movement and, 75; technol-
    ogy of, 8, 194n20
plagiarism, 37–38, 200n30
Plascencia, Salvador, 10–11
"The Poet and the Peasant" (Elmar;
    Suppé), 67
The Portrait of a Lady (James), 97,
    104, 184
postcolonial studies, 182
post-critique debates, 19–20
Price, Irene Goldman, 168
The Princess Casamassima (James):
    Conrad's *Secret Agent* and, 110–11;
    Davis's *Waiting for the Verdict* and,
    11; demographic realism and, 93;
    intimacy, political, 115–17; reform
    and aestheticism in, 94–96; suffering
    under domination, value of, 108–12
problem novels, 155–56, 159, 171
progress, notion of, 4, 16–17, 188
Progressive Era, 4–14, 54, 96, 192
protest novels, 124–25, 188
Proust, Marcel, 18–19, 168
Puckett, Kent, 94–95

Quiring, Ana, 175

"Race Prejudice and the Negro Artist" (Johnson), 130–31
Raiford, Leigh, 149
The Rainbow (Lawrence), 78
Rancière, Jacques, 2, 19
realism: aesthetic, 9, 12–19, 197n56; celebrity reform, 33–34; Chopin and, 64–65; critical positions on, 13–14; definitions of, 10–11, 196n56; demographic, 93, 99–104, 108, 120; French, 2; Jameson on, 2–3; modernism and, 3, 11; photographic, 65–74; reform and, 7–10; satirical, 81–82; sentimental, 29–30, 107, 181; subjectlessness and, 2; things, interiority, and identity in, 97; Wharton and relationship between literature and world, 166–67. *See also* reform realism
Red Apples (Courbet), 71
Redmond, Charles, 131
The Reef (Wharton), 162
reform: about, 4–7; aesthetic critique of, 14–15; mass culture and, 4; realism and, 7–10
"Reformers: A Hymn of Hate" (Parker), 14
reform realism: aesthetic realism and, 14; defined, 9; direct address and, 109–10; legacy of, 188–92; as literary instrument, 10. *See also specific authors*
Rich, Adrienne, 112–13
Rieff, David, 188, 190
Riis, Jacob, 8, 195n28
Robbins, Sarah Ruffing, 31
Roberts, Brian Russell, 129
Robinson, Bill, 137–38
Robinson Crusoe (Defoe), 10–11
Roderick Hudson (James), 94, 104–5
Rodriguez, Dylan, 191–92
Rohrbach, Augusta, 109, 143, 188
Roosevelt, Teddy, 154
Rose, Jane Atteridge, 37, 39
Rowland, Beryl, 210n18
Rubin, Gayle, 62

Ruth Hall (Fern), 31–32
Ryan, Susan, 4–5, 14–15, 34

Saint-Amour, Paul, 200n30
Sale, Maggie, 131
"Sally Parson's Duty" (Cooke), 109
Sánchez, María Carla, 5–6
Sargent, John Singer, 1
satirical realism, 81–82
Save the Children, 40–41, *41*
scandals, 34
Schapiro, Meyer, 71, 206n33
Schocket, Eric, 44–45, 202n74
Schweitzer, Ivy, 84
Scott, Geoffrey, 166–67
The Second Book of Negro Spirituals (Johnson), 132, 137
The Second Life (Davis), 36
The Secret Agent (Conrad), 110–11
Seitler, Dana, 30, 52, 54–55
Sekora, John, 139–40
self-conscious intimacy, 113–15
sentimental realism: Berlant on sentimentality, 107; Davis's "Life in the Iron-Mills" and, 29–30; James and, 107; Wharton and, 181
sentimental reform fiction, 6–7
Shaeffer, Helen Woodward, 37–38
"A Shameful Affair" (Chopin), 72, 73
"The Shame of America" ad, 149–51, *150*
Showalter, Elaine, 77, 220n72
Silent Protest Parade (New York, 1917), 145–47
Silver, Andrew, 54
Sinclair, Upton: *The Jungle*, 7, 194n16; *Mammonart*, 126; *Oil*, 155
Singley, Carol, 16
slave narratives, 139–40, 143
slavery and enslaved persons, 45–50
Slum Stories of London (Nevinson), 10
Social Purity movement, 5, 64, 75–83, 88
social science, 7–8
Society for the Prevention of Cruelty to Animals, 164
sociopolitical identity, 18

Sofer, Naomi, 198n5
Sollors, Werner, 140
Sontag, Susan, 182
The Souls of Black Folk (Du Bois), 125, 143–44
The Sound and the Fury (Faulkner), 170
Stanton, Elizabeth Cady, 77
Steinbeck, John, 5
Stevens, Hugh, 210n18
Stevenson, Robert Louis, 33
The Story of Avis (Phelps), 67
Stowe, Harriet Beecher: celebrity and, 40; daguerreotyping, 12; Davis and, 31–32; direct address and, 109; model of fictional activism, 110; scandals, 34; *Uncle Tom's Cabin*, 6–7, 31, 40, 45–46, 194n12
Stratton, Matthew, 12–13
Stutfield, Hugh E. M., 86–87
Sullivan, James William, 9–10
Suppé, Franz von, 67

Taylor, Andrew, 118
Temple, Shirley, 138
Tenement Tales of New York (Sullivan), 10
Tester, Keith, 41
"The Tree of Knowledge" (*The New Review*), 78–79
Thirty Years of Lynching in the United States, 1889–1918 (Paul Finkelman), 147–51
This Side of Paradise (Fitzgerald), 170
TOMS shoes, 188–89, 222n116
Torrence, Ridgeley, 136
Toth, Emily, 64–65, 76–77, 206n33
Towheed, Shafquat, 220n72
The Tragic Muse (James), 104
Trilling, Lionel, 13, 95
Tufescu, Florina, 200n30
Twain, Mark, 33, 140
Twilight Sleep (Wharton), 12, 162, 218n26
"two-colored rule" in vaudeville, 137–38
Tyrrell, Henry, 73

Uncle Tom's Cabin (Stowe), 6–7, 31, 40, 45–46, 194n12

The Valley of Decision (Wharton), 171, 219n50
Van Vechten, Carl, 126–27, 136, 144–45
vaudeville, 137–38
"La Vénus d'Ille" (Mérimée), 67
"The Vice of Reading" (Wharton), 173
Vita-Finzi, Penelope, 218n14
Vizetelly, Henry, 76, 79–80
Vogler, Candace, 112–13

Waiting for the Verdict (Davis), 11, 202n74
Walker, David, 131
Walker, Nancy, 208n67
Warner, Susan, 10–11
Warren, Kenneth, 15–16, 127, 129–30, 135
Weber, Brenda, 31–32
Weld, Theodore D., 45–46
Wells, Ida B., 149–50
Wharton, Edith: American Hostels for Refugees and, 179–80, 189; beauty and political struggle, tension between, 158; Children of Flanders Rescue Committee and, 180; as critic, 19; dismissals of, 156–57; expatriation to France, 162, 169, 178; Flaubert and, 193n2; garment factor established by, 189; the historical novel and, 171; Johnson on, 128; Land of Letters and, 18–19, 167–69, 173–77, 187–88; literature and world, relationship between, 166–67; "making up" in childhood, 167; metaphor and, 183–87; Mitchell's "rest cure" and, 209n76; modernism and, 219n48; philanthropy as hypocrisy and, 162; politics of, 157; the problem novel and, 155–56, 159, 171; on progress, 16–17; reading program and library of, 166, 168, 218n31, 219n38; as transitional figure, 21; war relief work, 178–80, 189
—works: *The Age of Innocence*, 170–72, 176; *The Art of Fiction*, 12, 193n2; *A Backward Glance*, 155, 168; *The Book of the Homeless* (anthology), 180–82, 186–88; *The Custom of the Country*, 172–76; *The Decoration of Houses*

—works (*continued*)
(with Codman), 184–86; *Ethan Frome*, 128; *Fighting France*, 178, 182; *The Fruit of the Tree*, 155–56, 158–62; "The Fulness of Life," 185; *The Gods Arrive*, 172; *The House of Mirth*, 167, 172, 176–78, 186; *Hudson River Bracketed*, 14, 162–64, 170, 172–73; *The Marne*, 165; *The Reef*, 162; review of Scott's *The Architecture of Humanism*, 166–67; *Twilight Sleep*, 12, 162, 218n26; *The Valley of Decision*, 171, 219n50; "The Vice of Reading," 173; *The Writing of Fiction*, 171
Wheatley, Phillis, 135
White, Richard, 5
White, Walter, 123, 125, 149, 216–17n92
Whitman, Walt, 174
The Wide, Wide World (Warner), 10–11
Wiggins, "Blind Tom" (Thomas Bethune), 48–49
Wilde, Oscar, 76, 200n30
Wilson, Ivy, 131

"Wiser Than a God" (Chopin), 63, 68
Wolff, Cynthia Griffin, 166, 205n20
Wolstenhome, Susan, 65, 76–77
Womack, Autumn, 100, 142, 149–50
The Woman Who Dares (Gestefeld), 88
The Woman Who Did (Allen), 77–78
"Women in Literature" (Davis), 34
Wood, Mary, 96
Wright, Richard, 124, 129
The Writing of Fiction (Wharton), 171
Wurzelbacher, Samuel ("Joe the Plumber"), 100

Yaeger, Patricia, 85, 205n20
"The Yellow Wall-Paper" (Gilman), 7, 208n76

"Zampa" (Hérold), 67
Zola, Émile: Cézanne and, 206n33; Chopin and, 71–72, 79; James and, 1; *Lourdes*, 15, 65; *L'Oeuvre*, 71; Riis compared to, 8